execute.txt
Procedure to follow :
===
01.Buy the suitable licensed turboC 64 bit version.
02.This must be for Windows 10 64 bit.
03.Extract it and get turboC 64 bit.
04.Run setup.exe within it.
05.C:\TURBOC\ may the directory.
06.In that there is BIN directory.
07.Place *.EXE in C:\TURBOC\BIN\.
08.Run *.EXE from C:\TURBOC\BIN\.
09.Copy the relavent files into C:\TURBOC\BIN\.
10.Set path appropriately.
===

*

genco.c
/* General Compiler */
#include<stdio.h>
#include<conio.h>
#include<stdlib.h>
#include<string.h>
/* --------------- global declarations --------------- */
FILE huge *fpt,*fpt1,*fpt2,*fpt3,*fpt4,*fpt5,*fpt6,*fpt7,*fpt8,*fpt9,*fpt10;
   /* --- */
char ch,tim[9],date2[9],date[11],time2[12],st[41],fname[12],sign,curpos[81];
int a,b,c,d,e,f,g,h,i,j,k,l,m,n,o,p,q,r,s,u,v,w,x,y,z;
struct comm{char command[81];};struct comm com;
char vars1[101][81],vars2[101][81],str2[101][81],str3[101][81];
int var[101],labelvar[101][81],flag[101],count[101];
/* --- */
main(int argc,char *argv[])
{
var[50]=0;
fflush(stdin);
strcpy(fname,argv[1]);
fpt=fopen(fname,"r+");
if(fpt==NULL){
printf("The file not opened.Exiting...");
getch();
exit(1);
}
/* --- */
fpt1=fopen("command.dbm","wb+");
while(fscanf(fpt,"%s",com.command)!=EOF){
fwrite(&com.command,sizeof(com.command),1,fpt1);
}

```c
fclose(fpt1);
fpt1=fopen("command.dbm","rb+");
fpt3=fopen("declare.dat","w+");
while(fread(&com.command,sizeof(com.command),1,fpt1)==1){
if(strcmp(com.command,"declare")==0){
while(fread(&com.command,sizeof(com.command),1,fpt1)==1){
if(strcmp(com.command,"endst")!=0)fprintf(fpt3,"%s\n",com.command);
else goto label1;
}
}
}
label1:
fclose(fpt1);
fpt1=fopen("command.dbm","rb+");
fpt2=fopen("gencos.dat","r+");
j=0;
while(fread(&com.command,sizeof(com.command),1,fpt1)==1){
rewind(fpt2);
while(fscanf(fpt2,"%s",str2[0])!=EOF){
if(strcmp(str2[0],com.command)==0)goto label2;
else {
rewind(fpt3);
while(fscanf(fpt3,"%s",str3[0])!=EOF){
if(strcmp(str3[0],com.command)==0)goto label2;
}
}
}
strcpy(vars1[j++],com.command);
label2:k=0;
}
strcpy(vars1[j],"\0");
printf("The following maybe errors...\n");
for(k=0;strcmp(vars1[k],"\0")!=0;k++){printf("%s\t",vars1[k]);}
fcloseall();
}

*
gencos.dat
all
open
for
fresh
writeread
insert
read
oneofto
gofor
```

begining
fileseek
filetell
forward
filesize
increment
decrement
system
begin
endst
end
if
then
endif
goto
labelit
comment
message
anyval
anyvar
line
space
cat
endcat
storeval
char
endchar
storevar
lt
gt
eq
ne
le
ge
dump
addint
addnum
subint
subnum
mulint
mulnum
divint
divnum
power
factorial
of
ofend

substring
from
to
into
length
instring
occurence
in
charofint
intofchar
tointeger
tonumber
round
webrep
direct
inport
outport
indirect
call
function
endcall
getkey
getrowcol
get
getpassword
cascade
declare
and
setvideomode
text
graph
gotorowcol
is
drop
absolute
addconst
default
notnull
check
maybe
apowerx
avg
character
cnt
directly
convertcase
copyfile

decode
del
deletefile
dropconst
unique
emptyfile
greater
initcap
leftpad
upto
with
lefttrim
lesser
max
min
polynomial
power
replace
rightpad
righttrim
sum
tolower
toupper
varsize
rightpad
righttrim
at
putmat
getmat
delmat
filesize
toascii
tovalue
testit
convert
command.dbm
source.tmp
datafile.dat
csv
wsv
administer
let
system
manager
username
password
change

passwords
to
specify
drop
dropall
increment
decrement
fileopen
curdri
status
setdisk
decrec
selectall
display
selectif
applylogic
electrec
recnums
recstats
daysbet
dateat
dayat
dateform
timesbet
timestamp
splittimestamp
initcap
convertcase
toupper
tolower
varsize
lefttrim
righttrim
leftpad
rightpad
replace
character
decode
absolute
min
max
cnt
unique
del
recnums
recstats
convertdate

converttime

*

addintq.rmf
declare somex somey somez endst
begin
storeval somex eq +987654321 endst
storeval somey eq +123456789 endst
dump somez eq addint of somex somey ofend endst
message anyvar somez endst
storeval somex eq +987654321 endst
storeval somey eq -123456789 endst
dump somez eq addint of somex somey ofend endst
message anyvar somez endst
storeval somex eq -987654321 endst
storeval somey eq +123456789 endst
dump somez eq addint of somex somey ofend endst
message anyvar somez endst
storeval somex eq -987654321 endst
storeval somey eq -123456789 endst
dump somez eq addint of somex somey ofend endst
message anyvar somez endst
end

*

```
handles.c
#include<stdio.h>
main()
{
char *path="";
/* file handles */
int countx=0xffffff;
printf("62280 file handles are ready for your programming!!!\n",countx);
asm mov ah,67h;
asm mov bx,countx;
asm int 21h;
asm mov ax,4c00h;
asm int 21h;
}
```


*

```
mml.c
/* Multi-machine Multi-user Language(MML) */
#include<stdio.h>
#include<conio.h>
#include<stdlib.h>
```

```c
#include<string.h>
#include<dos.h>
#include<graphics.h>
#include<time.h>
#include<dir.h>
/* --------------- global declarations -------------- */
FILE huge *fpt,*fpt1,*fpt2,*fpt3,*fpt5,*fpt9,
            *fpt10,*fpt11,*fpt12,*fpt14,*fpt15;
    /* ------------------------------------------------------------------ */
time_t t;
char *complement(char *);
char *addint(char *,char *);
char *addnum(char *,char *);
char *subint(char *,char *);
char *subnum(char *,char *);
char *mulint2(void);
char *divint2(void);
char *substring(char *,int,int);
char *varcompare();
char *varappend();
int *strcomp(char *,char *);
int *fpt3myfputs(char *,FILE *);
char *increment_bucket();
char *decrement_bucket();
char *timeit(char *);
void convert_date(void);
void convert_time(void);
char ch,tim[9],date2[9],date[11],time2[12],st[41],fname[12],fname2[12],
    sign,sign3,curpos[81],logic[6][41];
int a,b,c,d,e,f,g,h,i,j,k,l,m,n,o,p,q,r,s,u,v,w,x,y,z,*addr;
int io,co,ip,dp,ts,kkk,day2,mon2;
struct comm{char command[81];};struct comm com;
char vars1[101][81],vars2[101][81],str2[101][81],str3[101][81],\
    res[81],filename[81],*twodarr[81],*mat,checkarr[31][81],curr_bucket[13];
int var[101],labelvar[101][81],flag[101],count[101],currdisk,drivenum,*diadd;
long int lfpt[101],li,li1,li2,li3,ri,place,place1,place2,place3,liq,lir,lis,lit,liu,liv;
int ESCAPE=1,UPARROW=72,DNARROW=80,drive=2;
union REGS regs;struct SREGS segregs;struct REGPACK reg;
int gdriver=DETECT,grmode,errorcode;
int midx,midy,radius=100;
char sign,ch,date1[11],/*date2[11],*/st1[11],st2[11],st3[11],d1[11],d2[11],
                                st4[11],st5[11],st6[11],s1[11],s2[11];
int mon,dummy,day1,day2,mon1,mon2,yea1,yea2,days;
char
sign,ch,ch1,ch2,str1[11],str2a[11],date1[11],/*date2[11],*/st1[11],st2[11],st3[11],
st4[11],st5[11],st6[11],d1[11],d2[11],year[11],yea2a[11],mon2a[11],day2a[11];
int days,mons,yea,mon,day,days1,days2,currdisk,prevdisk,nextdisk,created;
```

```c
char sign,ch,date1[11],/*date2[11],*/st1[11],st2[11],st3[11],d1[11],d2[11],
st4[11],st5[11],st6[11],s1[11],s2[11],timestamp[31],today[11],weekday[11];
int u,num1,totday,curday,mon,dummy,day1,day2,mon1,mon2,yea1,yea2,days;
char form1[81],form2[81],cent[81],cent2[81];
char dd[12],mm[12],yy[12],mon3[12],yyyy[12],number[5],namepart[5];
long double doub1,doub2,doub3,sum,diff,prod,divres,power;
long int lin1,lint2,lint3;
char str[81],fname1[13],fnameprior[13];
time_t t;
/* ----------------------------------------------- */
main(int argc,char *argv[])
{
/* Prior to this programme,the handles programme must be run */
mountall();
currdisk=drivenum=2;
ri=0;
var[50]=0;
fflush(stdin);
strcpy(fname,argv[1]);
strcpy(fname2,fname);
/*clrscr();*/
i=0;flag[13]=0;
fpt=fopen(fname2,"r+");
if(fpt==NULL){
printf("CBL file not opened.Exiting...");
getch();
exit(1);
}
fpt1=fopen("command.dbm","wb+");
while(fscanf(fpt,"%s",com.command)!=EOF){
if(strcmp(com.command,"execute")==0){
fscanf(fpt,"%s",com.command);
fpt2=fopen("source.tmp","r+");
while(fscanf(fpt2,"%s",com.command)!=EOF){
fwrite(&com.command,sizeof(com.command),1,fpt1);
}
fclose(fpt2);
fscanf(fpt,"%s",com.command);
fscanf(fpt,"%s",com.command);
}
fwrite(&com.command,sizeof(com.command),1,fpt1);
}
rewind(fpt1);
fpt5=fopen("report.htm","w+");
fpt10=fopen("temp.dat","w+");
fpt14=fopen("constrai.var","r+");
if(fpt14==NULL)fpt14=fopen("constrai.var","w+");
```

```c
nullifyvars();
strcpy(vars1[0],"dummy");strcpy(vars2[0],"tummy");
/*i=0;*/flag[100]=0;kkk=0;flag[56]=0;
beg:
/*putchar('\n');*/
for( ;!feof(fpt1);i++){
for(j=0;j<=101;j++)nullify(str2[j]);
for(j=0;j<=101;j++)nullify(str3[j]);
if(flag[100]==1){fread(&com.command,sizeof(com.command),1,fpt1);}
fread(&com.command,sizeof(com.command),1,fpt1);
/*printf("-%s-",com.command);*/
if(strcmp(com.command,"begin")==0){goto end;}
/* ---------------------------------------------------- */
else if(strcmp(com.command,"comment")==0){
while(fread(&com.command,sizeof(com.command),1,fpt1)==1){
if(strcmp(com.command,"endst")==0){goto end;}
}
}
/* ---------------------------------------------------- */
else if(strcmp(com.command,"message")==0){
fread(&com.command,sizeof(com.command),1,fpt1);
    if(strcmp(com.command,"cat")==0){
fread(&com.command,sizeof(com.command),1,fpt1);
while(strcmp(com.command,"endcat")!=0)
{
printf("%s ",com.command);
fread(&com.command,sizeof(com.command),1,fpt1);
}
}
else if(strcmp(com.command,"line")==0){putchar('\n');}
else if(strcmp(com.command,"space")==0){
fread(&com.command,sizeof(com.command),1,fpt1);
for(var[10]=0;var[10]<=atoi(com.command);var[10]++)putchar(' ');
}
else if(strcmp(com.command,"anyval")==0)
{fread(&com.command,sizeof(com.command),1,fpt1);printf("%s
",com.command);}
else if(strcmp(com.command,"anyvar")==0){
fread(&com.command,sizeof(com.command),1,fpt1);
strcpy(str3[50],com.command);varcompare();strcpy(str2[10],str3[52]);
printf("%s ",str2[10]);
}
else if(strcmp(com.command,"tab")==0){}
fread(&com.command,sizeof(com.command),1,fpt1);
goto end;
}
/* ---------------------------------------------------- */
```

```c
else if(strcmp(com.command,"get")==0){
fread(&com.command,sizeof(com.command),1,fpt1);
strcpy(str2[0],com.command);
gets(str2[1]);
if(strcmp(str2[1],"\0")==0)strcpy(str2[1],"NIL");
strcpy(str3[56],str2[0]);strcpy(str3[58],str2[1]);varappend();
fread(&com.command,sizeof(com.command),1,fpt1);
goto end;
}
/* ------------------------------------------------------ */
else if(strcmp(com.command,"getpassword")==0){
fread(&com.command,sizeof(com.command),1,fpt1);
strcpy(str2[61],com.command);
for(k=0;(ch=getch())!=13;k++)str2[62][k]=ch;str2[62][k]='\0';
if(strcmp(str2[62],"\0")==0)strcpy(str2[62],"NIL");
strcpy(str3[56],str2[61]);strcpy(str3[58],str2[62]);varappend();
fread(&com.command,sizeof(com.command),1,fpt1);
goto end;
}
/* ------------------------------------------------------ */
else if(strcmp(com.command,"storeval")==0){
k=0;
fread(&com.command,sizeof(com.command),1,fpt1);
strcpy(str2[0],com.command);
fread(&com.command,sizeof(com.command),1,fpt1); /* eq */
while(1){
fread(&com.command,sizeof(com.command),1,fpt1);
if(strcmp(com.command,"char")==0){
strcpy(str2[1],"\0");
while(1){
fread(&com.command,sizeof(com.command),1,fpt1);
strcpy(str2[2],com.command);
if(strcmp(com.command,"endchar")==0){
if(k<=0)strcpy(str2[1],"NIL");
else str2[1][strlen(str2[1])-1]='\0';
goto label999;
}
else {
++k;
strcat(str2[1],str2[2]);
strcat(str2[1]," ");
}
}
}
else {strcpy(str2[1],com.command);goto label999;}
}
label999:
```

```
strcpy(str3[56],str2[0]);strcpy(str3[58],str2[1]);varappend();
fread(&com.command,sizeof(com.command),1,fpt1);
goto end;
}
/* ---------------------------------------------------- */
else if(strcmp(com.command,"storevar")==0){
fread(&com.command,sizeof(com.command),1,fpt1);
strcpy(str2[10],com.command);
fread(&com.command,sizeof(com.command),1,fpt1);
fread(&com.command,sizeof(com.command),1,fpt1);
strcpy(str2[1],com.command);
strcpy(str3[50],str2[1]);varcompare();strcpy(str2[19],str3[52]);
strcpy(str3[56],str2[10]);strcpy(str3[58],str2[19]);varappend();
fread(&com.command,sizeof(com.command),1,fpt1);
goto end;
}
/* ---------------------------------------------------- */
else if(strcmp(com.command,"goto")==0){
fread(&com.command,sizeof(com.command),1,fpt1);
strcpy(labelvar[var[3]],com.command);
rewind(fpt1);
for(i=0;!feof(fpt1);i++){
fread(&com.command,sizeof(com.command),1,fpt1);
if(strcmp(com.command,"labelit")==0){
fread(&com.command,sizeof(com.command),1,fpt1);
if(strcmp(com.command,labelvar[var[3]])==0)goto end;
}
}
goto end;
}
/* ------------------------------------------------------- */
else if(strcmp(com.command,"if")==0){
flag[0]=0;
fread(&com.command,sizeof(com.command),1,fpt1);
strcpy(str2[0],com.command);
fread(&com.command,sizeof(com.command),1,fpt1);
strcpy(str2[1],com.command);
fread(&com.command,sizeof(com.command),1,fpt1);
strcpy(str2[2],com.command);
fread(&com.command,sizeof(com.command),1,fpt1);
fread(&com.command,sizeof(com.command),1,fpt1);
strcpy(str2[3],com.command);
strcpy(str3[50],str2[0]);varcompare();strcpy(str3[2],str3[52]);
strcpy(str3[50],str2[2]);varcompare();strcpy(str3[12],str3[52]);
if(strcmp(str2[1],"gt")==0){
if(str3[2][0]=='+'&&str3[12][0]=='+'){
flag[1]=0;
```

```
for(k=0;str3[2][k]!='\0';k++)if(str3[2][k]=='.'){flag[1]=1;break;}
flag[2]=0;
for(y=0;str3[12][y]!='\0';y++)if(str3[12][y]=='.'){flag[2]=1;break;}
if(flag[1]==1&&flag[2]==1){
if(k==y){if(strcmp(str3[2],str3[12])>0)flag[0]=1;}
else if(k>y)flag[0]=1;
else flag[0]=0;
}
else if(flag[1]==0&&flag[2]==0){
if(strcomp(str3[2],str3[12])==+1)flag[0]=1;
else flag[0]=0;
}
}
else if(str3[2][0]=='-'&&str3[12][0]=='-'){
flag[1]=0;
for(k=0;str3[2][k]!='\0';k++)if(str3[2][k]=='.'){flag[1]=1;break;}
flag[2]=0;
for(y=0;str3[12][y]!='\0';y++)if(str3[12][y]=='.'){flag[2]=1;break;}
if(flag[1]==1&&flag[2]==1){
if(k==y){if(strcmp(str3[2],str3[12])<0)flag[0]=1;}
else if(k<y)flag[0]=1;
else flag[0]=0;
}
else if(flag[1]==0&&flag[2]==0){
if(strcomp(str3[2],str3[12])==-1)flag[0]=1;
else flag[0]=0;
}
}
else if(str3[2][0]=='+'&&str3[12][0]=='-'){
flag[0]=1;
}
else if(str3[2][0]=='-'&&str3[12][0]=='+'){
flag[0]=0;
}
else if(strcmp(str3[2],str3[12])>0)flag[0]=1;
}
else if(strcmp(str2[1],"lt")==0){
if(str3[2][0]=='+'&&str3[12][0]=='+'){
flag[1]=0;
for(k=0;str3[2][k]!='\0';k++)if(str3[2][k]=='.'){flag[1]=1;break;}
flag[2]=0;
for(y=0;str3[12][y]!='\0';y++)if(str3[12][y]=='.'){flag[2]=1;break;}
if(flag[1]==1&&flag[2]==1){
if(k==y){if(strcmp(str3[2],str3[12])<0)flag[0]=1;}
else if(k<y)flag[0]=1;
else flag[0]=0;
}
```

```c
else if(flag[1]==0&&flag[2]==0){
if(strcomp(str3[2],str3[12])==-1)flag[0]=1;
else flag[0]=0;
}
}
else if(str3[2][0]=='-'&&str3[12][0]=='-'){
flag[1]=0;
for(k=0;str3[2][k]!='\0';k++)if(str3[2][k]=='.'){flag[1]=1;break;}
flag[2]=0;
for(y=0;str3[12][y]!='\0';y++)if(str3[12][y]=='.'){flag[2]=1;break;}
if(flag[1]==1&&flag[2]==1){
if(k==y){if(strcmp(str3[2],str3[12])>0)flag[0]=1;}
else if(k>y)flag[0]=1;
else flag[0]=0;
}
else if(flag[1]==0&&flag[2]==0){
if(strcomp(str3[2],str3[12])==+1)flag[0]=1;
else flag[0]=0;
}
}
else if(str3[2][0]=='+'&&str3[12][0]=='-'){
flag[0]=0;
}
else if(str3[2][0]=='-'&&str3[12][0]=='+'){
flag[0]=1;
}
else if(strcmp(str3[2],str3[12])<0)flag[0]=1;
}
else if(strcmp(str2[1],"eq")==0){
if(strcmp(str3[2],str3[12])==0)flag[0]=1;
}
else if(strcmp(str2[1],"ge")==0){
if(str3[2][0]=='+'&&str3[12][0]=='+'){
flag[1]=0;
for(k=0;str3[2][k]!='\0';k++)if(str3[2][k]=='.'){flag[1]=1;break;}
flag[2]=0;
for(y=0;str3[12][y]!='\0';y++)if(str3[12][y]=='.'){flag[2]=1;break;}
if(flag[1]==1&&flag[2]==1){
if(k==y){if(strcmp(str3[2],str3[12])>=0)flag[0]=1;}
else if(k>y)flag[0]=1;
else flag[0]=0;
}
else if(flag[1]==0&&flag[2]==0){
if(strcomp(str3[2],str3[12])==1||strcomp(str3[2],str3[12])==0)flag[0]=1;
else flag[0]=0;
}
}
}
```

```c
else if(str3[2][0]=='-'&&str3[12][0]=='-'){
flag[1]=0;
for(k=0;str3[2][k]!='\0';k++)if(str3[2][k]=='.'){flag[1]=1;break;}
flag[2]=0;
for(y=0;str3[12][y]!='\0';y++)if(str3[12][y]=='.'){flag[2]=1;break;}
if(flag[1]==1&&flag[2]==1){
if(k==y){if(strcmp(str3[2],str3[12])<=0)flag[0]=1;}
else if(k<y)flag[0]=1;
else flag[0]=0;
}
else if(flag[1]==0&&flag[2]==0){
if(strcomp(str3[2],str3[12])==-1||strcomp(str3[2],str3[12])==0)flag[0]=1;
else flag[0]=0;
}
}
else if(str3[2][0]=='+'&&str3[12][0]=='-'){
flag[0]=1;
}
else if(str3[2][0]=='-'&&str3[12][0]=='+'){
flag[0]=0;
}
else if(strcmp(str3[2],str3[12])>=0)flag[0]=1;
}
else if(strcmp(str2[1],"le")==0){
if(str3[2][0]=='+'&&str3[12][0]=='+'){
flag[1]=0;
for(k=0;str3[2][k]!='\0';k++)if(str3[2][k]=='.'){flag[1]=1;break;}
flag[2]=0;
for(y=0;str3[12][y]!='\0';y++)if(str3[12][y]=='.'){flag[2]=1;break;}
if(flag[1]==1&&flag[2]==1){
if(k==y){if(strcmp(str3[2],str3[12])<=0)flag[0]=1;}
else if(k<y)flag[0]=1;
else flag[0]=0;
}
else if(flag[1]==0&&flag[2]==0){
if(strcomp(str3[2],str3[12])==-1||strcomp(str3[2],str3[12])==0)flag[0]=1;
else flag[0]=0;
}
}
else if(str3[2][0]=='-'&&str3[12][0]=='-'){
flag[1]=0;
for(k=0;str3[2][k]!='\0';k++)if(str3[2][k]=='.'){flag[1]=1;break;}
flag[2]=0;
for(y=0;str3[12][y]!='\0';y++)if(str3[12][y]=='.'){flag[2]=1;break;}
if(flag[1]==1&&flag[2]==1){
if(k==y){if(strcmp(str3[2],str3[12])>=0)flag[0]=1;}
else if(k>y)flag[0]=1;
```

```c
else flag[0]=0;
}
else if(flag[1]==0&&flag[2]==0){
if(strcomp(str3[2],str3[12])==1||strcomp(str3[2],str3[12])==0)flag[0]=1;
else flag[0]=0;
}
}
else if(str3[2][0]=='+'&&str3[12][0]=='-'){
flag[0]=0;
}
else if(str3[2][0]=='-'&&str3[12][0]=='+'){
flag[0]=1;
}
else if(strcmp(str3[2],str3[12])<=0)flag[0]=1;
}
else if(strcmp(str2[1],"ne")==0){
if(strcmp(str3[2],str3[12])!=0)flag[0]=1;
}
if(flag[0]==1){goto end;}
else if(flag[0]==0){
while(!feof(fpt1)){
fread(&com.command,sizeof(com.command),1,fpt1);
strcpy(str2[4],com.command);
if(strcmp(com.command,"endif")==0){
fread(&com.command,sizeof(com.command),1,fpt1);
if(strcmp(com.command,str2[3])==0)goto end;
}
}
}
}
/* ----------------------------------------------------------- */
else if(strcmp(com.command,"writefile")==0){
fread(&com.command,sizeof(com.command),1,fpt1);
strcpy(str2[77],com.command);
fread(&com.command,sizeof(com.command),1,fpt1);
fread(&com.command,sizeof(com.command),1,fpt1);
strcpy(str2[78],com.command);
strcpy(str3[50],str2[77]);varcompare();strcpy(str2[67],str3[52]);
strcpy(str3[50],str2[78]);varcompare();strcpy(str2[68],str3[52]);
fclose(fpt10);
fpt10=fopen(str2[68],"a+");
if(fpt10==NULL)fpt10=fopen(str2[68],"w+");
if(str2[67][0]=='#'){
str2[67][0]='+';
/*fprintf(fpt10,"%c",atoi(str2[67]));*/putc(atoi(str2[67]),fpt10);
str2[67][0]='#';
}
```

```
else /*fprintf(fpt10,"%s",str2[67]);*/putc(str2[67][0],fpt10);
fread(&com.command,sizeof(com.command),1,fpt1);
goto end;
}
/* ---------------------------------------------------------- */
else if(strcmp(com.command,"readfile")==0){
fread(&com.command,sizeof(com.command),1,fpt1);
strcpy(str2[77],com.command);
fread(&com.command,sizeof(com.command),1,fpt1);
fread(&com.command,sizeof(com.command),1,fpt1);
strcpy(str2[78],com.command);
if(flag[56]==1)goto label11211;
/*strcpy(str3[50],str2[77]);varcompare();strcpy(str2[67],str3[52]);*/
strcpy(str3[50],str2[78]);varcompare();strcpy(str2[68],str3[52]);
fclose(fpt10);
fpt10=fopen(str2[68],"r+");
fseek(fpt10,ri,SEEK_SET);
/*
k=0;
while((ch=getc(fpt10))!='\n'&&ch!=EOF)
{str2[69][k++]=ch;str2[69][k]='\0';}
*/
ch=getc(fpt10);
str2[69][0]=ch;str2[69][1]='\0';
ri=ftell(fpt10);
if(ch==EOF)flag[56]=1;
strcpy(str3[56],str2[77]);strcpy(str3[58],str2[69]);varappend();
goto label11212;
label11211:
strcpy(str2[69],"EOF");
strcpy(str3[56],str2[77]);strcpy(str3[58],str2[69]);varappend();
label11212:
fread(&com.command,sizeof(com.command),1,fpt1);
goto end;
}
/* ---------------------------------------------------------- */
else if(strcmp(com.command,"fileseek")==0){
fread(&com.command,sizeof(com.command),1,fpt1); /* filename */
strcpy(str2[51],com.command);
strcpy(str3[50],str2[51]);varcompare();strcpy(str2[61],str3[52]);
fclose(fpt10);
fpt10=fopen(str2[61],"r+");
fread(&com.command,sizeof(com.command),1,fpt1); /* for */
/* begining,ending,back,forth */
fread(&com.command,sizeof(com.command),1,fpt1);
if(strcmp(com.command,"begining")==0){
fseek(fpt10,0L,SEEK_SET);
```

```c
}
else if(strcmp(com.command,"ending")==0){
fseek(fpt10,0L,SEEK_END);
}
if(strcmp(com.command,"back")==0){
fseek(fpt10,ri,SEEK_SET);fseek(fpt10,-1L,SEEK_CUR);
}
if(strcmp(com.command,"forth")==0){
fseek(fpt10,ri,SEEK_SET);fseek(fpt10,1L,SEEK_CUR);
}
ri=ftell(fpt10);
fread(&com.command,sizeof(com.command),1,fpt1);
goto end;
}
/* ----------------------------------------------------------- */
else if(strcmp(com.command,"fileopen")==0){
fread(&com.command,sizeof(com.command),1,fpt1); /* filename */
strcpy(str2[51],com.command);
strcpy(str3[50],str2[51]);varcompare();strcpy(str2[61],str3[52]);
fpt10=fopen(str2[61],"r+");
if(fpt10==NULL)fpt10=fopen(str2[61],"w+");
fread(&com.command,sizeof(com.command),1,fpt1);
goto end;
}
/* ----------------------------------------------------------- */
else if(strcmp(com.command,"fileclose")==0){
fread(&com.command,sizeof(com.command),1,fpt1); /* filename */
strcpy(str2[51],com.command);
strcpy(str3[50],str2[51]);varcompare();strcpy(str2[61],str3[52]);
fclose(fpt10);
fread(&com.command,sizeof(com.command),1,fpt1);
goto end;
}
/* ----------------------------------------------------------- */
else if(strcmp(com.command,"filetell")==0){
fread(&com.command,sizeof(com.command),1,fpt1); /* filename */
strcpy(str2[51],com.command);
strcpy(str3[50],str2[51]);varcompare();strcpy(str2[61],str3[52]);
fread(&com.command,sizeof(com.command),1,fpt1); /* into */
fread(&com.command,sizeof(com.command),1,fpt1); /* somelong */
strcpy(str2[52],com.command);
fclose(fpt10);
fpt10=fopen(str2[61],"r+");
fseek(fpt10,ri,SEEK_SET);
ri=ftell(fpt10);
sprintf(str2[77],"%li",ri);
str2[76][0]='+';
```

```c
strcat(str2[76],str2[77]);
strcpy(str3[56],str2[52]);strcpy(str3[58],str2[76]);varappend();
fread(&com.command,sizeof(com.command),1,fpt1);
goto end;
}
/* ------------------------------------------------------------ */
else if(strcmp(com.command,"open")==0){
fclose(fpt3);flag[20]=0;
fread(&com.command,sizeof(com.command),1,fpt1);
strcpy(str2[50],com.command);
strcpy(str3[50],str2[50]);varcompare();strcpy(str2[0],str3[52]);
fread(&com.command,sizeof(com.command),1,fpt1);
fread(&com.command,sizeof(com.command),1,fpt1);
strcpy(str2[91],com.command);
fread(&com.command,sizeof(com.command),1,fpt1);
fread(&com.command,sizeof(com.command),1,fpt1);
strcpy(str2[55],com.command);
strcpy(str3[50],str2[55]);varcompare( );strcpy(str2[65],str3[52]);
fread(&com.command,sizeof(com.command),1,fpt1);
strcpy(str2[86],com.command);
currdisk=drivenum;
if(strcmp(str2[91],"fresh")==0){
fpt3=fopen(str2[0],"w+");
if(fpt3==NULL)strcpy(str2[87],"notopened");
else strcpy(str2[87],"opened");
flag[20]=1;
}
else if(strcmp(str2[91],"writeread")==0){
fpt3=fopen(str2[0],"r+");
if(fpt3==NULL)strcpy(str2[87],"notopened");
else strcpy(str2[87],"opened");
flag[20]=2;
}
strcpy(filename,str2[0]);
place=ftell(fpt3);
sprintf(str2[96],"%i",drivenum);
str2[97][0]='+';
strcat(str2[97],str2[96]);
strcpy(str3[56],str2[55]);strcpy(str3[58],str2[97]);varappend();
strcpy(str3[56],str2[86]);strcpy(str3[58],str2[87]);varappend();
fread(&com.command,sizeof(com.command),1,fpt1);
goto end;
}
/* ------------------------------------------------------------ */
else if(strcmp(com.command,"insert")==0){
fread(&com.command,sizeof(com.command),1,fpt1);
strcpy(str2[1],com.command);
```

```c
strcpy(str3[50],str2[1]);varcompare();strcpy(str2[31],str3[52]);
fclose(fpt3);
fpt3=fopen(filename,"r+");
fseek(fpt3,0L,SEEK_END);
myfputs(str2[31],fpt3);
prasan9:
place=ftell(fpt3);
fread(&com.command,sizeof(com.command),1,fpt1);
goto end;
}
/* -------------------------------------------------------- */
else if(strcmp(com.command,"read")==0){
fread(&com.command,sizeof(com.command),1,fpt1);
strcpy(str2[51],com.command);
fclose(fpt3);
fpt3=fopen(filename,"r+");
fseek(fpt3,place,SEEK_SET);
myfgets(str2[14],fpt3);if(feof(fpt3))goto prasanna12;
place=ftell(fpt3);
prasanna12:
if(strcmp(str2[14],"\0")==0){
fread(&com.command,sizeof(com.command),1,fpt1); /* oneofto */
fread(&com.command,sizeof(com.command),1,fpt1);  /* labelname */
strcpy(labelvar[var[4]],com.command);
rewind(fpt1);
for(i=0;!feof(fpt1);i++){
fread(&com.command,sizeof(com.command),1,fpt1);
if(strcmp(com.command,"labelit")==0){
fread(&com.command,sizeof(com.command),1,fpt1);
if(strcmp(com.command,labelvar[var[4]])==0)goto end;
}
}
}
strcpy(str3[56],str2[51]);strcpy(str3[58],str2[14]);varappend();
fread(&com.command,sizeof(com.command),1,fpt1);
goto end;
}
/* -------------------------------------------------------- */
else if(strcmp(com.command,"fileseek2")==0){
fread(&com.command,sizeof(com.command),1,fpt1);
strcpy(str2[1],com.command);
strcpy(str3[50],str2[1]);varcompare();strcpy(str2[31],str3[52]);
fclose(fpt3);
fpt3=fopen(filename,"r+");
lfpt[2]=atol(str2[31]);
if(lfpt[2]==0)goto gvnr1;
lfpt[1]=0;
```

```c
while(1){
myfgets(str2[33],fpt3);if(feof(fpt3))break;
++lfpt[1];
if(lfpt[1]>=lfpt[2])break;
}
gvnr1:
place=ftell(fpt3);
fread(&com.command,sizeof(com.command),1,fpt1);
goto end;
}
/* ---------------------------------------------------------- */
else if(strcmp(com.command,"filetell2")==0){
fread(&com.command,sizeof(com.command),1,fpt1);
strcpy(str2[1],com.command);
/*place=ftell(fpt3);*/
if(place==0){lfpt[2]=0;goto prasanna11;}
fclose(fpt3);
fpt3=fopen(filename,"r+");
lfpt[2]=0;
while(1){
myfgets(str2[11],fpt3);if(feof(fpt3))break;
lfpt[1]=ftell(fpt3);
++lfpt[2];
if(lfpt[1]==place)break;
}
prasanna11:
sprintf(str3[33],"%li",lfpt[2]);
strcpy(str3[34],"+");strcat(str3[34],str3[33]);
strcpy(str3[56],str2[1]);strcpy(str3[58],str3[34]);varappend();
place=ftell(fpt3);
fread(&com.command,sizeof(com.command),1,fpt1);
goto end;
}
/* ---------------------------------------------------------- */
else if(strcmp(com.command,"longseek")==0){
fread(&com.command,sizeof(com.command),1,fpt1);
strcpy(str2[1],com.command);
strcpy(str3[50],str2[1]);varcompare();strcpy(str2[31],str3[52]);
fclose(fpt3);
fpt3=fopen(filename,"r+");
lfpt[2]=atol(str2[31]);
fseek(fpt3,lfpt[2],SEEK_SET);
place=ftell(fpt3);
fread(&com.command,sizeof(com.command),1,fpt1);
goto end;
}
/* ---------------------------------------------------------- */
```

```c
else if(strcmp(com.command,"longtell")==0){
fread(&com.command,sizeof(com.command),1,fpt1);
strcpy(str2[1],com.command);
lfpt[1]=ftell(fpt3);
sprintf(str3[33],"%li",lfpt[1]);
strcpy(str3[34],"+");strcat(str3[34],str3[33]);
strcpy(str3[56],str2[1]);strcpy(str3[58],str3[34]);varappend();
place=ftell(fpt3);
fread(&com.command,sizeof(com.command),1,fpt1);
goto end;
}
/* -------------------------------------------------------- */
else if(strcmp(com.command,"forward")==0){
fread(&com.command,sizeof(com.command),1,fpt1);
strcpy(str2[0],com.command);
strcpy(str3[50],str2[0]);varcompare();strcpy(str2[1],str3[52]);
fclose(fpt3);
fpt3=fopen(filename,"r+");
fseek(fpt3,place,SEEK_SET);
lfpt[1]=atol(str2[1]);
lfpt[2]=0;
while(1){
myfgets(str2[11],fpt3);
if(feof(fpt3))break;
++lfpt[2];
if(lfpt[2]==lfpt[1])break;
}
place=ftell(fpt3);
fread(&com.command,sizeof(com.command),1,fpt1);
goto end;
}
/* -------------------------------------------------------- */
else if(strcmp(com.command,"gofor")==0){
fread(&com.command,sizeof(com.command),1,fpt1);
   if(strcmp(com.command,"begining")==0)
{
fseek(fpt3,0L,SEEK_SET);
}
place=ftell(fpt3);
fread(&com.command,sizeof(com.command),1,fpt1);
goto end;
}
/* -------------------------------------------------------- */
else if(strcmp(com.command,"increment")==0){
fread(&com.command,sizeof(com.command),1,fpt1);
strcpy(str3[41],com.command);
strcpy(str3[50],str3[41]);varcompare();strcpy(str3[51],str3[52]);
```

```
strcpy(curr_bucket,str3[51]);
strcpy(str3[61],increment_bucket());
strcpy(str3[56],str3[41]);strcpy(str3[58],str3[61]);varappend();
fread(&com.command,sizeof(com.command),1,fpt1);
goto end;
}
/* ------------------------------------------------------------ */
else if(strcmp(com.command,"decrement")==0){
fread(&com.command,sizeof(com.command),1,fpt1);
strcpy(str3[41],com.command);
strcpy(str3[50],str3[41]);varcompare();strcpy(str3[51],str3[52]);
strcpy(curr_bucket,str3[51]);
strcpy(str3[61],decrement_bucket());
strcpy(str3[56],str3[41]);strcpy(str3[58],str3[61]);varappend();
fread(&com.command,sizeof(com.command),1,fpt1);
goto end;
}
/* ------------------------------------------------------------ */
else if(strcmp(com.command,"filesize")==0){
fread(&com.command,sizeof(com.command),1,fpt1);
fread(&com.command,sizeof(com.command),1,fpt1);
strcpy(str2[51],com.command);
strcpy(str3[50],str2[51]);varcompare();strcpy(str2[61],str3[52]);
fread(&com.command,sizeof(com.command),1,fpt1);
fread(&com.command,sizeof(com.command),1,fpt1);
strcpy(str2[52],com.command);
strcpy(str3[50],str2[51]);varcompare();strcpy(str2[61],str3[52]);
fclose(fpt15);
fpt15=fopen(str2[61],"r+");
if(fpt15==NULL)goto end2;
fseek(fpt15,0L,SEEK_END);
li3=ftell(fpt15);
sprintf(str2[62],"%li",li3);
str2[63][0]='+';
strcat(str2[63],str2[62]);
strcpy(str3[56],str2[52]);strcpy(str3[58],str2[63]);varappend();
fclose(fpt15);
fread(&com.command,sizeof(com.command),1,fpt1);
goto end;
}
/* ------------------------------------------------------------ */
else if(strcmp(com.command,"setdisk")==0){
fread(&com.command,sizeof(com.command),1,fpt1); /* disknumber */
strcpy(str2[51],com.command);
strcpy(str3[50],str2[51]);varcompare();strcpy(str2[61],str3[52]);
setdisk(atoi(str2[61]));
drivenum=atoi(str2[61]);
```

```c
fread(&com.command,sizeof(com.command),1,fpt1);
goto end;
}
/* -------------------------------------------------------- */
else if(strcmp(com.command,"dump")==0){
fread(&com.command,sizeof(com.command),1,fpt1);
strcpy(str2[13],com.command);
fread(&com.command,sizeof(com.command),1,fpt1); /* eq */
fread(&com.command,sizeof(com.command),1,fpt1);
    if(strcmp(com.command,"addint")==0){
fread(&com.command,sizeof(com.command),1,fpt1);/* of */
fread(&com.command,sizeof(com.command),1,fpt1);
strcpy(str2[10],com.command);
strcpy(str3[50],str2[10]);varcompare();strcpy(str2[1],str3[52]);
strcpy(str3[1],str2[1]);
fread(&com.command,sizeof(com.command),1,fpt1);
strcpy(str2[10],com.command);
strcpy(str3[50],str2[10]);varcompare();strcpy(str2[1],str3[52]);
strcpy(str3[2],str2[1]);
strcpy(str2[101],str3[1]);intlesstomore();strcpy(str2[1],str2[100]);
strcpy(str2[101],str3[2]);intlesstomore();strcpy(str2[2],str2[100]);
strcpy(str2[14],addint(str2[1],str2[2]));
strcpy(str2[101],str2[14]);intmoretoless();strcpy(str2[24],str2[100]);
strcpy(str3[56],str2[13]);strcpy(str3[58],str2[24]);varappend();
fread(&com.command,sizeof(com.command),1,fpt1); /* ofend */
fread(&com.command,sizeof(com.command),1,fpt1);
goto end;
}
else if(strcmp(com.command,"addnum")==0){
fread(&com.command,sizeof(com.command),1,fpt1);/* of */
fread(&com.command,sizeof(com.command),1,fpt1);
strcpy(str2[10],com.command);
strcpy(str3[50],str2[10]);varcompare();strcpy(str2[1],str3[52]);
strcpy(str3[1],str2[1]);
fread(&com.command,sizeof(com.command),1,fpt1);
strcpy(str2[10],com.command);
strcpy(str3[50],str2[10]);varcompare();strcpy(str2[1],str3[52]);
strcpy(str3[2],str2[1]);
if(strcmp(str3[1],"+0.0")==0)
{strcpy(str2[14],str3[2]);goto label101010;}
else if(strcmp(str3[1],"-0.0")==0)
{strcpy(str2[14],str3[2]);goto label101010;}
else if(strcmp(str3[2],"+0.0")==0)
{strcpy(str2[14],str3[1]);goto label101010;}
else if(strcmp(str3[2],"-0.0")==0)
{strcpy(str2[14],str3[1]);goto label101010;}
strcpy(str2[101],str3[1]);numlesstomore();strcpy(str2[1],str2[100]);
```

```
strcpy(str2[101],str3[2]);numlesstomore();strcpy(str2[2],str2[100]);
strcpy(str2[14],addnum(str2[1],str2[2]));
strcpy(str2[101],str2[14]);nummoretoless();strcpy(str2[99],str2[100]);
strcpy(str3[56],str2[13]);strcpy(str3[58],str2[99]);varappend();
goto label101020;
label101010:
strcpy(str3[56],str2[13]);strcpy(str3[58],str2[14]);varappend();
label101020:
fread(&com.command,sizeof(com.command),1,fpt1); /* ofend */
fread(&com.command,sizeof(com.command),1,fpt1);
goto end;
}
else if(strcmp(com.command,"subint")==0){
fread(&com.command,sizeof(com.command),1,fpt1);/* of */
fread(&com.command,sizeof(com.command),1,fpt1);
strcpy(str2[10],com.command);
strcpy(str3[50],str2[10]);varcompare();strcpy(str2[1],str3[52]);
strcpy(str3[1],str2[1]);
fread(&com.command,sizeof(com.command),1,fpt1);
strcpy(str2[10],com.command);
strcpy(str3[50],str2[10]);varcompare();strcpy(str2[1],str3[52]);
strcpy(str3[2],str2[1]);
strcpy(str2[101],str3[1]);
intlesstomore();
strcpy(str2[1],str2[100]);
strcpy(str2[101],str3[2]);
intlesstomore();
strcpy(str2[2],str2[100]);
strcpy(str2[14],subint(str2[1],str2[2]));
strcpy(str2[101],str2[14]);intmoretoless();strcpy(str2[99],str2[100]);
strcpy(str3[56],str2[13]);strcpy(str3[58],str2[99]);varappend();
fread(&com.command,sizeof(com.command),1,fpt1); /* ofend */
fread(&com.command,sizeof(com.command),1,fpt1);
goto end;
}
else if(strcmp(com.command,"subnum")==0){
fread(&com.command,sizeof(com.command),1,fpt1);/* of */
fread(&com.command,sizeof(com.command),1,fpt1);
strcpy(str2[10],com.command);
strcpy(str3[50],str2[10]);varcompare();strcpy(str2[1],str3[52]);
strcpy(str3[1],str2[1]);
fread(&com.command,sizeof(com.command),1,fpt1);
strcpy(str2[10],com.command);
strcpy(str3[50],str2[10]);varcompare();strcpy(str2[1],str3[52]);
strcpy(str3[2],str2[1]);
strcpy(str2[101],str3[1]);
numlesstomore();
```

```c
strcpy(str2[1],str2[100]);
strcpy(str2[101],str3[2]);
numlesstomore();
strcpy(str2[2],str2[100]);
strcpy(str2[14],subnum(str2[1],str2[2]));
strcpy(str2[101],str2[14]);nummoretoless();strcpy(str2[99],str2[100]);
strcpy(str3[56],str2[13]);strcpy(str3[58],str2[99]);varappend();
fread(&com.command,sizeof(com.command),1,fpt1); /* ofend */
fread(&com.command,sizeof(com.command),1,fpt1);
goto end;
}
else if(strcmp(com.command,"mulint")==0){
fread(&com.command,sizeof(com.command),1,fpt1);/* of */
fread(&com.command,sizeof(com.command),1,fpt1);
strcpy(str2[10],com.command);
strcpy(str3[50],str2[10]);varcompare();strcpy(str2[1],str3[52]);
strcpy(str3[1],str2[1]);
fread(&com.command,sizeof(com.command),1,fpt1);
strcpy(str2[10],com.command);
strcpy(str3[50],str2[10]);varcompare();strcpy(str2[1],str3[52]);
strcpy(str3[2],str2[1]);
if(str3[1][0]==str3[2][0])sign='+';else sign='-';
if(strcmp(str3[1],"+0")==0&&strcmp(str3[2],"+0")==0)
{strcpy(str2[22],"+0");str2[22][0]=sign;
strcpy(str2[99],str2[22]);goto label123123;}
else if(strcmp(str3[1],"+0")==0&&strcmp(str3[2],"-0")==0)
{strcpy(str2[22],"-0");str2[22][0]=sign;
strcpy(str2[99],str2[22]);goto label123123;}
else if(strcmp(str3[1],"-0")==0&&strcmp(str3[2],"+0")==0)
{strcpy(str2[22],"-0");str2[22][0]=sign;
strcpy(str2[99],str2[22]);goto label123123;}
else if(strcmp(str3[1],"-0")==0&&strcmp(str3[2],"-0")==0)
{strcpy(str2[22],"+0");str2[22][0]=sign;
strcpy(str2[99],str2[22]);goto label123123;}
if(strcmp(str3[1],"+1")==0)
{strcpy(str2[22],str3[2]);str2[22][0]=sign;
strcpy(str2[99],str2[22]);goto label123123;}
else if(strcmp(str3[1],"-1")==0)
{strcpy(str2[22],str3[2]);str2[22][0]=sign;
strcpy(str2[99],str2[22]);goto label123123;}
else if(strcmp(str3[2],"+1")==0)
{strcpy(str2[22],str3[1]);str2[22][0]=sign;
strcpy(str2[99],str2[22]);goto label123123;}
else if(strcmp(str3[2],"-1")==0)
{strcpy(str2[22],str3[1]);str2[22][0]=sign;
strcpy(str2[99],str2[22]);goto label123123;}
strcpy(str2[101],str3[1]);
```

```
intlesstomore();
strcpy(str2[1],str2[100]);
strcpy(str2[101],str3[2]);
intlesstomore();
strcpy(str2[2],str2[100]);
if(str2[1][0]!=str2[2][0])sign='-';else sign='+';
strcpy(str2[31],str2[1]);strcpy(str2[32],str2[2]);
mulint2();
str2[22][0]=sign;str2[22][80]='\0';
strcpy(str2[101],str2[22]);intmoretoless();strcpy(str2[99],str2[100]);
label123123:
strcpy(str3[56],str2[13]);strcpy(str3[58],str2[99]);varappend();
fread(&com.command,sizeof(com.command),1,fpt1); /* ofend */
fread(&com.command,sizeof(com.command),1,fpt1);
goto end;
}
else if(strcmp(com.command,"mulnum")==0){
fread(&com.command,sizeof(com.command),1,fpt1);/* of */
fread(&com.command,sizeof(com.command),1,fpt1);
strcpy(str2[10],com.command);
strcpy(str3[50],str2[10]);varcompare();strcpy(str2[1],str3[52]);
strcpy(str3[1],str2[1]);
fread(&com.command,sizeof(com.command),1,fpt1);
strcpy(str2[10],com.command);
strcpy(str3[50],str2[10]);varcompare();strcpy(str2[1],str3[52]);
strcpy(str3[2],str2[1]);
if(str3[1][0]==str3[2][0])sign='+';
else sign='-';
if(strcmp(str3[1],"+0.0")==0||strcmp(str3[1],"-0.0")==0||\
  strcmp(str3[2],"+0.0")==0||strcmp(str3[2],"-0.0")==0)
  {strcpy(str2[98],"+0.0");str2[98][0]=sign;goto labellab;}
/* ---------------------------------------- */
for(k=0;str3[1][k]!='.';k++)str2[1][k]=str3[1][k];
j=k;++k;
for( ;str3[1][k]!='\0';k++)str2[1][k-1]=str3[1][k];
str2[1][k-1]='\0';
count[1]=k-j-1;
for(k=0;str3[2][k]!='.';k++)str2[2][k]=str3[2][k];
j=k;++k;
for( ;str3[2][k]!='\0';k++)str2[2][k-1]=str3[2][k];
str2[2][k-1]='\0';
count[2]=k-j-1;
/* ---------------------------------------- */
strcpy(str2[101],str2[1]);intlesstomore();strcpy(str3[1],str2[100]);
strcpy(str2[101],str2[2]);intlesstomore();strcpy(str3[2],str2[100]);
/* ---------------------------------------- */
if(str3[1][0]!=str3[2][0])sign='-';else sign='+';
```

```c
str3[1][0]=str3[2][0]='+';
strcpy(str2[31],str3[1]);strcpy(str2[32],str3[2]);
/* ------------------------------------------ */
strcpy(str2[1],str3[1]);strcpy(str2[2],str3[2]);
mulint2();
/* -------------------------------------------------- */
if((count[1]+count[2])>=strlen(str2[22])){
b=0;
for(a=strlen(str2[22])-1;a>=1;a--)
{str2[86][b++]=str2[22][a];}
for(y=0;y<=((count[1]+count[2])-strlen(str2[22]));y++)str2[86][b++]='0';
str2[86][b++]='.';str2[86][b++]='0';
str2[86][b++]=sign;str2[86][b]='\0';
/*printf("%s ",str2[86]);getch();*/
b=0;
for(a=strlen(str2[86])-1;a>=0;a--)str2[92][b++]=str2[86][a];
str2[92][b]='\0';
strcpy(str3[56],str2[13]);strcpy(str3[58],str2[92]);varappend();
goto labellab2;
}
/* -------------------------------------------------- */
t=0;
for(k=strlen(str2[22])-1;k>=0;k--)str2[90][t++]=str2[22][k];
str2[90][t]='\0';
/*printf("%s ",str2[90]);getch();*/
for(k=0;k<count[1]+count[2];k++)str2[91][k]=str2[90][k];
str2[91][k]='.';
for(++k;k<=strlen(str2[90]);k++)str2[91][k]=str2[90][k-1];
str2[91][k]='\0';
/*printf("%s ",str2[91]);getch();*/
t=0;
for(k=strlen(str2[91])-1;k>=0;k--)str2[92][t++]=str2[91][k];
str2[92][t]='\0';
decimate(str2[92],12);
strcpy(str3[56],str2[13]);strcpy(str3[58],str2[92]);varappend();
goto labellab2;
labellab:
for(y=0;str2[98][y]!='\0';y++);
str2[98][y+1]='\0';
str2[98][y]='0';str2[98][--y]='.';str2[98][--y]='0';str2[98][--y]=sign;
strcpy(str2[99],"\0");
str2[99][0]=str2[98][y];
str2[99][1]=str2[98][++y];
str2[99][2]=str2[98][++y];
str2[99][3]=str2[98][++y];
str2[99][4]=str2[98][++y];
decimate(str2[99],12);
```

```
strcpy(str3[56],str2[13]);strcpy(str3[58],str2[99]);varappend();
labellab2:
fread(&com.command,sizeof(com.command),1,fpt1); /* ofend */
fread(&com.command,sizeof(com.command),1,fpt1);
goto end;
}
else if(strcmp(com.command,"divint")==0){
fread(&com.command,sizeof(com.command),1,fpt1);/* of */
fread(&com.command,sizeof(com.command),1,fpt1);
strcpy(str2[10],com.command);
strcpy(str3[50],str2[10]);varcompare();strcpy(str2[1],str3[52]);
strcpy(str3[1],str2[1]);
fread(&com.command,sizeof(com.command),1,fpt1);
strcpy(str2[10],com.command);
strcpy(str3[50],str2[10]);varcompare();strcpy(str2[1],str3[52]);
strcpy(str3[2],str2[1]);
if(str3[1][0]!=str3[2][0])sign='-';else sign='+';
if(strcmp(str3[2],"+1")==0)
{strcpy(str2[99],str3[1]);str2[99][0]=sign;goto labelaxbx2;}
else if(strcmp(str3[2],"-1")==0)
{strcpy(str2[99],str3[1]);str2[99][0]=sign;goto labelaxbx2;}
if(strcmp(str3[2],"+0")==0&&strcmp(str3[1],"+0")==0)
{strcpy(str2[99],"+IND");str2[99][0]=sign;goto labelaxbx2;}
else if(strcmp(str3[2],"+0")==0&&strcmp(str3[1],"-0")==0)
{strcpy(str2[99],"+IND");str2[99][0]=sign;goto labelaxbx2;}
else if(strcmp(str3[2],"-0")==0&&strcmp(str3[1],"+0")==0)
{strcpy(str2[99],"+IND");str2[99][0]=sign;goto labelaxbx2;}
else if(strcmp(str3[2],"-0")==0&&strcmp(str3[1],"-0")==0)
{strcpy(str2[99],"+IND");str2[99][0]=sign;goto labelaxbx2;}
if(strcmp(str3[2],"+0")==0&&strcmp(str3[1],"+0")!=0)
{strcpy(str2[99],"+INF");str2[99][0]=sign;goto labelaxbx2;}
else if(strcmp(str3[2],"+0")==0&&strcmp(str3[1],"-0")!=0)
{strcpy(str2[99],"+INF");str2[99][0]=sign;goto labelaxbx2;}
else if(strcmp(str3[2],"-0")==0&&strcmp(str3[1],"+0")!=0)
{strcpy(str2[99],"+INF");str2[99][0]=sign;goto labelaxbx2;}
else if(strcmp(str3[2],"-0")==0&&strcmp(str3[1],"-0")!=0)
{strcpy(str2[99],"+INF");str2[99][0]=sign;goto labelaxbx2;}
/* ------------------------------------------ */
strcpy(str2[101],str3[1]);intlesstomore();strcpy(str2[1],str2[100]);
strcpy(str2[101],str3[2]);intlesstomore();strcpy(str2[2],str2[100]);
/* ------------------------------------------ */
if(str2[1][0]!=str2[2][0])sign='-';else sign='+';
str2[1][0]=str2[2][0]='+';
strcpy(str2[31],str2[1]);strcpy(str2[32],str2[2]);
/* ------------------------------------------ */
divint2();
labelaxbx:
```

```
strcpy(str2[101],str2[32]);intmoretoless();strcpy(str2[99],str2[100]);
str2[99][0]=sign;/**/
labelaxbx2:
strcpy(str3[56],str2[13]);strcpy(str3[58],str2[99]);varappend();
fread(&com.command,sizeof(com.command),1,fpt1); /* ofend */
fread(&com.command,sizeof(com.command),1,fpt1);
goto end;
}
else if(strcmp(com.command,"divnum")==0){
/* only plus sign is accepted for both */
fread(&com.command,sizeof(com.command),1,fpt1);/* of */
fread(&com.command,sizeof(com.command),1,fpt1);
strcpy(str2[10],com.command);
strcpy(str3[50],str2[10]);varcompare();strcpy(str2[1],str3[52]);
strcpy(str3[1],str2[1]);
fread(&com.command,sizeof(com.command),1,fpt1);
strcpy(str2[11],com.command);
strcpy(str3[50],str2[11]);varcompare();strcpy(str2[2],str3[52]);
strcpy(str3[2],str2[2]);
/*printf("11.%s %s ",str3[1],str3[2]);getch();*/
if(str3[1][0]!=str3[2][0])sign='-';else sign='+';
sign3=sign;
if(strcmp(str3[2],"+1.0")==0)
{strcpy(str2[97],str3[1]);str2[97][0]=sign;goto label54345;}
else if(strcmp(str3[2],"-1.0")==0)
{strcpy(str2[97],str3[1]);str2[97][0]=sign;goto label54345;}
if(strcmp(str3[2],"+0.0")==0&&strcmp(str3[1],"+0.0")==0)
{strcpy(str2[97],"+IND");str2[97][0]=sign;goto label54345;}
else if(strcmp(str3[2],"+0.0")==0&&strcmp(str3[1],"-0.0")==0)
{strcpy(str2[97],"+IND");str2[97][0]=sign;goto label54345;}
else if(strcmp(str3[2],"-0.0")==0&&strcmp(str3[1],"+0.0")==0)
{strcpy(str2[97],"+IND");str2[97][0]=sign;goto label54345;}
else if(strcmp(str3[2],"-0.0")==0&&strcmp(str3[1],"-0.0")==0)
{strcpy(str2[97],"+IND");str2[97][0]=sign;goto label54345;}
if(strcmp(str3[2],"+0.0")==0&&str3[1][0]=='+')
{strcpy(str2[97],"+INF");str2[97][0]=sign;goto label54345;}
else if(strcmp(str3[2],"+0.0")==0&&str3[1][0]=='-')
{strcpy(str2[97],"-INF");str2[97][0]=sign;goto label54345;}
else if(strcmp(str3[2],"-0.0")==0&&str3[1][0]=='+')
{strcpy(str2[97],"-INF");str2[97][0]=sign;goto label54345;}
else if(strcmp(str3[2],"-0.0")==0&&str3[1][0]=='-')
{strcpy(str2[97],"+INF");str2[97][0]=sign;goto label54345;}
if(strcmp(str3[1],"+0.0")==0)
{strcpy(str2[97],"+0.0");str2[97][0]=sign;goto label54345;}
else if(strcmp(str3[1],"-0.0")==0)
{strcpy(str2[97],"-0.0");str2[97][0]=sign;goto label54345;}
/* --------------------------------------------- */
```

```
/* ----------------------------------------- */
for(k=0;str3[1][k]!='.';k++)str2[1][k]=str3[1][k];
j=k;++k;
for( ;str3[1][k]!='\0';k++)str2[1][k-1]=str3[1][k];
str2[1][k-1]='\0';
count[1]=k-j-1;
for(k=0;str3[2][k]!='.';k++)str2[2][k]=str3[2][k];
j=k;++k;
for( ;str3[2][k]!='\0';k++)str2[2][k-1]=str3[2][k];
str2[2][k-1]='\0';
count[2]=k-j-1;
/* ----------------------------------------- */
/*printf(" %i %i ",count[1],count[2]);getch();*/
str2[1][0]='+';str2[2][0]='+';sign='+';
var[7]=0;
g=0;
flag[6]=0;
flag[15]=0;
strcpy(str2[41],str2[1]);
strcpy(str2[42],str2[2]);
u=0;for(t=0;str2[1][t]!='\0';t++)if(str2[1][t]!='.')str2[51][u++]=str2[1][t];
str2[51][u]='\0';
u=0;for(t=0;str2[2][t]!='\0';t++)if(str2[2][t]!='.')str2[52][u++]=str2[2][t];
str2[52][u]='\0';
/*printf("%s %s ",str2[51],str2[52]);getch();*/
strcpy(str2[1],str2[51]);strcpy(str2[2],str2[52]);
strcpy(str2[101],str2[1]);intlesstomore();strcpy(str3[51],str2[100]);
strcpy(str2[101],str2[2]);intlesstomore();strcpy(str3[52],str2[100]);
strcpy(str3[66],str3[51]);
strcpy(str3[67],str3[52]);
strcpy(str2[1],str3[51]);
strcpy(str2[2],str3[52]);
if(strcmp(str2[1],str2[2])<0)flag[6]=1;
divint2();
strcpy(str2[101],str2[32]);intmoretoless();strcpy(str3[37],str2[100]);
strcpy(str2[7],str3[37]);
strcat(str2[7],".");
str3[37][0]='+';
/*strcat(str3[37],".");*/
strcpy(str2[50],str3[37]);
strcpy(str2[101],str2[2]);intmoretoless();strcpy(str3[38],str2[100]);
nagar4:
strcpy(str2[1],str3[38]);
strcpy(str2[2],str3[37]);
/*printf("12.%s %s ",str2[1],str2[2]);getch();*/
mulint2();
strcpy(str2[101],str2[22]);intlesstomore();strcpy(str3[22],str2[100]);
```

```c
strcpy(str2[101],str2[51]);intlesstomore();strcpy(str3[51],str2[100]);
/*printf("13.%s %s ",str3[51],str3[22]);getch();*/
strcpy(str2[45],subint(str3[51],str3[22]));
/*printf("14.%s ",str2[45]);getch();*/
nagar2:
/*printf("new#..%s ",str2[45]);getch();*/
strcpy(str2[101],str2[45]);intmoretoless();strcpy(str2[46],str2[100]);
/*printf("%s ",str2[46]);*/
if(strcmp(str2[46],"+0")==0){
/*printf("%s %s ",str2[51],str2[52]);*/
if(strcmp(str2[51],str2[52])==0){strcpy(str2[97],"+1.0");goto label54345;}
else strcpy(str2[46],"+1");
}
strcat(str2[46],"0");
/*printf("#.%s ",str2[46]);getch();*/
strcpy(str2[101],str2[46]);intlesstomore();strcpy(str2[47],str2[100]);
/*printf(">.%s %s ",str2[47],str3[67]);getch();*/
strcpy(str2[73],str2[47]);
if(strcmp(str2[73],str3[67])<0){
strcpy(str2[45],str2[47]);
strcat(str2[7],"+0");
++g;
goto nagar2;
}
else {
strcpy(str2[1],"+1");
strcpy(str2[3],"+1");
strcpy(str2[101],str2[1]);intlesstomore();strcpy(str2[77],str2[100]);
strcpy(str2[101],str2[3]);intlesstomore();strcpy(str2[78],str2[100]);
nagar3:
strcpy(str2[2],str3[67]);
mulint2();
strcpy(str2[101],str2[22]);intlesstomore();strcpy(str2[48],str2[100]);
/*printf("15.%s %s ",str2[73],str2[48]);getch();*/
if(strcmp(str2[48],str2[73])<0){
strcpy(str2[49],addint(str2[77],str2[78]));
/*printf("16.%s ",str2[49]);getch();*/
strcpy(str2[101],str2[49]);intmoretoless();strcpy(str2[1],str2[100]);
strcpy(str2[77],str2[49]);
goto nagar3;
}
else {
strcpy(str3[68],subint(str2[49],str2[78]));
/*printf("17.%s ",str3[68]);getch();*/
strcpy(str2[101],str3[68]);intmoretoless();strcpy(str2[8],str2[100]);
strcat(str2[7],str2[8]);
strcpy(str2[45],subint(str2[48],str3[67]));
```

```
/*printf("@.%s ",str2[45]);getch();*/
strcpy(str2[69],subint(str2[73],str2[45]));
/*printf("@@.%s ",str2[69]);getch();*/
strcpy(str2[45],str2[69]);
complement(str3[67]);
str3[67][0]='+';
++var[7];if(var[7]<=20)goto nagar2;else goto nagar5;
}
}
nagar5:
u=0;
str2[10][u]=sign;
for(l=1;str2[7][l]!='\0';l++){
if(str2[7][l]!='+'&&str2[7][l]!='-')str2[10][++u]=str2[7][l];
}
str2[10][u]='\0';
b=0;
for(a=0;a<strlen(str2[10]);a++)if(str2[10][a]=='.')break;
count[3]=a;
/*printf("^.%i ",count[3]);*/
b=0;
for(a=0;a<strlen(str2[10]);a++)if(str2[10][a]!='.')str2[11][b++]=str2[10][a];
str2[11][b]='\0';
/*printf("%s ",str2[11]);getch();*/
count[4]=count[3]-(count[1]-count[2]);
b=0;
for(a=0;a<strlen(str2[11]);a++){
if(a!=count[4])str2[12][b++]=str2[11][a];
else {str2[12][b++]='.';str2[12][b++]=str2[11][a];}
}
str2[12][b]='\0';
/*printf("^^.%s ",str2[12]);getch();*/
b=0;
for(a=0;a<strlen(str2[12]);a++){
if(a==1){if(str2[12][a]!='0')str2[97][b++]=str2[12][a];}
else str2[97][b++]=str2[12][a];
}
str2[97][b]='\0';
for(a=0;str2[97][a]!='.';a++)str2[12][a]=str2[97][a];
str2[12][a++]='.';
for(b=0;b<12;b++)str2[12][a+b]=str2[97][a+b];
str2[12][a+b]='\0';
if(str2[12][1]=='.'){
strcpy(str2[14],"+0.");
strcpy(str2[15],substring(str2[12],2,strlen(str2[12])));
strcat(str2[14],str2[15]);
}
```

```
else strcpy(str2[14],str2[12]);
strcpy(str2[97],str2[14]);
/* ------------------------------------------------ */
label54345:
str2[7][0]='+';str2[7][1]='0';str2[7][2]='\0';
if(str2[97][1]=='0'){
str2[7][2]='.';
for(u=0;str2[97][u]!='.';u++);
for(v=2;str2[97][u]!='\0';u++)str2[7][++v]=str2[97][u+1];str2[7][++v]='\0';
}
else {strcpy(str2[7],str2[97]);}
str2[7][0]=sign3;
fclose(fpt2);
strcpy(str3[56],str2[13]);strcpy(str3[58],str2[7]);varappend();
fread(&com.command,sizeof(com.command),1,fpt1); /* ofend */
fread(&com.command,sizeof(com.command),1,fpt1);
goto end;
}
}
/* -------------------------------------------------------- */
else if(strcmp(com.command,"power")==0){
fread(&com.command,sizeof(com.command),1,fpt1); /* of */
fread(&com.command,sizeof(com.command),1,fpt1);
strcpy(str2[61],com.command);
fread(&com.command,sizeof(com.command),1,fpt1); /* to */
fread(&com.command,sizeof(com.command),1,fpt1);
strcpy(str2[62],com.command);
fread(&com.command,sizeof(com.command),1,fpt1); /* into */
fread(&com.command,sizeof(com.command),1,fpt1);
strcpy(str2[63],com.command);
strcpy(str3[50],str2[61]);varcompare();strcpy(str2[81],str3[52]);
strcpy(str3[50],str2[62]);varcompare();strcpy(str2[82],str3[52]);
if(strcmp(str2[81],"+0.0")==0||strcmp(str2[81],"-0.0")==0)
{strcpy(str3[4],"+0.0");goto label12321;}
if(strcmp(str2[82],"+1")==0){strcpy(str3[4],str2[81]);goto label12321;}
if(strcmp(str2[82],"+0.0")==0){strcpy(str3[4],"+1");goto label12321;}
else if(strcmp(str2[82],"-0.0")==0){strcpy(str3[4],"+1");goto label12321;}
strcpy(str2[101],str2[82]);intlesstomore();strcpy(str2[77],str2[100]);
strcpy(str2[101],"+0");intlesstomore();strcpy(str2[85],str2[100]);
strcpy(str2[101],"+1");intlesstomore();strcpy(str2[86],str2[100]);
strcpy(str2[101],"+1");intlesstomore();strcpy(str2[90],str2[100]);
/* ----------------------------------------------- */
strcpy(str2[97],str2[81]);
while(1){
strcpy(str2[85],addint(str2[85],str2[90]));
if(strcmp(str2[85],str2[77])==0)break;
strcpy(str3[1],str2[81]);strcpy(str3[2],str2[97]);
```

```c
for(k=0;str3[1][k]!='.';k++)str2[1][k]=str3[1][k];
j=k;++k;
for( ;str3[1][k]!='\0';k++)str2[1][k-1]=str3[1][k];
str2[1][k-1]='\0';
count[1]=k-j-1;
for(k=0;str3[2][k]!='.';k++)str2[2][k]=str3[2][k];
j=k;++k;
for( ;str3[2][k]!='\0';k++)str2[2][k-1]=str3[2][k];
str2[2][k-1]='\0';
count[2]=k-j-1;
/* -------------------------------------- */
strcpy(str2[101],str2[1]);intlesstomore();strcpy(str3[1],str2[100]);
strcpy(str2[101],str2[2]);intlesstomore();strcpy(str3[2],str2[100]);
/* -------------------------------------- */
if(str3[1][0]!=str3[2][0])sign='-';else sign='+';
str3[1][0]=str3[2][0]='+';
strcpy(str2[31],str3[1]);strcpy(str2[32],str3[2]);
/* -------------------------------------- */
strcpy(str2[1],str3[1]);strcpy(str2[2],str3[2]);
strcpy(str2[101],str3[1]);intmoretoless();strcpy(str2[1],str2[100]);
strcpy(str2[101],str3[2]);intmoretoless();strcpy(str2[2],str2[100]);
strcpy(str2[21],"\0");
mulint2();
strcpy(str2[101],str2[22]);intlesstomore();strcpy(str2[21],str2[100]);
strcpy(str2[81],str2[21]);
}
/* ------------------------------------------------ */
var[0]=count[1]*atoi(str2[82]);
strcpy(str3[3],"\0");
strcpy(str2[101],str2[21]);intmoretoless();strcpy(str3[3],str2[100]);
for(k=0;str3[3][k]!='\0';k++);
for(y=0;y<k-var[0];y++)str3[4][y]=str3[3][y];
str3[4][y++]='.';
for( ;y<=k;y++)str3[4][y]=str3[3][y-1];
str3[4][y]='\0';
for(y=0;str3[4][y]!='.';y++);
str3[4][y+13]='\0';
label12321:
strcpy(str3[56],str2[63]);strcpy(str3[58],str3[4]);varappend();
fread(&com.command,sizeof(com.command),1,fpt1);
goto end;
}
/* ---------------------------------------------------- */
else if(strcmp(com.command,"factorial")==0){
fread(&com.command,sizeof(com.command),1,fpt1); /* of */
fread(&com.command,sizeof(com.command),1,fpt1);
strcpy(str2[61],com.command);
```

```c
fread(&com.command,sizeof(com.command),1,fpt1); /* into */
fread(&com.command,sizeof(com.command),1,fpt1);
strcpy(str2[62],com.command);
strcpy(str3[50],str2[61]);varcompare();strcpy(str2[81],str3[52]);
if(strcmp(str2[81],"+0")==0){strcpy(str2[96],"+1");goto label123456;}
if(strcmp(str2[81],"+1")==0){strcpy(str2[96],"+1");goto label123456;}
strcpy(str2[101],str2[81]);intlesstomore();strcpy(str2[82],str2[100]);
strcpy(str2[101],"+0");intlesstomore();strcpy(str2[83],str2[100]);
strcpy(str2[101],"+1");intlesstomore();strcpy(str2[84],str2[100]);
strcpy(str2[101],"+2");intlesstomore();strcpy(str2[88],str2[100]);
strcpy(str2[24],str2[84]);
strcpy(str2[96],str2[82]);
sign='+';
while(1){
strcpy(str2[85],subint(str2[82],str2[84]));
strcpy(str2[84],str2[24]);
str2[82][0]=str2[84][0]='+';
if(strcmp(str2[82],str2[88])<=0)break;
strcpy(str2[1],str2[96]);
for(k=0;k<=79;k++)str2[2][k]=str2[85][k];str2[2][80]='\0';
str2[1][80]=str2[2][80]='\0';
str2[1][1]=str2[2][1]='0';
strcpy(str2[101],str2[1]);intmoretoless();strcpy(str2[76],str2[100]);
strcpy(str2[101],str2[2]);intmoretoless();strcpy(str2[77],str2[100]);
strcpy(str2[1],str2[76]);
strcpy(str2[2],str2[77]);
mulint2();
/*str2[22][0]=sign;*/
/*str2[22][80]='\0';*/
strcpy(str2[101],str2[22]);intlesstomore();strcpy(str2[96],str2[100]);
/*strcpy(str2[96],str2[22]);*/
strcpy(str2[82],str2[85]);
str2[96][80]=str2[82][80]='\0';
strcpy(str2[84],str2[24]);
}
label123456:
strcpy(str2[101],str2[96]);intmoretoless();strcpy(str2[90],str2[100]);
strcpy(str3[56],str2[62]);strcpy(str3[58],str2[90]);varappend();
fread(&com.command,sizeof(com.command),1,fpt1);
goto end;
}
/* ---------------------------------------------------------- */
else if(strcmp(com.command,"intofchar")==0){
fread(&com.command,sizeof(com.command),1,fpt1);
fread(&com.command,sizeof(com.command),1,fpt1);
strcpy(str2[61],com.command);
fread(&com.command,sizeof(com.command),1,fpt1);
```

```
fread(&com.command,sizeof(com.command),1,fpt1);
strcpy(str2[62],com.command);
strcpy(str3[50],str2[61]);varcompare();strcpy(str2[81],str3[52]);
k=str2[81][0];sprintf(str2[83],"%i",k);
str2[82][0]='+';str2[82][1]='\0';strcat(str2[82],str2[83]);
strcpy(str3[56],str2[62]);strcpy(str3[58],str2[82]);varappend();
fread(&com.command,sizeof(com.command),1,fpt1);
goto end;
}
/* ---------------------------------------------------------- */
else if(strcmp(com.command,"charofint")==0){
fread(&com.command,sizeof(com.command),1,fpt1); /* of */
fread(&com.command,sizeof(com.command),1,fpt1);
strcpy(str2[61],com.command);
fread(&com.command,sizeof(com.command),1,fpt1); /* into */
fread(&com.command,sizeof(com.command),1,fpt1);
strcpy(str2[62],com.command);
strcpy(str3[50],str2[61]);varcompare();strcpy(str2[81],str3[52]);
sscanf(str2[81],"%i",&k);
ch=k;
str2[82][0]=ch;str2[82][1]='\0';
strcpy(str3[56],str2[62]);strcpy(str3[58],str2[82]);varappend();
fread(&com.command,sizeof(com.command),1,fpt1);
goto end;
}
/* ---------------------------------------------------------- */
else if(strcmp(com.command,"webrep")==0){
fread(&com.command,sizeof(com.command),1,fpt1);
fclose(fpt5);
fpt5=fopen("report.htm","a+");
if(strcmp(com.command,"cat")==0){
while(1){
fread(&com.command,sizeof(com.command),1,fpt1);
if(strcmp(com.command,"endcat")!=0){
fprintf(fpt5,"%s ",com.command);
}
else {goto label0001;}
}
}
else if(strcmp(com.command,"anyval")==0){
fread(&com.command,sizeof(com.command),1,fpt1);
fprintf(fpt5,"%s",com.command);
goto label0001;
}
else if(strcmp(com.command,"anyvar")==0){
fread(&com.command,sizeof(com.command),1,fpt1);
strcpy(str2[51],com.command);
```

```c
strcpy(str3[50],str2[51]);varcompare();strcpy(str2[52],str3[52]);
fprintf(fpt5,"%s",str2[52]);
goto label0001;
}
else if(strcmp(com.command,"line")==0){fprintf(fpt5,"\n");}
else if(strcmp(com.command,"space")==0){
fread(&com.command,sizeof(com.command),1,fpt1);
for(j=0;j<=atoi(com.command);j++)fprintf(fpt5," ");
}
label0001:
fread(&com.command,sizeof(com.command),1,fpt1);
goto end;
}
/* --------------------------------------------------------- */
else if(strcmp(com.command,"call")==0){
fread(&com.command,sizeof(com.command),1,fpt1); /* funname */
strcpy(str2[0],com.command);
fread(&com.command,sizeof(com.command),1,fpt1); /* endst */
lfpt[var[50]]=ftell(fpt1);
while(fread(&com.command,sizeof(com.command),1,fpt1)==1){
if(strcmp(com.command,"function")==0){
fread(&com.command,sizeof(com.command),1,fpt1); /* funname */
if(strcmp(com.command,str2[0])==0){
fread(&com.command,sizeof(com.command),1,fpt1); /* is */
goto end;
}
}
}
}
else if(strcmp(com.command,"endcall")==0){
fseek(fpt1,lfpt[var[50]],SEEK_SET);goto end;
}
/* --------------------------------------------------------- */
else if(strcmp(com.command,"substring")==0){
fread(&com.command,sizeof(com.command),1,fpt1);
strcpy(str2[61],com.command);
fread(&com.command,sizeof(com.command),1,fpt1);/* from */
if(strcmp(com.command,"from")==0){
fread(&com.command,sizeof(com.command),1,fpt1);
strcpy(str2[62],com.command);
fread(&com.command,sizeof(com.command),1,fpt1);/* to */
fread(&com.command,sizeof(com.command),1,fpt1);
strcpy(str2[63],com.command);
fread(&com.command,sizeof(com.command),1,fpt1);/* into */
fread(&com.command,sizeof(com.command),1,fpt1);
strcpy(str2[64],com.command);
strcpy(str3[50],str2[61]);varcompare();strcpy(str2[81],str3[52]);
```

```c
if(strcmp(str2[81],"NIL")==0){strcpy(str2[85],"NIL");goto labelnil;}
strcpy(str3[50],str2[62]);varcompare();strcpy(str2[82],str3[52]);
strcpy(str3[50],str2[63]);varcompare();strcpy(str2[83],str3[52]);
sscanf(str2[82],"%i",&var[0]);sscanf(str2[83],"%i",&var[1]);
if(var[1]==var[0]){str2[85][0]=str2[81][var[0]-1];str2[85][1]='\0';}
else {
k=0;
for(y=var[0];y<var[1];y++)
str2[85][k++]=str2[81][y];
str2[85][k]='\0';
}
labelnil:
strcpy(str3[56],str2[64]);strcpy(str3[58],str2[85]);varappend();
}
else if(strcmp(com.command,"length")==0){
fread(&com.command,sizeof(com.command),1,fpt1);
fread(&com.command,sizeof(com.command),1,fpt1);
strcpy(str2[62],com.command);
strcpy(str3[50],str2[61]);varcompare();strcpy(str2[81],str3[52]);
if(strcmp(str2[81],"NIL")==0){k=0;goto labelk;}
for(k=0;str2[81][k]!='\0';k++);
labelk:
itoa(k,str2[82],10);
strcpy(str2[90],"\0");strcat(str2[90],"+");strcat(str2[90],str2[82]);
strcpy(str3[56],str2[62]);strcpy(str3[58],str2[90]);varappend();
}
fread(&com.command,sizeof(com.command),1,fpt1);
goto end;
}
/* ---------------------------------------------------------- */
/* instring of somey from +5 occurence +4 in somex into somez endst */
else if(strcmp(com.command,"instring")==0){
strcpy(str2[61],"\0");strcpy(str2[81],"\0");
strcpy(str2[62],"\0");strcpy(str2[82],"\0");
strcpy(str2[63],"\0");strcpy(str2[83],"\0");
strcpy(str2[64],"\0");strcpy(str2[84],"\0");
fread(&com.command,sizeof(com.command),1,fpt1); /* of */
fread(&com.command,sizeof(com.command),1,fpt1);
strcpy(str2[61],com.command);
fread(&com.command,sizeof(com.command),1,fpt1);/* from */
fread(&com.command,sizeof(com.command),1,fpt1);
strcpy(str2[62],com.command);
fread(&com.command,sizeof(com.command),1,fpt1);/* occurence */
fread(&com.command,sizeof(com.command),1,fpt1);
strcpy(str2[63],com.command);
fread(&com.command,sizeof(com.command),1,fpt1);/* in */
fread(&com.command,sizeof(com.command),1,fpt1);
```

```c
strcpy(str2[64],com.command);
fread(&com.command,sizeof(com.command),1,fpt1);/* into */
fread(&com.command,sizeof(com.command),1,fpt1);
strcpy(str2[65],com.command);
strcpy(str3[50],str2[61]);varcompare();strcpy(str2[81],str3[52]);
strcpy(str3[50],str2[62]);varcompare();strcpy(str2[82],str3[52]);
strcpy(str3[50],str2[63]);varcompare();strcpy(str2[83],str3[52]);
strcpy(str3[50],str2[64]);varcompare();strcpy(str2[84],str3[52]);
var[0]=0;
for(y=0;str2[84][y]!='\0';y++)if(y>=atoi(str2[82]))break;
for( ;str2[84][y]!='\0';y++){
if(str2[84][y]==str2[81][0])++var[0];
if(var[0]>=atoi(str2[83]))break;
}
strcpy(str2[85],"\0");
sprintf(str2[85],"%i",y+1);
strcpy(str2[86],"\0");
str2[86][0]='+';str2[86][1]='\0';strcat(str2[86],str2[85]);
strcpy(str3[56],str2[65]);strcpy(str3[58],str2[86]);varappend();
fread(&com.command,sizeof(com.command),1,fpt1);
goto end;
}
/* ------------------------------------------------------------ */
else if(strcmp(com.command,"cascade")==0){
fread(&com.command,sizeof(com.command),1,fpt1);
strcpy(str2[61],com.command);
fread(&com.command,sizeof(com.command),1,fpt1); /* and */
fread(&com.command,sizeof(com.command),1,fpt1);
strcpy(str2[62],com.command);
fread(&com.command,sizeof(com.command),1,fpt1); /* into */
fread(&com.command,sizeof(com.command),1,fpt1);
strcpy(str2[63],com.command);
strcpy(str3[50],str2[61]);varcompare();strcpy(str2[81],str3[52]);
strcpy(str3[50],str2[62]);varcompare();strcpy(str2[82],str3[52]);
strcpy(str3[50],str2[63]);varcompare();strcpy(str2[83],str3[52]);
for(y=0;str2[81][y]!='\0';y++);
for(k=0;str2[82][k]!='\0';k++)str2[81][y++]=str2[82][k];
str2[81][y]='\0';
strcpy(str3[56],str2[63]);strcpy(str3[58],str2[81]);varappend();
fread(&com.command,sizeof(com.command),1,fpt1);
goto end;
}
/* ------------------------------------------------------------ */
else if(strcmp(com.command,"getkey")==0){
fread(&com.command,sizeof(com.command),1,fpt1); /* scancode */
strcpy(str2[51],com.command);
fread(&com.command,sizeof(com.command),1,fpt1); /* asciicode */
```

```c
strcpy(str2[52],com.command);
str2[53][0]='+';str2[54][0]='+';
regs.h.ah=0x00;int86(0x16,&regs,&regs);
itoa(regs.h.ah,str3[59],10);
strcat(str2[53],str3[59]);
strcpy(str3[58],str2[53]);strcpy(str3[56],str2[51]);varappend();
fclose(fpt2);
itoa(regs.h.al,str3[60],10);
strcat(str2[54],str3[60]);
strcpy(str3[58],str2[54]);strcpy(str3[56],str2[52]);varappend();
fclose(fpt2);
fread(&com.command,sizeof(com.command),1,fpt1);
goto end;
}
/* ----------------------------------------------------------- */
else if(strcmp(com.command,"setvideomode")==0){
fread(&com.command,sizeof(com.command),1,fpt1);
strcpy(str2[51],com.command);
if(strcmp(str2[51],"graph")==0){
regs.h.ah=0x00;regs.h.al=0x0e;int86(0x10,&regs,&regs);
}
else if(strcmp(str2[51],"text")==0){
regs.h.ah=0x00;regs.h.al=0x03;int86(0x10,&regs,&regs);
}
fread(&com.command,sizeof(com.command),1,fpt1);
goto end;
}
/* ----------------------------------------------------------- */
else if(strcmp(com.command,"system")==0){
fread(&com.command,sizeof(com.command),1,fpt1);
strcpy(str2[61],com.command);
strcpy(str3[50],str2[61]);varcompare();strcpy(str2[64],str3[52]);
system(str2[64]);
fread(&com.command,sizeof(com.command),1,fpt1);
goto end;
}
/* ----------------------------------------------------------- */
else if(strcmp(com.command,"timestamp")==0){
fread(&com.command,sizeof(com.command),1,fpt1);
fread(&com.command,sizeof(com.command),1,fpt1);
strcpy(str2[4],com.command);
time(&t);
strcpy(str2[64],ctime(&t));str2[64][24]='\0';
strcpy(str3[56],str2[4]);strcpy(str3[58],str2[64]);varappend();
fread(&com.command,sizeof(com.command),1,fpt1);
goto end;
}
```

```c
/* ----------------------------------------------------------- */
else if(strcmp(com.command,"floor")==0){
fread(&com.command,sizeof(com.command),1,fpt1);
fread(&com.command,sizeof(com.command),1,fpt1);
strcpy(str2[4],com.command);
strcpy(str3[50],str2[4]);varcompare();strcpy(str2[64],str3[52]);
for(y=0;str2[64][y]!='.';y++);
str2[64][y]='\0';
strcpy(str3[56],str2[4]);strcpy(str3[58],str2[64]);varappend();
fread(&com.command,sizeof(com.command),1,fpt1);
goto end;
}
/* ----------------------------------------------------------- */
else if(strcmp(com.command,"ceil")==0){
fread(&com.command,sizeof(com.command),1,fpt1);
fread(&com.command,sizeof(com.command),1,fpt1);
strcpy(str2[4],com.command);
strcpy(str3[50],str2[4]);varcompare();strcpy(str2[64],str3[52]);
for(y=0;str2[64][y]!='.';y++);
str2[64][y]='\0';
strcpy(str2[101],str2[64]);intlesstomore();strcpy(str2[65],str2[100]);
strcpy(str2[33],"+1");
strcpy(str2[101],str2[33]);intlesstomore();strcpy(str2[34],str2[100]);
strcpy(str2[65],addint(str2[65],str2[34]));
strcpy(str2[101],str2[65]);intmoretoless();strcpy(str2[77],str2[100]);
strcpy(str3[56],str2[4]);strcpy(str3[58],str2[77]);varappend();
fread(&com.command,sizeof(com.command),1,fpt1);
goto end;
}
/* ----------------------------------------------------------- */
else if(strcmp(com.command,"round")==0){
fread(&com.command,sizeof(com.command),1,fpt1);
fread(&com.command,sizeof(com.command),1,fpt1);
strcpy(str3[0],com.command);
strcpy(str3[50],str3[0]);varcompare();strcpy(str3[60],str3[52]);
fread(&com.command,sizeof(com.command),1,fpt1);
fread(&com.command,sizeof(com.command),1,fpt1);
strcpy(str3[1],com.command);
strcpy(str3[50],str3[1]);varcompare();strcpy(str3[61],str3[52]);
strcpy(str2[101],str3[60]);numlesstomore();strcpy(str3[77],str2[100]);
strcpy(str3[60],str3[77]);
sign=str3[60][0];
strcpy(str3[63],substring(str3[60],1,strlen(str3[60])));
for(k=0;str3[63][k]!='.';k++);
o=k;
ch=str3[63][k+1+atoi(str3[61])];
flag[47]=0;
```

```c
if(ch>='5'){
m=0;
for(l=0;l<=k+atoi(str3[61]);l++)if(str3[63][l]!='.')str3[64][m++]=str3[63][l];
str3[64][m]='\0';
roun:
--k;
if(str3[64][k+atoi(str3[61])]>='9'){
str3[64][k+atoi(str3[61])]='0';
if(k+atoi(str3[61])-1>=0){
if(str3[64][k+atoi(str3[61])-1]=='9')goto roun;
else {
    str3[64][k+atoi(str3[61])-1]+=1;
    strcpy(str3[62],str3[64]);
str3[69][0]=sign;
for(k=1;k<=0;k++)str3[69][k]=str3[62][k-1];
str3[69][k++]='.';
for( ;k<0+atoi(str3[61]);k++)str3[69][k]=str3[62][k+1];
str3[69][k]='\0';
strcpy(str3[62],str3[69]);
    goto rounend2;
    }
}
else {
    flag[47]=1;
    if(sign=='+')strcpy(str3[68],"+");
    else if(sign=='-')strcpy(str3[68],"-");
    strcat(str3[68],"1");
for(k=1;k<=0+1;k++)str3[68][k+1]=str3[64][k];
str3[68][k++]='.';
if(atoi(str3[61])==1){str3[68][k++]='0';goto rounendbef;}
else if(atoi(str3[61])==0)
{str3[68][k-2]='0';str3[68][k-1]='.';str3[68][k]='0';++k;goto rounendbef;}
for( ;k<0+atoi(str3[61]);k++)str3[68][k]=str3[64][k];
rounendbef:
str3[68][k]='\0';
    goto rounend;
    }
}
else {
    str3[64][k+atoi(str3[61])]+=1;
    str3[64][k+atoi(str3[61])+1]='\0';
    strcpy(str3[62],str3[64]);
str3[69][0]=sign;
for(k=1;k<=0;k++)str3[69][k]=str3[62][k-1];
str3[69][k++]='.';
if(atoi(str3[61])==0){str3[69][k]='0';str3[69][k+1]='\0';goto sujay;}
for( ;k<0+atoi(str3[61])+2;k++)str3[69][k]=str3[62][k-2];
```

```c
str3[69][k]='\0';
sujay:
strcpy(str3[62],str3[69]);
    goto rounend2;
    }
}
else {
for(l=0;l<=k+1+atoi(str3[61]);l++)str3[62][l]=str3[60][l];
str3[62][l]='\0';
goto rounend2;
}
rounend:
strcpy(str3[62],str3[68]);
rounend2:
fread(&com.command,sizeof(com.command),1,fpt1);
strcpy(str2[101],str3[62]);nummoretoless();strcpy(str3[77],str2[100]);
strcpy(str3[62],str3[77]);
for(o=0;str3[62][o]!='.';o++);
if(str3[62][++o]=='\0'){str3[62][o]='0';str3[62][++o]='\0';}
fread(&com.command,sizeof(com.command),1,fpt1);
strcpy(str3[2],com.command);
strcpy(str3[56],str3[2]);strcpy(str3[58],str3[62]);varappend();
fread(&com.command,sizeof(com.command),1,fpt1);
goto end;
}
/* ----------------------------------------------------------- */
else if(strcmp(com.command,"direct")==0){
fread(&com.command,sizeof(com.command),1,fpt1);
if(strcmp(com.command,"inport")==0){
fread(&com.command,sizeof(com.command),1,fpt1); /* portnum */
strcpy(str2[61],com.command);
fread(&com.command,sizeof(com.command),1,fpt1); /* into */
fread(&com.command,sizeof(com.command),1,fpt1);
strcpy(str2[62],com.command);
strcpy(str3[50],str2[61]);varcompare();strcpy(str2[71],str3[52]);
k=inportb(atoi(str2[71]));
itoa(k,str2[82],16);
str2[41][0]='+';str2[41][1]='\0';
strcat(str2[41],str2[82]);
strcpy(str2[82],str2[41]);
strcpy(str3[56],str2[62]);strcpy(str3[58],str2[82]);varappend();
fread(&com.command,sizeof(com.command),1,fpt1);
goto end;
}
else if(strcmp(com.command,"outport")==0){
fread(&com.command,sizeof(com.command),1,fpt1); /* somey */
strcpy(str2[61],com.command);
```

```c
fread(&com.command,sizeof(com.command),1,fpt1); /* to */
fread(&com.command,sizeof(com.command),1,fpt1); /* portnum */
strcpy(str2[62],com.command);
strcpy(str3[50],str2[61]);varcompare();strcpy(str2[71],str3[52]);
strcpy(str3[50],str2[62]);varcompare();strcpy(str2[72],str3[52]);
outportb(atoi(str2[72]),atoi(str2[71]));
fread(&com.command,sizeof(com.command),1,fpt1);
goto end;
}
}
/* ---------------------------------------------------------- */
else if(strcmp(com.command,"indirect")==0){
fread(&com.command,sizeof(com.command),1,fpt1);
if(strcmp(com.command,"inport")==0){
fread(&com.command,sizeof(com.command),1,fpt1);
strcpy(str2[61],com.command);
fread(&com.command,sizeof(com.command),1,fpt1);
fread(&com.command,sizeof(com.command),1,fpt1);
strcpy(str2[62],com.command);
strcpy(str3[50],str2[61]);varcompare();strcpy(str2[71],str3[52]);
regs.x.dx=atoi(str2[71]);
k=inportb(regs.x.dx);
regs.h.al=k;
itoa(regs.h.al,str2[82],10);
str2[41][0]='+';str2[41][1]='\0';
strcat(str2[41],str2[82]);
strcpy(str2[82],str2[41]);
strcpy(str3[56],str2[62]);strcpy(str3[58],str2[82]);varappend();
fread(&com.command,sizeof(com.command),1,fpt1);
goto end;
}
else if(strcmp(com.command,"outport")==0){
fread(&com.command,sizeof(com.command),1,fpt1);
strcpy(str2[61],com.command);
fread(&com.command,sizeof(com.command),1,fpt1);
fread(&com.command,sizeof(com.command),1,fpt1);
strcpy(str2[62],com.command);
strcpy(str3[50],str2[61]);varcompare();strcpy(str2[71],str3[52]);
strcpy(str3[50],str2[62]);varcompare();strcpy(str2[72],str3[52]);
regs.h.al=atoi(str2[71]);
regs.x.dx=atoi(str2[72]);
outportb(regs.x.dx,regs.h.al);
fread(&com.command,sizeof(com.command),1,fpt1);
goto end;
}
}
/* ---------------------------------------------------------- */
```

```c
else if(strcmp(com.command,"addconst")==0){
fread(&com.command,sizeof(com.command),1,fpt1); /* type */
strcpy(str2[80],com.command);
fread(&com.command,sizeof(com.command),1,fpt1); /* hashed/normal */
strcpy(str2[81],com.command);
fread(&com.command,sizeof(com.command),1,fpt1); /* to */
fread(&com.command,sizeof(com.command),1,fpt1); /* somex */
strcpy(str2[82],com.command);
fclose(fpt14);
fpt14=fopen("constrai.var","r+");
if(fpt14==NULL)fpt14=fopen("constrai.var","w+");
fseek(fpt14,0L,SEEK_END);
myfputs(str2[82],fpt14);
myfputs(str2[80],fpt14);
myfputs(str2[81],fpt14);
myfputs("~",fpt14);
fclose(fpt14);
fread(&com.command,sizeof(com.command),1,fpt1);
goto end;
}
/* ---------------------------------------------------------- */
else if(strcmp(com.command,"dropconst")==0){
fread(&com.command,sizeof(com.command),1,fpt1); /* type */
strcpy(str2[80],com.command);
fread(&com.command,sizeof(com.command),1,fpt1); /* hashed/normal */
strcpy(str2[81],com.command);
fread(&com.command,sizeof(com.command),1,fpt1); /* from */
fread(&com.command,sizeof(com.command),1,fpt1); /* somex */
strcpy(str2[82],com.command);
fclose(fpt10);
fpt10=fopen("temp.dat","w+");
fclose(fpt14);
fpt14=fopen("constrai.var","r+");
while(1){
if(feof(fpt14))goto prasanna3;
li3=ftell(fpt14);
myfgets(str2[85],fpt14);if(feof(fpt14))goto prasanna3;
if(strcmp(str2[85],str2[82])==0){
myfgets(str2[86],fpt14);if(feof(fpt14))goto prasanna3;
if(strcmp(str2[86],str2[80])==0){
myfgets(str2[87],fpt14);if(feof(fpt14))goto prasanna3;
if(strcmp(str2[87],str2[81])==0){
myfgets(str2[88],fpt14);if(feof(fpt14))goto prasanna3;
goto prasanna2;
}
else goto prasanna1;
}
```

```
else goto prasanna1;
}
prasanna1:
fseek(fpt14,li3,SEEK_SET);
while(!feof(fpt14)){
myfgets(str2[89],fpt14);if(feof(fpt14))goto prasanna3;
myfputs(str2[89],fpt10);
if(strcmp(str2[89],"~")==0)goto prasanna2;
}
prasanna2:
continue;
}
prasanna3:
fclose(fpt10);
fpt10=fopen("temp.dat","r+");
fclose(fpt14);
fpt14=fopen("constrai.var","w+");
while((ch=getc(fpt10))!=EOF)putc(ch,fpt14);
fclose(fpt14);
fclose(fpt10);
fread(&com.command,sizeof(com.command),1,fpt1);
goto end;
}
/* ------------------------------------------------------- */
else if(strcmp(com.command,"printit")==0){
fread(&com.command,sizeof(com.command),1,fpt1);
strcpy(str2[61],com.command);
strcpy(str3[50],str2[61]);varcompare();strcpy(str2[81],str3[52]);
fread(&com.command,sizeof(com.command),1,fpt1); /* and */
fread(&com.command,sizeof(com.command),1,fpt1);
strcpy(str2[62],com.command);
strcpy(str3[50],str2[62]);varcompare();strcpy(str2[82],str3[52]);
for(t=0;str2[81][t]!='\0';t++){
/* print a char in color */
regs.h.ah=9;
regs.h.al=str2[81][t];
regs.h.bh=0;
regs.h.bl=atoi(str2[82]);
regs.x.cx=1;
int86(0x10,&regs,&regs);
/* get the cursor */
regs.h.ah=3;
regs.h.bh=0;
int86(0x10,&regs,&regs);
r=regs.h.dh;
c=regs.h.dl;
/* set the cursor */
```

```c
regs.h.ah=2;
regs.h.bh=0;
regs.h.dh=r;
regs.h.dl=++c;
int86(0x10,&regs,&regs);
}
fread(&com.command,sizeof(com.command),1,fpt1);
goto end;
}
/* ---------------------------------------------------------- */
else if(strcmp(com.command,"spaceit")==0){
fread(&com.command,sizeof(com.command),1,fpt1);
strcpy(str2[61],com.command);
strcpy(str3[50],str2[61]);varcompare();strcpy(str2[81],str3[52]);
fread(&com.command,sizeof(com.command),1,fpt1); /* and */
fread(&com.command,sizeof(com.command),1,fpt1);
strcpy(str2[62],com.command);
strcpy(str3[50],str2[62]);varcompare();strcpy(str2[82],str3[52]);
for(t=0;t<atoi(str2[81]);t++){
/* print a char in color */
regs.h.ah=9;
regs.h.al=' ';
regs.h.bh=0;
regs.h.bl=atoi(str2[82]);
regs.x.cx=1;
int86(0x10,&regs,&regs);
/* get the cursor */
regs.h.ah=3;
regs.h.bh=0;
int86(0x10,&regs,&regs);
r=regs.h.dh;
c=regs.h.dl;
/* set the cursor */
regs.h.ah=2;
regs.h.bh=0;
regs.h.dh=r;
regs.h.dl=++c;
int86(0x10,&regs,&regs);
}
fread(&com.command,sizeof(com.command),1,fpt1);
goto end;
}
/* ---------------------------------------------------------- */
else if(strcmp(com.command,"putmem")==0){
fread(&com.command,sizeof(com.command),1,fpt1); /* segaddr */
strcpy(str2[3],com.command);
strcpy(str3[50],str2[3]);varcompare();strcpy(str3[31],str3[52]);
```

```c
sscanf(str3[31],"%i",&s);
fread(&com.command,sizeof(com.command),1,fpt1);
strcpy(str2[5],com.command);
strcpy(str3[50],str2[5]);varcompare();strcpy(str3[51],str3[52]);/* for len */
regs.x.ax=s;
reg.r_ds=regs.x.ax;
reg.r_di=str3[51];
for(q=0;q<strlen(str3[51]);q++){
diadd=reg.r_di;
++reg.r_di;
++diadd;
}
*diadd='\0';
fread(&com.command,sizeof(com.command),1,fpt1);
goto end;
}
/* ---------------------------------------------------- */
else if(strcmp(com.command,"getmem")==0){
fread(&com.command,sizeof(com.command),1,fpt1); /* segaddr */
strcpy(str2[3],com.command);
strcpy(str3[50],str2[3]);varcompare();strcpy(str3[31],str3[52]);
sscanf(str3[31],"%i",&s);
fread(&com.command,sizeof(com.command),1,fpt1); /* string */
strcpy(str2[4],com.command);
strcpy(str3[50],str2[4]);varcompare();strcpy(str3[41],str3[52]);
sscanf(str3[41],"%i",&o);
fread(&com.command,sizeof(com.command),1,fpt1);
strcpy(str2[5],com.command); /* output */
regs.x.ax=s;
reg.r_ds=regs.x.ax;
reg.r_di=str3[41];
for(q=0; ;q++){
diadd=reg.r_di;
str3[51][q]=*diadd;
if(str3[51][q]=='\0')break;
++reg.r_di;
++diadd;
}
str3[51][q]='\0';
strcpy(str3[56],str2[5]);strcpy(str3[58],str3[51]);varappend();
fread(&com.command,sizeof(com.command),1,fpt1);
goto end;
}
/* ---------------------------------------------------- */
else if(strcmp(com.command,"testit")==0){
fread(&com.command,sizeof(com.command),1,fpt1); /* type */
strcpy(str2[83],com.command);
```

```c
fread(&com.command,sizeof(com.command),1,fpt1); /* data */
strcpy(str2[64],com.command);
strcpy(str3[50],str2[64]);varcompare();strcpy(str2[84],str3[52]);
fread(&com.command,sizeof(com.command),1,fpt1); /* into */
fread(&com.command,sizeof(com.command),1,fpt1); /* retval */
strcpy(str2[66],com.command);
/**/
flag[11]=1;
if(strcmp(str2[83],"integer")==0){
if(str2[84][0]=='+'||str2[84][0]=='-'){
for(u=1;str2[84][u]!='\0';u++){
if(str2[84][u]<'0'||str2[84][u]>'9'){flag[11]=0;goto naga11;}
else if(str2[84][u]=='.'){flag[11]=0;goto naga11;}
}
}
else {flag[11]=0;goto naga11;}
}
else if(strcmp(str2[83],"number")==0){
k=0;
if(str2[84][0]=='+'||str2[84][0]=='-'){
for(u=1;str2[84][u]!='\0';u++){
if(str2[84][u]=='.'){++k;if(k>1){flag[11]=0;goto naga11;} else flag[11]=1;}
else {
if(str2[84][u]<'0'||str2[84][u]>'9'){flag[11]=0;goto naga11;}
                                        else {flag[11]=1;}
}
}
if(k==0){flag[11]=0;goto naga11;}
}
else {flag[11]=0;goto naga11;}
}
else if(strcmp(str2[83],"string")==0){
if(str2[84][0]!='+'&&str2[84][0]!='-')flag[11]=1;
else {flag[11]=0;goto naga11;}
}
naga11:
if(flag[11]==1)strcpy(str2[73],"valid");
else if(flag[11]==0)strcpy(str2[73],"invalid");
strcpy(str3[56],str2[66]);strcpy(str3[58],str2[73]);varappend();
fread(&com.command,sizeof(com.command),1,fpt1);
goto end;
}
/* ------------------------------------------------------- */
else if(strcmp(com.command,"unique")==0){/*10*/
fread(&com.command,sizeof(com.command),1,fpt1); /* of */
fread(&com.command,sizeof(com.command),1,fpt1); /* someq */
strcpy(str2[60],com.command);
```

```c
strcpy(str3[50],str2[60]);varcompare();strcpy(str2[80],str3[52]);
fread(&com.command,sizeof(com.command),1,fpt1); /* filename */
strcpy(str2[61],com.command);
strcpy(str3[50],str2[61]);varcompare();strcpy(str2[81],str3[52]);
fread(&com.command,sizeof(com.command),1,fpt1); /* recname */
strcpy(str2[62],com.command);
strcpy(str3[50],str2[62]);varcompare();strcpy(str2[82],str3[52]);
fread(&com.command,sizeof(com.command),1,fpt1); /* type */
strcpy(str2[63],com.command);
strcpy(str3[50],str2[63]);varcompare();strcpy(str2[83],str3[52]);
fread(&com.command,sizeof(com.command),1,fpt1); /* offset */
strcpy(str2[64],com.command);
strcpy(str3[50],str2[64]);varcompare();strcpy(str2[84],str3[52]);
fread(&com.command,sizeof(com.command),1,fpt1); /* reclen */
strcpy(str2[65],com.command);
strcpy(str3[50],str2[65]);varcompare();strcpy(str2[85],str3[52]);
fread(&com.command,sizeof(com.command),1,fpt1); /* into */
fread(&com.command,sizeof(com.command),1,fpt1); /* someg */
strcpy(str2[66],com.command);
/**/
fclose(fpt13);
fpt13=fopen(str2[81],"r+");
li3=0;
while(!feof(fpt13)){/*11*/
myfgets(str2[51],fpt13);++li3;
if(li3==atol(str2[84]))break;
}/*11*/
strcpy(str3[1],str2[51]);
if(strcmp(str3[1],str2[80])==0)
{/*12*/
goto labelvar22;
}/*12*/
while(!feof(fpt13)){/*13*/
li3=0;
while(!feof(fpt13)){/*14*/
myfgets(str2[51],fpt13);++li3;
if(li3==atol(str2[85]))break;
}/*14*/
strcpy(str3[2],str2[51]);
if(strcmp(str3[2],str2[80])==0)
{/*15*/
goto labelvar22;
}/*15*/
}/*13*/
labelvar11:
strcpy(str3[56],str2[66]);strcpy(str3[58],"unique");varappend();
goto labelvar33;
```

```c
labelvar22:
strcpy(str3[56],str2[66]);strcpy(str3[58],"notunique");varappend();
labelvar33:
fclose(fpt13);
fread(&com.command,sizeof(com.command),1,fpt1);
goto end;
}/*20*/
/**/
/* -------------------------------------------------------- */
else if(strcmp(com.command,"del")==0){
fread(&com.command,sizeof(com.command),1,fpt1); /* of */
fread(&com.command,sizeof(com.command),1,fpt1); /* filename */
strcpy(str2[61],com.command);
strcpy(str3[50],str2[61]);varcompare();strcpy(str2[81],str3[52]);
fread(&com.command,sizeof(com.command),1,fpt1); /* colname */
strcpy(str2[62],com.command);
strcpy(str3[50],str2[62]);varcompare();strcpy(str2[82],str3[52]);
fread(&com.command,sizeof(com.command),1,fpt1); /* offset */
strcpy(str2[63],com.command);
strcpy(str3[50],str2[63]);varcompare();strcpy(str2[83],str3[52]);
fread(&com.command,sizeof(com.command),1,fpt1); /* reclen */
strcpy(str2[64],com.command);
strcpy(str3[50],str2[64]);varcompare();strcpy(str2[84],str3[52]);
/**/
fclose(fpt13);
fpt13=fopen(str2[81],"r+");
fclose(fpt10);
fpt10=fopen("temp.dat","w+");
for( ; ; ){
li3=0;
while(1){
myfgets(str2[51],fpt13);if(feof(fpt13))goto labelxxx;
++li3;
if(li3!=atol(str2[83]))
{myfputs(str2[51],fpt10);if(li3==atol(str2[84]))goto labelxxx0;}
}
labelxxx0:
continue;
}
labelxxx:
fclose(fpt13);
fclose(fpt10);
fpt10=fopen("temp.dat","r+");
fpt13=fopen(str2[81],"w+");
while((ch=getc(fpt10))!=EOF)putc(ch,fpt13);
fclose(fpt10);
fclose(fpt13);
```

```c
fread(&com.command,sizeof(com.command),1,fpt1);
goto end;
}
/* -------------------------------------------------------- */
else if(strcmp(com.command,"daysbet")==0){
fread(&com.command,sizeof(com.command),1,fpt1);
strcpy(str2[0],com.command);
fread(&com.command,sizeof(com.command),1,fpt1);
strcpy(str2[1],com.command);
fread(&com.command,sizeof(com.command),1,fpt1); /* into */
fread(&com.command,sizeof(com.command),1,fpt1); /* sign */
strcpy(str2[2],com.command);
fread(&com.command,sizeof(com.command),1,fpt1); /* days */
strcpy(str2[3],com.command);
strcpy(str3[50],str2[0]);varcompare();strcpy(str2[60],str3[52]);
strcpy(str3[50],str2[1]);varcompare();strcpy(str2[61],str3[52]);
/*clrscr();*/
/* ------------------------------------- */
/* get the dates,months,years of dates */
day1=atoi(substring(str2[60],0,1));
day2=atoi(substring(str2[61],0,1));
mon1=atoi(substring(str2[60],3,4));
mon2=atoi(substring(str2[61],3,4));
strcpy(s1,substring(str2[60],6,9));
sscanf(s1,"%i",&yea1);
strcpy(s2,substring(str2[61],6,9));
sscanf(s2,"%i",&yea2);
/* decide the lesser date */
sign='+';
if(yea1>yea2)
{strcpy(d1,str2[61]);strcpy(d2,str2[60]);sign='-';
dummy=day1;day1=day2;day2=dummy;
dummy=mon1;mon1=mon2;mon2=dummy;
dummy=yea1;yea1=yea2;yea2=dummy;}
else if(yea1<yea2){strcpy(d2,str2[61]);strcpy(d1,str2[60]);}
else {
if(mon1>mon2)
{strcpy(d1,str2[61]);strcpy(d2,str2[60]);sign='-';
dummy=day1;day1=day2;day2=dummy;
dummy=mon1;mon1=mon2;mon2=dummy;
dummy=yea1;yea1=yea2;yea2=dummy;}
else if(mon1<mon2){strcpy(d1,str2[60]);strcpy(d2,str2[61]);}
else {
if(day1>day2)
{strcpy(d1,str2[61]);strcpy(d2,str2[60]);sign='-';
dummy=day1;day1=day2;day2=dummy;
dummy=mon1;mon1=mon2;mon2=dummy;
```

```c
dummy=yea1;yea1=yea2;yea2=dummy;}
else if(day1<day2){strcpy(d2,str2[61]);strcpy(d1,str2[60]);}
else {
strcpy(d1,str2[60]);strcpy(d2,str2[61]);
}
}
}
/* now,find the difference between the dates */
days=0;
if(yea1==yea2)
{
if(mon1==mon2)
{
if(day1==day2)
{
}
else {
days=day1-day2;
days=abs(days);
}
}
else {
--mon2;
if(mon1==1)days=31-day1;
else if(mon1==2)days=28-day1;
else if(mon1==3)days=31-day1;
else if(mon1==4)days=30-day1;
else if(mon1==5)days=31-day1;
else if(mon1==6)days=30-day1;
else if(mon1==7)days=31-day1;
else if(mon1==8)days=31-day1;
else if(mon1==9)days=30-day1;
else if(mon1==10)days=31-day1;
else if(mon1==11)days=30-day1;
else if(mon1==12)days=31-day1;
if(yea1/4*4==yea1)days+=1;
label101:
++mon1;
if(mon1==1)days+=31;
else if(mon1==2)days+=28;
else if(mon1==3)days+=31;
else if(mon1==4)days+=30;
else if(mon1==5)days+=31;
else if(mon1==6)days+=30;
else if(mon1==7)days+=31;
else if(mon1==8)days+=31;
else if(mon1==9)days+=30;
```

```
else if(mon1==10)days+=31;
else if(mon1==11)days+=30;
else if(mon1==12)days+=31;
if(mon1<mon2)goto label101;
days+=day2;
}
}
else {
if(mon1==1)days=31-day1;
else if(mon1==2)days=28-day1;
else if(mon1==3)days=31-day1;
else if(mon1==4)days=30-day1;
else if(mon1==5)days=31-day1;
else if(mon1==6)days=30-day1;
else if(mon1==7)days=31-day1;
else if(mon1==8)days=31-day1;
else if(mon1==9)days=30-day1;
else if(mon1==10)days=31-day1;
else if(mon1==11)days=30-day1;
else if(mon1==12)days=31-day1;
if(yea1/4*4==yea1)if(mon1<3)days+=1;
label103:
++mon1;
if(mon1==1)days+=31;
else if(mon1==2)days+=28;
else if(mon1==3)days+=31;
else if(mon1==4)days+=30;
else if(mon1==5)days+=31;
else if(mon1==6)days+=30;
else if(mon1==7)days+=31;
else if(mon1==8)days+=31;
else if(mon1==9)days+=30;
else if(mon1==10)days+=31;
else if(mon1==11)days+=30;
else if(mon1==12)days+=31;
if(mon1<12)goto label103;
label102:++yea1;
if(yea1<yea2){days+=365;if(yea1/4*4==yea1)days+=1;goto label102;}
if(mon2==1)days+=0;
else if(mon2==2)days+=31;
else if(mon2==3)days+=59;
else if(mon2==4)days+=90;
else if(mon2==5)days+=120;
else if(mon2==6)days+=151;
else if(mon2==7)days+=181;
else if(mon2==8)days+=212;
else if(mon2==9)days+=243;
```

```c
else if(mon2==10)days+=273;
else if(mon2==11)days+=304;
else if(mon2==12)days+=334;
if(yea2/4*4==yea2)if(mon2>=3)days+=1;
days+=day2;
}
str2[81][0]=sign;str2[81][1]='\0';
sprintf(str2[80],"%i",days);
str2[82][0]='+';strcat(str2[82],str2[80]);
/* ------------------------------------------------ */
strcpy(str3[56],str2[2]);strcpy(str3[58],str2[81]);varappend();
strcpy(str3[56],str2[3]);strcpy(str3[58],str2[82]);varappend();
fread(&com.command,sizeof(com.command),1,fpt1);
goto end;
}
/* ---------------------------------------------------------- */
else if(strcmp(com.command,"putmat")==0){
fread(&com.command,sizeof(com.command),1,fpt1);
strcpy(str2[0],com.command);
strcpy(str3[50],str2[0]);varcompare();strcpy(str3[0],str3[52]);
fclose(fpt9);
fpt9=fopen(str3[0],"r+");
if(fpt9==NULL)fpt9=fopen(str3[0],"w+");
fseek(fpt9,0L,SEEK_END);
fread(&com.command,sizeof(com.command),1,fpt1);
strcpy(str2[0],com.command);
strcpy(str3[50],str2[0]);varcompare();strcpy(str2[80],str3[52]);
myfputs(str2[80],fpt9);
fread(&com.command,sizeof(com.command),1,fpt1);
strcpy(str2[1],com.command);
strcpy(str3[50],str2[1]);varcompare();strcpy(str2[81],str3[52]);
myfputs(str2[81],fpt9);
sscanf(str2[81],"%i",&var[11]);
for(u=0;u<var[11];u++){
fread(&com.command,sizeof(com.command),1,fpt1);
strcpy(str2[2],com.command);
strcpy(str3[50],str2[2]);varcompare();strcpy(str2[82],str3[52]);
myfputs(str2[82],fpt9);
}
fread(&com.command,sizeof(com.command),1,fpt1);
strcpy(str2[3],com.command);
strcpy(str3[50],str2[3]);varcompare();strcpy(str2[83],str3[52]);
myfputs(str2[83],fpt9);
strcpy(str2[84],"&");
myfputs(str2[84],fpt9);
fclose(fpt9);
fread(&com.command,sizeof(com.command),1,fpt1);
```

```c
goto end;
}
/* -------------------------------------------------------- */
else if(strcmp(com.command,"getmat")==0){
flag[10]=0;v=0;u=0;
fread(&com.command,sizeof(com.command),1,fpt1);
strcpy(str2[0],com.command);
strcpy(str3[50],str2[0]);varcompare();strcpy(str3[0],str3[52]);
fclose(fpt9);
fpt9=fopen(str3[0],"r+");
if(fpt9==NULL)fpt9=fopen(str3[0],"w+");
fseek(fpt9,0L,SEEK_SET);
while(1){
fread(&com.command,sizeof(com.command),1,fpt1);
if(strcmp(com.command,"endst")==0){strcpy(str2[3],str2[u-1]);}
if(strcmp(com.command,"endst")==0)break;
strcpy(str2[u],com.command);
strcpy(str3[50],str2[u]);varcompare();strcpy(str2[u+50],str3[52]);
++u;
}
while(1){
while(1){
myfgets(str3[v+50],fpt9);if(feof(fpt9))goto matrix1;
if(strcmp(str3[v+50],"&")==0)break;
++v;
}
u=0;v=0;
while(1){
if(strcmp(str3[v+2+50],"&")!=0){
if(strcmp(str2[u+50],str3[v+50])==0){
++u;++v;
}
else {flag[10]=1;break;}
}
else break;
}
if(flag[10]==0){
revseek(fpt9);revseek(fpt9);
myfgets(str2[90],fpt9);if(feof(fpt9))goto matrix1;
strcpy(str3[56],str2[3]);strcpy(str3[58],str2[90]);varappend();
goto matrix1;
}
flag[10]=0;
}
matrix1:
fclose(fpt9);
goto end;
```

```c
}
/* ---------------------------------------------------------- */
else if(strcmp(com.command,"delmat")==0){
li=0;
flag[10]=0;v=0;u=0;
fclose(fpt10);
fpt10=fopen("temp.dat","w+");
fread(&com.command,sizeof(com.command),1,fpt1);
strcpy(str2[0],com.command);
strcpy(str3[50],str2[0]);varcompare();strcpy(str3[0],str3[52]);
fclose(fpt9);
fpt9=fopen(str3[0],"r+");
if(fpt9==NULL)fpt9=fopen(str3[0],"w+");
fseek(fpt9,0L,SEEK_SET);
while(1){
fread(&com.command,sizeof(com.command),1,fpt1);
if(strcmp(com.command,"endst")==0)break;
strcpy(str2[u],com.command);
strcpy(str3[50],str2[u]);varcompare();strcpy(str2[u+50],str3[52]);
++u;
}
while(1){
u=0;v=0;
li1=ftell(fpt9);/*printf("li1.%li ",li1);*/
while(1){
myfgets(str3[v+50],fpt9);if(feof(fpt9))goto matrix11;
/*printf("%s ",str3[v+50]);*/
if(strcmp(str3[v+50],"&")==0)
{li2=ftell(fpt9);/*printf("li2.%li ",li2);*/goto matrix44;}
else ++v;
}
matrix44:
u=0;v=0;
while(1){
/*printf("->%s %s ",str2[u+50],str3[v+50]);*/
if(strcmp(str2[u+50],str3[v+50])==0){
++u;++v;
if(strcmp(str3[v+1+50],"&")==0)/*goto matrix11;*/
{
/*printf("matched");*/
/*li1,li2*/
fclose(fpt9);
fclose(fpt10);
fpt9=fopen(str3[0],"r+");
fpt10=fopen("temp.dat","w+");
li3=0;
while((ch=getc(fpt9))!=EOF){
```

```c
if(li3>=li1&&li3<li2){++li3;}
else {putc(ch,fpt10);++li3;}
}
fclose(fpt10);
fclose(fpt9);
fpt9=fopen(str3[0],"w+");
fpt10=fopen("temp.dat","r+");
while((ch=getc(fpt10))!=EOF)putc(ch,fpt9);
goto matrix11;
}
}
else {
while(1){
myfgets(str2[70],fpt9);if(feof(fpt9))goto matrix11;
if(strcmp(str2[70],"&")==0)goto matrix22;
}
}
}
matrix22:
u=0;++v;
}
matrix11:
/*printf("li1.%li ",li1);printf("li2.%li ",li2);*/
fclose(fpt9);
fclose(fpt10);
goto end;
}
/* ----------------------------------------------------------- */
else if(strcmp(com.command,"dateat")==0){
fread(&com.command,sizeof(com.command),1,fpt1);
strcpy(str2[61],com.command);
fread(&com.command,sizeof(com.command),1,fpt1);
strcpy(str2[62],com.command);
fread(&com.command,sizeof(com.command),1,fpt1);
strcpy(str2[63],com.command);
fread(&com.command,sizeof(com.command),1,fpt1); /* into */
fread(&com.command,sizeof(com.command),1,fpt1);
strcpy(str2[64],com.command);
strcpy(str3[50],str2[61]);varcompare();strcpy(str2[71],str3[52]);
strcpy(str3[50],str2[62]);varcompare();strcpy(str2[72],str3[52]);
strcpy(str3[50],str2[63]);varcompare();strcpy(str2[73],str3[52]);
/* calculate the date */
strcpy(yea2a,substring(str2[71],6,9));
sscanf(yea2a,"%i",&yea);
strcpy(mon2a,substring(str2[71],3,4));
mon=atoi(mon2a);
strcpy(day2a,substring(str2[71],0,1));
```

```c
day=atoi(day2a);
sign=str2[72][0];
sscanf(str2[73],"%i",&days);
if(sign=='+')
{
label101ABC:
++day;
--days;
if(days<=0)
{goto end3;}
else
{
if(mon==1){if(day>31-1)goto label102ABC;else goto label101ABC;}
else if(mon==2)
{
if(yea/4*4!=yea){if(day>28-1)goto label102ABC;else goto label101ABC;}
else {if(day>29-1){goto label102ABC;} else goto label101ABC;}
}
else if(mon==3){if(day>31-1)goto label102ABC;else goto label101ABC;}
else if(mon==4){if(day>30-1)goto label102ABC;else goto label101ABC;}
else if(mon==5){if(day>31-1)goto label102ABC;else goto label101ABC;}
else if(mon==6){if(day>30-1)goto label102ABC;else goto label101ABC;}
else if(mon==7){if(day>31-1)goto label102ABC;else goto label101ABC;}
else if(mon==8){if(day>31-1)goto label102ABC;else goto label101ABC;}
else if(mon==9){if(day>30-1)goto label102ABC;else goto label101ABC;}
else if(mon==10){if(day>31-1)goto label102ABC;else goto label101ABC;}
else if(mon==11){if(day>30-1)goto label102ABC;else goto label101ABC;}
else if(mon==12){if(day>31-1)goto label102ABC;else goto label101ABC;}
else {
++yea;mon=1;day=0;goto label101ABC;
}
}
label102ABC:++mon;day=0;if(mon>12)goto label103ABC;else goto label101ABC;
label103ABC:++yea;mon=1;day=0;goto label101ABC;
}
else if(sign=='-')
{
label104ABC:
--day;
--days;
if(days<=0){goto end3;}
else
{
if(mon==1){if(day<1)goto label105ABC;else goto label104ABC;}
else if(mon==2){if(day<1)goto label105ABC;else goto label104ABC;}
else if(mon==3){if(day<1)goto label105ABC;else goto label104ABC;}
else if(mon==4){if(day<1)goto label105ABC;else goto label104ABC;}
```

```c
else if(mon==5){if(day<1)goto label105ABC;else goto label104ABC;}
else if(mon==6){if(day<1)goto label105ABC;else goto label104ABC;}
else if(mon==7){if(day<1)goto label105ABC;else goto label104ABC;}
else if(mon==8){if(day<1)goto label105ABC;else goto label104ABC;}
else if(mon==9){if(day<1)goto label105ABC;else goto label104ABC;}
else if(mon==10){if(day<1)goto label105ABC;else goto label104ABC;}
else if(mon==11){if(day<1)goto label105ABC;else goto label104ABC;}
else if(mon==12){if(day<1)goto label105ABC;else goto label104ABC;}
else {
--yea;mon=12;day=31;goto label104ABC;
}
}
label105ABC:
--mon;
if(mon==1)day=31;
else if(mon==2){if(yea/4*4==yea)day=29;else day=28;}
else if(mon==3)day=31;
else if(mon==4)day=30;
else if(mon==5)day=31;
else if(mon==6)day=30;
else if(mon==7)day=31;
else if(mon==8)day=30;
else if(mon==9)day=31;
else if(mon==10)day=31;
else if(mon==11)day=30;
else if(mon==12)day=31;
if(mon<1)goto label106ABC;else goto label104ABC;
label106ABC:
--yea;
mon=12;
day=31;
goto label104ABC;
}
end3:
str2[74][0]='\0';
sprintf(str2[75],"%i",day);
sprintf(str2[76],"%i",mon);
sprintf(str2[77],"%i",yea);
strcat(str2[74],str2[75]);strcat(str2[74],"-");
strcat(str2[74],str2[76]);strcat(str2[74],"-");
strcat(str2[74],str2[77]);
strcpy(str3[56],str2[64]);strcpy(str3[58],str2[74]);varappend();
fread(&com.command,sizeof(com.command),1,fpt1);
goto end;
}
/* ------------------------------------------------------- */
else if(strcmp(com.command,"dayat")==0){
```

```c
fread(&com.command,sizeof(com.command),1,fpt1);
strcpy(str2[0],com.command);
fread(&com.command,sizeof(com.command),1,fpt1); /* into */
fread(&com.command,sizeof(com.command),1,fpt1); /* days */
strcpy(str2[3],com.command);
strcpy(str3[50],str2[0]);varcompare();strcpy(str2[60],str3[52]);
/*clrscr();*/
day1=atoi(substring(str2[60],0,1));
mon1=atoi(substring(str2[60],3,4));
strcpy(s1,substring(str2[60],6,9));
sscanf(s1,"%i",&yea1);
/* todays timestamp */
time(&t);
strcpy(timestamp,ctime(&t));
strcpy(today,substring(timestamp,0,2));
strcpy(st1,substring(timestamp,4,6));
strcpy(st2,substring(timestamp,8,9));
strcpy(st3,substring(timestamp,19,23));
strcpy(date2,"\0");
if(strcmp(st1,"Jan")==0)strcpy(st4,"01");
else if(strcmp(st1,"Feb")==0)strcpy(st4,"02");
else if(strcmp(st1,"Mar")==0)strcpy(st4,"03");
else if(strcmp(st1,"Apr")==0)strcpy(st4,"04");
else if(strcmp(st1,"May")==0)strcpy(st4,"05");
else if(strcmp(st1,"Jun")==0)strcpy(st4,"06");
else if(strcmp(st1,"Jul")==0)strcpy(st4,"07");
else if(strcmp(st1,"Aug")==0)strcpy(st4,"08");
else if(strcmp(st1,"Sep")==0)strcpy(st4,"09");
else if(strcmp(st1,"Oct")==0)strcpy(st4,"10");
else if(strcmp(st1,"Nov")==0)strcpy(st4,"11");
else if(strcmp(st1,"Dec")==0)strcpy(st4,"12");
day2=atoi(st2);
mon2=atoi(st4);
sscanf(st3,"%i",&yea2);
sign='+';
if(yea1>yea2)
{strcpy(d1,str2[61]);strcpy(d2,str2[60]);sign='-';
dummy=day1;day1=day2;day2=dummy;
dummy=mon1;mon1=mon2;mon2=dummy;
dummy=yea1;yea1=yea2;yea2=dummy;}
else if(yea1<yea2){strcpy(d2,str2[61]);strcpy(d1,str2[60]);}
else {
if(mon1>mon2)
{strcpy(d1,str2[61]);strcpy(d2,str2[60]);sign='-';
dummy=day1;day1=day2;day2=dummy;
dummy=mon1;mon1=mon2;mon2=dummy;
dummy=yea1;yea1=yea2;yea2=dummy;}
```

```c
else if(mon1<mon2){strcpy(d1,str2[60]);strcpy(d2,str2[61]);}
else {
if(day1>day2)
{strcpy(d1,str2[61]);strcpy(d2,str2[60]);sign='-';
dummy=day1;day1=day2;day2=dummy;
dummy=mon1;mon1=mon2;mon2=dummy;
dummy=yea1;yea1=yea2;yea2=dummy;}
else if(day1<day2){strcpy(d2,str2[61]);strcpy(d1,str2[60]);}
else {
strcpy(d1,str2[60]);strcpy(d2,str2[61]);
}
}
}
/* now,find the difference between the dates */
days=0;
if(yea1==yea2)
{
if(mon1==mon2)
{
if(day1==day2)
{
}
else {
days=day1-day2;
days=abs(days);
}
}
else {
--mon2;
if(mon1==1)days=31-day1;
else if(mon1==2)days=28-day1;
else if(mon1==3)days=31-day1;
else if(mon1==4)days=30-day1;
else if(mon1==5)days=31-day1;
else if(mon1==6)days=30-day1;
else if(mon1==7)days=31-day1;
else if(mon1==8)days=31-day1;
else if(mon1==9)days=30-day1;
else if(mon1==10)days=31-day1;
else if(mon1==11)days=30-day1;
else if(mon1==12)days=31-day1;
if(yea1/4*4==yea1)days+=1;
label101A:
++mon1;
if(mon1==1)days+=31;
else if(mon1==2)days+=28;
else if(mon1==3)days+=31;
```

```
else if(mon1==4)days+=30;
else if(mon1==5)days+=31;
else if(mon1==6)days+=30;
else if(mon1==7)days+=31;
else if(mon1==8)days+=31;
else if(mon1==9)days+=30;
else if(mon1==10)days+=31;
else if(mon1==11)days+=30;
else if(mon1==12)days+=31;
if(mon1<mon2)goto label101A;
days+=day2;
}
}
else {
if(mon1==1)days=31-day1;
else if(mon1==2)days=28-day1;
else if(mon1==3)days=31-day1;
else if(mon1==4)days=30-day1;
else if(mon1==5)days=31-day1;
else if(mon1==6)days=30-day1;
else if(mon1==7)days=31-day1;
else if(mon1==8)days=31-day1;
else if(mon1==9)days=30-day1;
else if(mon1==10)days=31-day1;
else if(mon1==11)days=30-day1;
else if(mon1==12)days=31-day1;
if(yea1/4*4==yea1)if(mon1<3)days+=1;
label103A:
++mon1;
if(mon1==1)days+=31;
else if(mon1==2)days+=28;
else if(mon1==3)days+=31;
else if(mon1==4)days+=30;
else if(mon1==5)days+=31;
else if(mon1==6)days+=30;
else if(mon1==7)days+=31;
else if(mon1==8)days+=31;
else if(mon1==9)days+=30;
else if(mon1==10)days+=31;
else if(mon1==11)days+=30;
else if(mon1==12)days+=31;
if(mon1<12)goto label103A;
label102A:++yea1;
if(yea1<yea2){days+=365;if(yea1/4*4==yea1)days+=1;goto label102A;}
if(mon2==1)days+=0;
else if(mon2==2)days+=31;
else if(mon2==3)days+=59;
```

```c
else if(mon2==4)days+=90;
else if(mon2==5)days+=120;
else if(mon2==6)days+=151;
else if(mon2==7)days+=181;
else if(mon2==8)days+=212;
else if(mon2==9)days+=243;
else if(mon2==10)days+=273;
else if(mon2==11)days+=304;
else if(mon2==12)days+=334;
if(yea2/4*4==yea2)if(mon2>=3)days+=1;
days+=day2;
}
/* now calculate the day */
if(strcmp(today,"Mon")==0)curday=1;
else if(strcmp(today,"Tue")==0)curday=2;
else if(strcmp(today,"Wed")==0)curday=3;
else if(strcmp(today,"Thu")==0)curday=4;
else if(strcmp(today,"Fri")==0)curday=5;
else if(strcmp(today,"Sat")==0)curday=6;
else if(strcmp(today,"Sun")==0)curday=7;
days=days-(days/7*7);
if(sign=='-'){
totday=curday+days;
if(totday>7)totday-=7;
}
else if(sign=='+'){
totday=curday-days;
if(totday<1)totday+=7;
}
if(totday==1)strcpy(weekday,"Mon");
else if(totday==2)strcpy(weekday,"Tue");
else if(totday==3)strcpy(weekday,"Wed");
else if(totday==4)strcpy(weekday,"Thu");
else if(totday==5)strcpy(weekday,"Fri");
else if(totday==6)strcpy(weekday,"Sat");
else if(totday==7)strcpy(weekday,"Sun");
strcpy(str2[73],weekday);
strcpy(str3[56],str2[3]);strcpy(str3[58],str2[73]);varappend();
fread(&com.command,sizeof(com.command),1,fpt1);
goto end;
}
/* --------------------------------------------------------- */
else if(strcmp(com.command,"dateform")==0){
fread(&com.command,sizeof(com.command),1,fpt1); /* date1 */
strcpy(str2[61],com.command);
fread(&com.command,sizeof(com.command),1,fpt1); /* form1 */
strcpy(str2[62],com.command);
```

```c
fread(&com.command,sizeof(com.command),1,fpt1); /* centuary */
strcpy(str2[63],com.command);
fread(&com.command,sizeof(com.command),1,fpt1); /* form2 */
strcpy(str2[64],com.command);
fread(&com.command,sizeof(com.command),1,fpt1); /* into */
fread(&com.command,sizeof(com.command),1,fpt1); /* date2 */
strcpy(str2[65],com.command);
strcpy(str3[50],str2[61]);varcompare();strcpy(str2[71],str3[52]);
strcpy(str3[50],str2[62]);varcompare();strcpy(str2[72],str3[52]);
strcpy(str3[50],str2[63]);varcompare();strcpy(str2[73],str3[52]);
strcpy(str3[50],str2[64]);varcompare();strcpy(str2[74],str3[52]);
strcpy(date1,str2[71]);
strcpy(form1,str2[72]);
strcpy(cent,str2[73]);
strcpy(form2,str2[74]);
h=atoi(cent);
--h;
sprintf(cent2,"%i",h);
strcpy(date2,"\0");
if(strcmp(form1,"dd-mm-yy")==0){
if(strcmp(form2,"dd-mm-yy")==0){
strcpy(date2,date1);
}
else if(strcmp(form2,"dd-mon-yy")==0){
strcpy(dd,substring(date1,0,1));
strcpy(mm,substring(date1,3,4));
strcpy(yy,substring(date1,6,7));
strcat(date2,dd);
strcat(date2,"-");
if(strcmp(mm,"01")==0)strcpy(mm,"jan");
else if(strcmp(mm,"02")==0)strcpy(mm,"feb");
else if(strcmp(mm,"03")==0)strcpy(mm,"mar");
else if(strcmp(mm,"04")==0)strcpy(mm,"apr");
else if(strcmp(mm,"05")==0)strcpy(mm,"may");
else if(strcmp(mm,"06")==0)strcpy(mm,"jun");
else if(strcmp(mm,"07")==0)strcpy(mm,"jul");
else if(strcmp(mm,"08")==0)strcpy(mm,"aug");
else if(strcmp(mm,"09")==0)strcpy(mm,"sep");
else if(strcmp(mm,"10")==0)strcpy(mm,"oct");
else if(strcmp(mm,"11")==0)strcpy(mm,"nov");
else if(strcmp(mm,"12")==0)strcpy(mm,"dec");
strcat(date2,mm);
strcat(date2,"-");
strcat(date2,yy);
}
else if(strcmp(form2,"dd-mm-yyyy")==0){
strcpy(dd,substring(date1,0,1));
```

```c
strcpy(mm,substring(date1,3,4));
strcpy(yy,substring(date1,6,7));
strcat(date2,dd);
strcat(date2,"-");
strcat(date2,mm);
strcat(date2,"-");
strcat(date2,cent2);
strcat(date2,yy);
}
else if(strcmp(form2,"dd-mon-yyyy")==0){
strcpy(dd,substring(date1,0,1));
strcpy(mm,substring(date1,3,4));
strcpy(yy,substring(date1,6,7));
strcat(date2,dd);
strcat(date2,"-");
if(strcmp(mm,"01")==0)strcpy(mm,"jan");
else if(strcmp(mm,"02")==0)strcpy(mm,"feb");
else if(strcmp(mm,"03")==0)strcpy(mm,"mar");
else if(strcmp(mm,"04")==0)strcpy(mm,"apr");
else if(strcmp(mm,"05")==0)strcpy(mm,"may");
else if(strcmp(mm,"06")==0)strcpy(mm,"jun");
else if(strcmp(mm,"07")==0)strcpy(mm,"jul");
else if(strcmp(mm,"08")==0)strcpy(mm,"aug");
else if(strcmp(mm,"09")==0)strcpy(mm,"sep");
else if(strcmp(mm,"10")==0)strcpy(mm,"oct");
else if(strcmp(mm,"11")==0)strcpy(mm,"nov");
else if(strcmp(mm,"12")==0)strcpy(mm,"dec");
strcat(date2,mm);
strcat(date2,"-");
strcat(date2,cent2);
strcat(date2,yy);
}
}
else if(strcmp(form1,"dd-mon-yy")==0){
if(strcmp(form2,"dd-mm-yy")==0){
strcpy(dd,substring(date1,0,1));
strcpy(mm,substring(date1,3,5));
strcpy(yy,substring(date1,7,8));
strcat(date2,dd);
strcat(date2,"-");
if(strcmp(mm,"jan")==0)strcpy(mm,"01");
else if(strcmp(mm,"feb")==0)strcpy(mm,"02");
else if(strcmp(mm,"mar")==0)strcpy(mm,"03");
else if(strcmp(mm,"apr")==0)strcpy(mm,"04");
else if(strcmp(mm,"may")==0)strcpy(mm,"05");
else if(strcmp(mm,"jun")==0)strcpy(mm,"06");
else if(strcmp(mm,"jul")==0)strcpy(mm,"07");
```

```c
else if(strcmp(mm,"aug")==0)strcpy(mm,"08");
else if(strcmp(mm,"sep")==0)strcpy(mm,"09");
else if(strcmp(mm,"oct")==0)strcpy(mm,"10");
else if(strcmp(mm,"nov")==0)strcpy(mm,"11");
else if(strcmp(mm,"dec")==0)strcpy(mm,"12");
strcat(date2,mm);
strcat(date2,"-");
strcat(date2,yy);
}
else if(strcmp(form2,"dd-mon-yy")==0){
if(strcmp(form2,"dd-mon-yy")==0){
strcpy(date2,date1);
}
}
else if(strcmp(form2,"dd-mm-yyyy")==0){
strcpy(dd,substring(date1,0,1));
strcpy(mon3,substring(date1,3,5));
strcpy(yy,substring(date1,7,8));
strcat(date2,dd);
strcat(date2,"-");
if(strcmp(mon3,"jan")==0)strcpy(mm,"01");
else if(strcmp(mon3,"feb")==0)strcpy(mm,"02");
else if(strcmp(mon3,"mar")==0)strcpy(mm,"03");
else if(strcmp(mon3,"apr")==0)strcpy(mm,"04");
else if(strcmp(mon3,"may")==0)strcpy(mm,"05");
else if(strcmp(mon3,"jun")==0)strcpy(mm,"06");
else if(strcmp(mon3,"jul")==0)strcpy(mm,"07");
else if(strcmp(mon3,"aug")==0)strcpy(mm,"08");
else if(strcmp(mon3,"sep")==0)strcpy(mm,"09");
else if(strcmp(mon3,"oct")==0)strcpy(mm,"10");
else if(strcmp(mon3,"nov")==0)strcpy(mm,"11");
else if(strcmp(mon3,"dec")==0)strcpy(mm,"12");
strcat(date2,mm);
strcat(date2,"-");
strcat(date2,cent2);
strcat(date2,yy);
}
else if(strcmp(form2,"dd-mon-yyyy")==0){
strcpy(dd,substring(date1,0,1));
strcpy(mon3,substring(date1,3,5));
strcpy(yy,substring(date1,7,8));
strcat(date2,dd);
strcat(date2,"-");
strcat(date2,mon3);
strcat(date2,"-");
strcat(date2,cent2);
strcat(date2,yy);
```

```c
}
}
else if(strcmp(form1,"dd-mm-yyyy")==0){
if(strcmp(form2,"dd-mm-yy")==0){
strcpy(dd,substring(date1,0,1));
strcpy(mm,substring(date1,3,4));
strcpy(yy,substring(date1,8,9));
strcat(date2,dd);
strcat(date2,"-");
strcat(date2,mm);
strcat(date2,"-");
strcat(date2,yy);
}
else if(strcmp(form2,"dd-mon-yy")==0){
strcpy(dd,substring(date1,0,1));
strcpy(mm,substring(date1,3,4));
strcpy(yy,substring(date1,8,9));
strcat(date2,dd);
strcat(date2,"-");
if(strcmp(mm,"01")==0)strcpy(mm,"jan");
else if(strcmp(mm,"02")==0)strcpy(mm,"feb");
else if(strcmp(mm,"03")==0)strcpy(mm,"mar");
else if(strcmp(mm,"04")==0)strcpy(mm,"apr");
else if(strcmp(mm,"05")==0)strcpy(mm,"may");
else if(strcmp(mm,"06")==0)strcpy(mm,"jun");
else if(strcmp(mm,"07")==0)strcpy(mm,"jul");
else if(strcmp(mm,"08")==0)strcpy(mm,"aug");
else if(strcmp(mm,"09")==0)strcpy(mm,"sep");
else if(strcmp(mm,"10")==0)strcpy(mm,"oct");
else if(strcmp(mm,"11")==0)strcpy(mm,"nov");
else if(strcmp(mm,"12")==0)strcpy(mm,"dec");
strcat(date2,mm);
strcat(date2,"-");
strcat(date2,yy);
}
else if(strcmp(form2,"dd-mm-yyyy")==0){
strcpy(date2,date1);
}
else if(strcmp(form2,"dd-mon-yyyy")==0){
strcpy(dd,substring(date1,0,1));
strcpy(mm,substring(date1,3,4));
strcpy(yyyy,substring(date1,6,9));
strcat(date2,dd);
strcat(date2,"-");
if(strcmp(mm,"01")==0)strcpy(mm,"jan");
else if(strcmp(mm,"02")==0)strcpy(mm,"feb");
else if(strcmp(mm,"03")==0)strcpy(mm,"mar");
```

```c
else if(strcmp(mm,"04")==0)strcpy(mm,"apr");
else if(strcmp(mm,"05")==0)strcpy(mm,"may");
else if(strcmp(mm,"06")==0)strcpy(mm,"jun");
else if(strcmp(mm,"07")==0)strcpy(mm,"jul");
else if(strcmp(mm,"08")==0)strcpy(mm,"aug");
else if(strcmp(mm,"09")==0)strcpy(mm,"sep");
else if(strcmp(mm,"10")==0)strcpy(mm,"oct");
else if(strcmp(mm,"11")==0)strcpy(mm,"nov");
else if(strcmp(mm,"12")==0)strcpy(mm,"dec");
strcat(date2,mm);
strcat(date2,"-");
strcat(date2,yyyy);
}
}
else if(strcmp(form1,"dd-mon-yyyy")==0){
if(strcmp(form2,"dd-mm-yy")==0){
strcpy(dd,substring(date1,0,1));
strcpy(mon3,substring(date1,3,5));
strcpy(yy,substring(date1,9,10));
strcat(date2,dd);
strcat(date2,"-");
if(strcmp(mon3,"jan")==0)strcpy(mm,"01");
else if(strcmp(mon3,"feb")==0)strcpy(mm,"02");
else if(strcmp(mon3,"mar")==0)strcpy(mm,"03");
else if(strcmp(mon3,"apr")==0)strcpy(mm,"04");
else if(strcmp(mon3,"may")==0)strcpy(mm,"05");
else if(strcmp(mon3,"jun")==0)strcpy(mm,"06");
else if(strcmp(mon3,"jul")==0)strcpy(mm,"07");
else if(strcmp(mon3,"aug")==0)strcpy(mm,"08");
else if(strcmp(mon3,"sep")==0)strcpy(mm,"09");
else if(strcmp(mon3,"oct")==0)strcpy(mm,"10");
else if(strcmp(mon3,"nov")==0)strcpy(mm,"11");
else if(strcmp(mon3,"dec")==0)strcpy(mm,"12");
strcat(date2,mm);
strcat(date2,"-");
strcat(date2,yy);
}
else if(strcmp(form2,"dd-mon-yy")==0){
strcpy(dd,substring(date1,0,1));
strcpy(mm,substring(date1,3,5));
strcpy(yy,substring(date1,9,10));
strcat(date2,dd);
strcat(date2,"-");
strcat(date2,mm);
strcat(date2,"-");
strcat(date2,yy);
}
```

```c
else if(strcmp(form2,"dd-mm-yyyy")==0){
strcpy(dd,substring(date1,0,1));
strcpy(mon3,substring(date1,3,5));
strcpy(yy,substring(date1,9,10));
strcat(date2,dd);
strcat(date2,"-");
if(strcmp(mon3,"jan")==0)strcpy(mm,"01");
else if(strcmp(mon3,"feb")==0)strcpy(mm,"02");
else if(strcmp(mon3,"mar")==0)strcpy(mm,"03");
else if(strcmp(mon3,"apr")==0)strcpy(mm,"04");
else if(strcmp(mon3,"may")==0)strcpy(mm,"05");
else if(strcmp(mon3,"jun")==0)strcpy(mm,"06");
else if(strcmp(mon3,"jul")==0)strcpy(mm,"07");
else if(strcmp(mon3,"aug")==0)strcpy(mm,"08");
else if(strcmp(mon3,"sep")==0)strcpy(mm,"09");
else if(strcmp(mon3,"oct")==0)strcpy(mm,"10");
else if(strcmp(mon3,"nov")==0)strcpy(mm,"11");
else if(strcmp(mon3,"dec")==0)strcpy(mm,"12");
strcat(date2,mm);
strcat(date2,"-");
strcat(date2,cent2);
strcat(date2,yy);
}
else if(strcmp(form2,"dd-mon-yyyy")==0){
strcpy(date2,date1);
}
}
/* print */
strcat(date2,"\0");
strcpy(str2[76],date2);
strcpy(str3[56],str2[65]);strcpy(str3[58],str2[76]);varappend();
fread(&com.command,sizeof(com.command),1,fpt1);
goto end;
}
/* ------------------------------------------------------- */
else if(strcmp(com.command,"timesbet")==0){
fread(&com.command,sizeof(com.command),1,fpt1);
strcpy(str2[0],com.command);
strcpy(str3[50],str2[0]);varcompare();strcpy(str2[81],str3[52]);
fread(&com.command,sizeof(com.command),1,fpt1);
strcpy(str2[1],com.command);
strcpy(str3[50],str2[1]);varcompare();strcpy(str2[82],str3[52]);
fread(&com.command,sizeof(com.command),1,fpt1);
fread(&com.command,sizeof(com.command),1,fpt1);
strcpy(str2[31],com.command);
fread(&com.command,sizeof(com.command),1,fpt1);
strcpy(str2[32],com.command);
```

```
strcpy(str2[61],timeit(str2[81]));
strcpy(str2[62],timeit(str2[82]));
strcpy(str2[63],substring(str2[61],1,2));
strcpy(str2[64],substring(str2[61],3,4));
strcpy(str2[65],substring(str2[61],5,6));
strcpy(str2[73],substring(str2[62],1,2));
strcpy(str2[74],substring(str2[62],3,4));
strcpy(str2[75],substring(str2[62],5,6));
liq=atol(str2[63]);lir=atol(str2[64]);lis=atol(str2[65]);
lit=liq*3600+lir*60+lis;
liq=atol(str2[73]);lir=atol(str2[74]);lis=atol(str2[75]);
liu=liq*3600+lir*60+lis;
liv=abs(lit-liu);
sprintf(str2[76],"%li",liv);
if(strcmp(str2[61],str2[62])<0)strcpy(str2[22],"-");
else if(strcmp(str2[61],str2[62])>=0)strcpy(str2[22],"+");
strcpy(str3[56],str2[31]);strcpy(str3[58],str2[22]);varappend();
strcpy(str3[56],str2[32]);strcpy(str3[58],str2[76]);varappend();
fread(&com.command,sizeof(com.command),1,fpt1);
goto end;
}
/* ------------------------------------------------------- */
else if(strcmp(com.command,"splittimestamp")==0){
fread(&com.command,sizeof(com.command),1,fpt1);
strcpy(str2[60],com.command);
strcpy(str3[50],str2[60]);varcompare();strcpy(str2[80],str3[52]);
strcpy(str2[71],substring(str2[80],0,2));
strcpy(str2[72],substring(str2[80],4,6));
strcpy(str2[73],substring(str2[80],8,9));
strcpy(str2[74],substring(str2[80],11,12));
strcpy(str2[75],substring(str2[80],14,15));
strcpy(str2[76],substring(str2[80],17,18));
strcpy(str2[77],substring(str2[80],20,23));
fread(&com.command,sizeof(com.command),1,fpt1);
fread(&com.command,sizeof(com.command),1,fpt1);
strcpy(str2[61],com.command);
strcpy(str3[56],str2[61]);strcpy(str3[58],str2[71]);varappend();
fread(&com.command,sizeof(com.command),1,fpt1);
strcpy(str2[62],com.command);
strcpy(str3[56],str2[62]);strcpy(str3[58],str2[72]);varappend();
fread(&com.command,sizeof(com.command),1,fpt1);
strcpy(str2[63],com.command);
strcpy(str3[56],str2[63]);strcpy(str3[58],str2[73]);varappend();
fread(&com.command,sizeof(com.command),1,fpt1);
strcpy(str2[64],com.command);
strcpy(str3[56],str2[64]);strcpy(str3[58],str2[74]);varappend();
fread(&com.command,sizeof(com.command),1,fpt1);
```

```c
strcpy(str2[65],com.command);
strcpy(str3[56],str2[65]);strcpy(str3[58],str2[75]);varappend();
fread(&com.command,sizeof(com.command),1,fpt1);
strcpy(str2[66],com.command);
strcpy(str3[56],str2[66]);strcpy(str3[58],str2[76]);varappend();
fread(&com.command,sizeof(com.command),1,fpt1);
strcpy(str2[67],com.command);
strcpy(str3[56],str2[67]);strcpy(str3[58],str2[77]);varappend();
fread(&com.command,sizeof(com.command),1,fpt1);
goto end;
}
/* ------------------------------------------------------ */
else if(strcmp(com.command,"cnt")==0){
fread(&com.command,sizeof(com.command),1,fpt1); /* of */
fread(&com.command,sizeof(com.command),1,fpt1);
strcpy(str2[61],com.command);
strcpy(str3[50],str2[61]);varcompare();strcpy(str2[81],str3[52]);
fread(&com.command,sizeof(com.command),1,fpt1);
strcpy(str2[62],com.command);
strcpy(str3[50],str2[62]);varcompare();strcpy(str2[82],str3[52]);
fread(&com.command,sizeof(com.command),1,fpt1);
strcpy(str2[63],com.command);
strcpy(str3[50],str2[63]);varcompare();strcpy(str2[83],str3[52]);
fread(&com.command,sizeof(com.command),1,fpt1);
strcpy(str2[64],com.command);
strcpy(str3[50],str2[64]);varcompare();strcpy(str2[84],str3[52]);
fread(&com.command,sizeof(com.command),1,fpt1); /* into */
fread(&com.command,sizeof(com.command),1,fpt1);
strcpy(str2[65],com.command);
/**/
fclose(fpt13);
fpt13=fopen(str2[81],"r+");
li=0;
li3=0;
cow=0;
while((ch=getc(fpt13))!=EOF){
if((li3+1)==atol(str2[83])){++cow;break;}
else {
while((ch=getc(fpt13))!=',');
++li3;
if((li3+1)==atol(str2[83])){++cow;break;}
}
}
while(!feof(fpt13)){
li3=0;
while((ch=getc(fpt13))!=EOF){
if(ch==',')++li3;
```

```c
if((li3+1)==atol(str2[84])){++cow;break;}
}
}
--cow;
sprintf(str2[93],"%li",cow);
strcpy(str2[94],"+");
strcat(str2[94],str2[93]);
strcpy(str3[56],str2[65]);strcpy(str3[58],str2[94]);varappend();
fclose(fpt13);
fread(&com.command,sizeof(com.command),1,fpt1);
goto end;
}
/* ---------------------------------------------------------- */
else if(strcmp(com.command,"min")==0){
fread(&com.command,sizeof(com.command),1,fpt1); /* of */
fread(&com.command,sizeof(com.command),1,fpt1); /* filename */
strcpy(str2[61],com.command);
strcpy(str3[50],str2[61]);varcompare();strcpy(str2[81],str3[52]);
fread(&com.command,sizeof(com.command),1,fpt1); /* recname */
strcpy(str2[62],com.command);
strcpy(str3[50],str2[62]);varcompare();strcpy(str2[82],str3[52]);
fread(&com.command,sizeof(com.command),1,fpt1); /* type */
strcpy(str2[63],com.command);
strcpy(str3[50],str2[63]);varcompare();strcpy(str2[83],str3[52]);
fread(&com.command,sizeof(com.command),1,fpt1); /* offset */
strcpy(str2[64],com.command);
strcpy(str3[50],str2[64]);varcompare();strcpy(str2[84],str3[52]);
fread(&com.command,sizeof(com.command),1,fpt1); /* reclen */
strcpy(str2[65],com.command);
strcpy(str3[50],str2[65]);varcompare();strcpy(str2[85],str3[52]);
fread(&com.command,sizeof(com.command),1,fpt1); /* into */
fread(&com.command,sizeof(com.command),1,fpt1); /* somey */
strcpy(str2[66],com.command);
/**/
fclose(fpt13);
fpt13=fopen(str2[81],"r+");
li3=0;
while(!feof(fpt13)){
myfgets(str2[51],fpt13);++li3;
if(li3==atol(str2[84]))break;
}
strcpy(str2[71],str2[51]);

while(!feof(fpt13)){

li3=0;
while(!feof(fpt13)){
```

```
myfgets(str2[51],fpt13);++li3;
if(li3==atol(str2[85]))break;
}
strcpy(str2[72],str2[51]);
if(strcmp(str2[72],"\0")==0)goto naga1;
if(strcmp(str2[83],"integer")==0){
if(str2[71][0]=='+'&&str2[72][0]=='+'){
if(strlen(str2[71])==strlen(str2[72])){
if(strcomp(str2[71],str2[72])>0)strcpy(str2[73],str2[71]);
}
else if(strlen(str2[71])<strlen(str2[72]))strcpy(str2[73],str2[72]);
else if(strlen(str2[71])>strlen(str2[72]))strcpy(str2[73],str2[71]);
}
else if(str2[71][0]=='-'&&str2[72][0]=='-'){
if(strlen(str2[71])==strlen(str2[72])){
if(strcomp(str2[71],str2[72])<0)strcpy(str2[73],str2[71]);
}
else if(strlen(str2[71])>strlen(str2[72]))strcpy(str2[73],str2[72]);
else if(strlen(str2[71])<strlen(str2[72]))strcpy(str2[73],str2[71]);
}
else if(str2[71][0]=='-'&&str2[72][0]=='+'){
strcpy(str2[73],str2[72]);
}
else if(str2[71][0]=='+'&&str2[72][0]=='-'){
strcpy(str2[73],str2[71]);
}
}
else if(strcmp(str2[83],"string")==0){
if(strcomp(str2[71],str2[72])>0)strcpy(str2[73],str2[71]);
else strcpy(str2[73],str2[72]);
}
else if(strcmp(str2[83],"number")==0){
strcpy(str2[101],str2[71]);numlesstomore();strcpy(str2[1],str2[100]);
strcpy(str2[101],str2[72]);numlesstomore();strcpy(str2[2],str2[100]);
if(str2[1][0]=='+'&&str2[2][0]=='+'){
if(strcmp(str2[1],str2[2])<0)strcpy(str2[73],str2[71]);
else if(strcmp(str2[1],str2[2])>0)strcpy(str2[73],str2[72]);
else if(strcmp(str2[1],str2[2])==0)strcpy(str2[73],str2[71]);
}
else if(str2[1][0]=='-'&&str2[2][0]=='-'){
if(strcmp(str2[1],str2[2])>0)strcpy(str2[73],str2[71]);
else if(strcmp(str2[1],str2[2])<0)strcpy(str2[73],str2[72]);
else if(strcmp(str2[1],str2[2])==0)strcpy(str2[73],str2[71]);
}
else if(str2[1][0]=='-'&&str2[2][0]=='+')strcpy(str2[73],str2[71]);
else if(str2[1][0]=='+'&&str2[2][0]=='-')strcpy(str2[73],str2[72]);
}
```

```c
else if(strcmp(str2[83],"date")==0){
strcpy(str2[11],substring(str2[71],0,1));
strcpy(str2[12],substring(str2[71],3,4));
strcpy(str2[13],substring(str2[71],6,9));
strcat(str2[13],str2[12]);
strcat(str2[13],str2[11]);
strcpy(str2[21],substring(str2[72],0,1));
strcpy(str2[22],substring(str2[72],3,4));
strcpy(str2[23],substring(str2[72],6,9));
strcat(str2[23],str2[22]);
strcat(str2[23],str2[21]);
if(strcmp(str2[13],str2[23])==0)strcpy(str2[73],str2[13]);
else if(strcmp(str2[13],str2[23])>0)strcpy(str2[73],str2[23]);
else if(strcmp(str2[13],str2[23])<0)strcpy(str2[73],str2[13]);
strcpy(str2[74],"\0");
strcpy(str2[74],substring(str2[73],6,7));
strcat(str2[74],"-");
strcat(str2[74],substring(str2[73],4,5));
strcat(str2[74],"-");
strcat(str2[74],substring(str2[73],0,3));
strcpy(str2[73],str2[74]);
}
else if(strcmp(str2[83],"time")==0){
strcpy(str2[11],substring(str2[71],0,1));
strcpy(str2[12],substring(str2[71],3,4));
strcpy(str2[13],substring(str2[71],6,7));
strcpy(str2[14],substring(str2[71],9,10));
strcat(str2[14],str2[11]);
strcat(str2[14],str2[12]);
strcat(str2[14],str2[13]);
strcpy(str2[21],substring(str2[72],0,1));
strcpy(str2[22],substring(str2[72],3,4));
strcpy(str2[23],substring(str2[72],6,7));
strcpy(str2[24],substring(str2[72],9,10));
strcat(str2[24],str2[21]);
strcat(str2[24],str2[22]);
strcat(str2[24],str2[23]);
if(strcmp(str2[14],str2[24])==0)strcpy(str2[73],str2[14]);
else if(strcmp(str2[14],str2[24])>0)strcpy(str2[73],str2[24]);
else if(strcmp(str2[14],str2[24])<0)strcpy(str2[73],str2[14]);
strcpy(str2[74],"\0");
strcpy(str2[74],substring(str2[73],2,3));
strcat(str2[74],":");
strcat(str2[74],substring(str2[73],4,5));
strcat(str2[74],":");
strcat(str2[74],substring(str2[73],6,7));
strcat(str2[74],":");
```

```
strcat(str2[74],substring(str2[73],0,1));
strcpy(str2[73],str2[74]);
}
strcpy(str2[71],str2[73]);
}
naga1:
strcpy(str3[56],str2[66]);strcpy(str3[58],str2[73]);varappend();
fclose(fpt13);
fread(&com.command,sizeof(com.command),1,fpt1);
goto end;
}
/* -------------------------------------------------------- */
else if(strcmp(com.command,"max")==0){
fread(&com.command,sizeof(com.command),1,fpt1); /* of */
fread(&com.command,sizeof(com.command),1,fpt1); /* filename */
strcpy(str2[61],com.command);
strcpy(str3[50],str2[61]);varcompare();strcpy(str2[81],str3[52]);
fread(&com.command,sizeof(com.command),1,fpt1); /* recname */
strcpy(str2[62],com.command);
strcpy(str3[50],str2[62]);varcompare();strcpy(str2[82],str3[52]);
fread(&com.command,sizeof(com.command),1,fpt1); /* type */
strcpy(str2[63],com.command);
strcpy(str3[50],str2[63]);varcompare();strcpy(str2[83],str3[52]);
fread(&com.command,sizeof(com.command),1,fpt1); /* offset */
strcpy(str2[64],com.command);
strcpy(str3[50],str2[64]);varcompare();strcpy(str2[84],str3[52]);
fread(&com.command,sizeof(com.command),1,fpt1); /* reclen */
strcpy(str2[65],com.command);
strcpy(str3[50],str2[65]);varcompare();strcpy(str2[85],str3[52]);
fread(&com.command,sizeof(com.command),1,fpt1); /* into */
fread(&com.command,sizeof(com.command),1,fpt1); /* somey */
strcpy(str2[66],com.command);
/**/
fclose(fpt13);
fpt13=fopen(str2[81],"r+");
li3=0;
while(!feof(fpt13)){
myfgets(str2[51],fpt13);++li3;
if(li3==atol(str2[84]))break;
}
strcpy(str2[71],str2[51]);

while(!feof(fpt13)){

li3=0;
while(!feof(fpt13)){
myfgets(str2[51],fpt13);++li3;
```

```c
if(li3==atol(str2[85]))break;
}
strcpy(str2[72],str2[51]);
if(strcmp(str2[72],"\0")==0)goto naga2;
if(strcmp(str2[83],"integer")==0){
if(str2[71][0]=='+'&&str2[72][0]=='+'){
if(strlen(str2[71])==strlen(str2[72])){
if(strcomp(str2[71],str2[72])>0)strcpy(str2[73],str2[72]);
}
else if(strlen(str2[71])<strlen(str2[72]))strcpy(str2[73],str2[71]);
else if(strlen(str2[71])>strlen(str2[72]))strcpy(str2[73],str2[72]);
}
else if(str2[71][0]=='-'&&str2[72][0]=='-'){
if(strlen(str2[71])==strlen(str2[72])){
if(strcomp(str2[71],str2[72])<0)strcpy(str2[73],str2[72]);
}
else if(strlen(str2[71])>strlen(str2[72]))strcpy(str2[73],str2[71]);
else if(strlen(str2[71])<strlen(str2[72]))strcpy(str2[73],str2[72]);
}
else if(str2[71][0]=='-'&&str2[72][0]=='+'){
strcpy(str2[73],str2[71]);
}
else if(str2[71][0]=='+'&&str2[72][0]=='-'){
strcpy(str2[73],str2[72]);
}
}
else if(strcmp(str2[83],"string")==0){
if(strcomp(str2[71],str2[72])>0)strcpy(str2[73],str2[72]);
else strcpy(str2[73],str2[71]);
}
else if(strcmp(str2[83],"number")==0){
strcpy(str2[101],str2[71]);numlesstomore();strcpy(str2[1],str2[100]);
strcpy(str2[101],str2[72]);numlesstomore();strcpy(str2[2],str2[100]);
if(str2[1][0]=='+'&&str2[2][0]=='+'){
if(strcmp(str2[1],str2[2])<0)strcpy(str2[73],str2[72]);
else if(strcmp(str2[1],str2[2])>0)strcpy(str2[73],str2[71]);
else if(strcmp(str2[1],str2[2])==0)strcpy(str2[73],str2[72]);
}
else if(str2[1][0]=='-'&&str2[2][0]=='-'){
if(strcmp(str2[1],str2[2])>0)strcpy(str2[73],str2[72]);
else if(strcmp(str2[1],str2[2])<0)strcpy(str2[73],str2[71]);
else if(strcmp(str2[1],str2[2])==0)strcpy(str2[73],str2[72]);
}
else if(str2[1][0]=='-'&&str2[2][0]=='+')strcpy(str2[73],str2[72]);
else if(str2[1][0]=='+'&&str2[2][0]=='-')strcpy(str2[73],str2[71]);
}
else if(strcmp(str2[83],"date")==0){
```

```c
strcpy(str2[11],substring(str2[71],0,1));
strcpy(str2[12],substring(str2[71],3,4));
strcpy(str2[13],substring(str2[71],6,9));
strcat(str2[13],str2[12]);
strcat(str2[13],str2[11]);
strcpy(str2[21],substring(str2[72],0,1));
strcpy(str2[22],substring(str2[72],3,4));
strcpy(str2[23],substring(str2[72],6,9));
strcat(str2[23],str2[22]);
strcat(str2[23],str2[21]);
if(strcmp(str2[13],str2[23])==0)strcpy(str2[73],str2[23]);
else if(strcmp(str2[13],str2[23])>0)strcpy(str2[73],str2[13]);
else if(strcmp(str2[13],str2[23])<0)strcpy(str2[73],str2[23]);
strcpy(str2[74],"\0");
strcpy(str2[74],substring(str2[73],6,7));
strcat(str2[74],"-");
strcat(str2[74],substring(str2[73],4,5));
strcat(str2[74],"-");
strcat(str2[74],substring(str2[73],0,3));
strcpy(str2[73],str2[74]);
}
else if(strcmp(str2[83],"time")==0){
strcpy(str2[11],substring(str2[71],0,1));
strcpy(str2[12],substring(str2[71],3,4));
strcpy(str2[13],substring(str2[71],6,7));
strcpy(str2[14],substring(str2[71],9,10));
strcat(str2[14],str2[11]);
strcat(str2[14],str2[12]);
strcat(str2[14],str2[13]);
strcpy(str2[21],substring(str2[72],0,1));
strcpy(str2[22],substring(str2[72],3,4));
strcpy(str2[23],substring(str2[72],6,7));
strcpy(str2[24],substring(str2[72],9,10));
strcat(str2[24],str2[21]);
strcat(str2[24],str2[22]);
strcat(str2[24],str2[23]);
if(strcmp(str2[14],str2[24])==0)strcpy(str2[73],str2[24]);
else if(strcmp(str2[14],str2[24])>0)strcpy(str2[73],str2[14]);
else if(strcmp(str2[14],str2[24])<0)strcpy(str2[73],str2[24]);
strcpy(str2[74],"\0");
strcpy(str2[74],substring(str2[73],2,3));
strcat(str2[74],":");
strcat(str2[74],substring(str2[73],4,5));
strcat(str2[74],":");
strcat(str2[74],substring(str2[73],6,7));
strcat(str2[74],":");
strcat(str2[74],substring(str2[73],0,1));
```

```c
strcpy(str2[73],str2[74]);
}
strcpy(str2[71],str2[73]);
}
naga2:
strcpy(str3[56],str2[66]);strcpy(str3[58],str2[73]);varappend();
fclose(fpt13);
fread(&com.command,sizeof(com.command),1,fpt1);
goto end;
}
/* ---------------------------------------------------------- */
else if(strcmp(com.command,"initcap")==0){
fread(&com.command,sizeof(com.command),1,fpt1); /* of */
fread(&com.command,sizeof(com.command),1,fpt1);
strcpy(str2[61],com.command);
strcpy(str3[50],str2[61]);varcompare();strcpy(str2[81],str3[52]);
fread(&com.command,sizeof(com.command),1,fpt1); /* into */
fread(&com.command,sizeof(com.command),1,fpt1);
strcpy(str2[62],com.command);
if(str2[81][o]>=97&&str2[81][o]<=122)str2[81][o]-=32;
strcpy(str3[56],str2[62]);strcpy(str3[58],str2[81]);varappend();
fread(&com.command,sizeof(com.command),1,fpt1);
goto end;
}
/* ---------------------------------------------------------- */
else if(strcmp(com.command,"convertcase")==0){
fread(&com.command,sizeof(com.command),1,fpt1); /* of */
fread(&com.command,sizeof(com.command),1,fpt1);
strcpy(str2[61],com.command);
strcpy(str3[50],str2[61]);varcompare();strcpy(str2[81],str3[52]);
fread(&com.command,sizeof(com.command),1,fpt1); /* into */
fread(&com.command,sizeof(com.command),1,fpt1);
strcpy(str2[62],com.command);
for(o=0;str2[81][o]!='\0';o++){
if(str2[81][o]>=97&&str2[81][o]<=122)str2[81][o]-=32;
else if(str2[81][o]>=65&&str2[81][o]<=90)str2[81][o]+=32;
}
strcpy(str3[56],str2[62]);strcpy(str3[58],str2[81]);varappend();
fread(&com.command,sizeof(com.command),1,fpt1);
goto end;
}
/* ---------------------------------------------------------- */
else if(strcmp(com.command,"toupper")==0){
fread(&com.command,sizeof(com.command),1,fpt1); /* of */
fread(&com.command,sizeof(com.command),1,fpt1);
strcpy(str2[61],com.command);
strcpy(str3[50],str2[61]);varcompare();strcpy(str2[81],str3[52]);
```

```c
fread(&com.command,sizeof(com.command),1,fpt1); /* into */
fread(&com.command,sizeof(com.command),1,fpt1);
strcpy(str2[62],com.command);
for(o=0;str2[81][o]!='\0';o++){
if(str2[81][o]>=97&&str2[81][o]<=122)str2[81][o]-=32;
}
strcpy(str3[56],str2[62]);strcpy(str3[58],str2[81]);varappend();
fread(&com.command,sizeof(com.command),1,fpt1);
goto end;
}
/* --------------------------------------------------------- */
else if(strcmp(com.command,"tolower")==0){
fread(&com.command,sizeof(com.command),1,fpt1); /* of */
fread(&com.command,sizeof(com.command),1,fpt1);
strcpy(str2[61],com.command);
strcpy(str3[50],str2[61]);varcompare();strcpy(str2[81],str3[52]);
fread(&com.command,sizeof(com.command),1,fpt1); /* into */
fread(&com.command,sizeof(com.command),1,fpt1);
strcpy(str2[62],com.command);
for(o=0;str2[81][o]!='\0';o++){
if(str2[81][o]>=65&&str2[81][o]<=90)str2[81][o]+=32;
}
strcpy(str3[56],str2[62]);strcpy(str3[58],str2[81]);varappend();
fread(&com.command,sizeof(com.command),1,fpt1);
goto end;
}
/* --------------------------------------------------------- */
else if(strcmp(com.command,"varsize")==0){
fread(&com.command,sizeof(com.command),1,fpt1); /* of */
fread(&com.command,sizeof(com.command),1,fpt1);
strcpy(str2[61],com.command);
strcpy(str3[50],str2[61]);varcompare();strcpy(str2[81],str3[52]);
fread(&com.command,sizeof(com.command),1,fpt1); /* into */
fread(&com.command,sizeof(com.command),1,fpt1);
strcpy(str2[62],com.command);
u=strlen(str2[81]);
sprintf(str2[63],"%i",u);
strcpy(str2[64],"+");
strcat(str2[64],str2[63]);
strcpy(str3[56],str2[62]);strcpy(str3[58],str2[64]);varappend();
fread(&com.command,sizeof(com.command),1,fpt1);
goto end;
}
/* --------------------------------------------------------- */
else if(strcmp(com.command,"copyfile")==0){
fread(&com.command,sizeof(com.command),1,fpt1);
strcpy(str2[61],com.command);
```

```
strcpy(str3[50],str2[61]);varcompare();strcpy(str2[81],str3[52]);
fread(&com.command,sizeof(com.command),1,fpt1); /* to */
fread(&com.command,sizeof(com.command),1,fpt1);
strcpy(str2[62],com.command);
strcpy(str3[50],str2[62]);varcompare();strcpy(str2[82],str3[52]);
fclose(fpt14);
fpt14=fopen(str2[81],"r+");
fclose(fpt15);
fpt15=fopen(str2[82],"w+");
while((ch=getc(fpt14))!=EOF)putc(ch,fpt15);
fclose(fpt14);
fclose(fpt15);
fread(&com.command,sizeof(com.command),1,fpt1);
goto end;
}
/* ------------------------------------------------------- */
else if(strcmp(com.command,"emptyfile")==0){
fread(&com.command,sizeof(com.command),1,fpt1);
strcpy(str2[61],com.command);
strcpy(str3[50],str2[61]);varcompare();strcpy(str2[81],str3[52]);
fpt14=fopen(str2[81],"w+");
fclose(fpt14);
fread(&com.command,sizeof(com.command),1,fpt1);
goto end;
}
/* ------------------------------------------------------- */
else if(strcmp(com.command,"deletefile")==0){
fread(&com.command,sizeof(com.command),1,fpt1);
strcpy(str2[61],com.command);
strcpy(str3[50],str2[61]);varcompare();strcpy(str2[81],str3[52]);
strcpy(str2[82],"del ");
strcat(str2[82],str2[81]);
system(str2[82]);
fread(&com.command,sizeof(com.command),1,fpt1);
goto end;
}
/* ------------------------------------------------------- */
else if(strcmp(com.command,"lesser")==0){
fread(&com.command,sizeof(com.command),1,fpt1); /* of */
fread(&com.command,sizeof(com.command),1,fpt1); /* somex */
strcpy(str2[61],com.command);
strcpy(str3[50],str2[61]);varcompare();strcpy(str2[81],str3[52]);
fread(&com.command,sizeof(com.command),1,fpt1); /* somey */
strcpy(str2[62],com.command);
strcpy(str3[50],str2[62]);varcompare();strcpy(str2[82],str3[52]);
fread(&com.command,sizeof(com.command),1,fpt1); /* type */
strcpy(str2[63],com.command);
```

```c
strcpy(str3[50],str2[63]);varcompare();strcpy(str2[83],str3[52]);
fread(&com.command,sizeof(com.command),1,fpt1); /* into */
fread(&com.command,sizeof(com.command),1,fpt1); /* somez */
strcpy(str2[64],com.command);
/**/
strcpy(str2[71],str2[81]);strcpy(str2[72],str2[82]);
if(strcmp(str2[83],"integer")==0){
if(str2[71][0]=='+'&&str2[72][0]=='+'){
if(strlen(str2[71])==strlen(str2[72])){
if(strcomp(str2[71],str2[72])>0)strcpy(str2[73],str2[71]);
}
else if(strlen(str2[71])<strlen(str2[72]))strcpy(str2[73],str2[72]);
else if(strlen(str2[71])>strlen(str2[72]))strcpy(str2[73],str2[71]);
}
else if(str2[71][0]=='-'&&str2[72][0]=='-'){
if(strlen(str2[71])==strlen(str2[72])){
if(strcomp(str2[71],str2[72])<0)strcpy(str2[73],str2[71]);
}
else if(strlen(str2[71])>strlen(str2[72]))strcpy(str2[73],str2[72]);
else if(strlen(str2[71])<strlen(str2[72]))strcpy(str2[73],str2[71]);
}
else if(str2[71][0]=='-'&&str2[72][0]=='+'){
strcpy(str2[73],str2[72]);
}
else if(str2[71][0]=='+'&&str2[72][0]=='-'){
strcpy(str2[73],str2[71]);
}
}
else if(strcmp(str2[83],"string")==0){
if(strcomp(str2[71],str2[72])>0)strcpy(str2[73],str2[71]);
else strcpy(str2[73],str2[72]);
}
else if(strcmp(str2[83],"number")==0){
strcpy(str2[101],str2[71]);numlesstomore();strcpy(str2[1],str2[100]);
strcpy(str2[101],str2[72]);numlesstomore();strcpy(str2[2],str2[100]);
if(str2[1][0]=='+'&&str2[2][0]=='+'){
if(strcmp(str2[1],str2[2])<0)strcpy(str2[73],str2[71]);
else if(strcmp(str2[1],str2[2])>0)strcpy(str2[73],str2[72]);
else if(strcmp(str2[1],str2[2])==0)strcpy(str2[73],str2[71]);
}
else if(str2[1][0]=='-'&&str2[2][0]=='-'){
if(strcmp(str2[1],str2[2])>0)strcpy(str2[73],str2[71]);
else if(strcmp(str2[1],str2[2])<0)strcpy(str2[73],str2[72]);
else if(strcmp(str2[1],str2[2])==0)strcpy(str2[73],str2[71]);
}
else if(str2[1][0]=='-'&&str2[2][0]=='+')strcpy(str2[73],str2[71]);
else if(str2[1][0]=='+'&&str2[2][0]=='-')strcpy(str2[73],str2[72]);
```

```c
}
else if(strcmp(str2[83],"date")==0){
strcpy(str2[11],substring(str2[71],0,1));
strcpy(str2[12],substring(str2[71],3,4));
strcpy(str2[13],substring(str2[71],6,9));
strcat(str2[13],str2[12]);
strcat(str2[13],str2[11]);
strcpy(str2[21],substring(str2[72],0,1));
strcpy(str2[22],substring(str2[72],3,4));
strcpy(str2[23],substring(str2[72],6,9));
strcat(str2[23],str2[22]);
strcat(str2[23],str2[21]);
if(strcmp(str2[13],str2[23])==0)strcpy(str2[73],str2[13]);
else if(strcmp(str2[13],str2[23])>0)strcpy(str2[73],str2[23]);
else if(strcmp(str2[13],str2[23])<0)strcpy(str2[73],str2[13]);
strcpy(str2[74],"\0");
strcpy(str2[74],substring(str2[73],6,7));
strcat(str2[74],"-");
strcat(str2[74],substring(str2[73],4,5));
strcat(str2[74],"-");
strcat(str2[74],substring(str2[73],0,3));
strcpy(str2[73],str2[74]);
}
else if(strcmp(str2[83],"time")==0){
strcpy(str2[11],substring(str2[71],0,1));
strcpy(str2[12],substring(str2[71],3,4));
strcpy(str2[13],substring(str2[71],6,7));
strcpy(str2[14],substring(str2[71],9,10));
strcat(str2[14],str2[11]);
strcat(str2[14],str2[12]);
strcat(str2[14],str2[13]);
strcpy(str2[21],substring(str2[72],0,1));
strcpy(str2[22],substring(str2[72],3,4));
strcpy(str2[23],substring(str2[72],6,7));
strcpy(str2[24],substring(str2[72],9,10));
strcat(str2[24],str2[21]);
strcat(str2[24],str2[22]);
strcat(str2[24],str2[23]);
if(strcmp(str2[14],str2[24])==0)strcpy(str2[73],str2[14]);
else if(strcmp(str2[14],str2[24])>0)strcpy(str2[73],str2[24]);
else if(strcmp(str2[14],str2[24])<0)strcpy(str2[73],str2[14]);
strcpy(str2[74],"\0");
strcpy(str2[74],substring(str2[73],2,3));
strcat(str2[74],":");
strcat(str2[74],substring(str2[73],4,5));
strcat(str2[74],":");
strcat(str2[74],substring(str2[73],6,7));
```

```
strcat(str2[74],":");
strcat(str2[74],substring(str2[73],0,1));
strcpy(str2[73],str2[74]);
}
strcpy(str3[56],str2[64]);strcpy(str3[58],str2[73]);varappend();
fread(&com.command,sizeof(com.command),1,fpt1);
goto end;
}
/* --------------------------------------------------------- */
else if(strcmp(com.command,"greater")==0){
fread(&com.command,sizeof(com.command),1,fpt1); /* of */
fread(&com.command,sizeof(com.command),1,fpt1); /* somex */
strcpy(str2[61],com.command);
strcpy(str3[50],str2[61]);varcompare();strcpy(str2[81],str3[52]);
fread(&com.command,sizeof(com.command),1,fpt1); /* somey */
strcpy(str2[62],com.command);
strcpy(str3[50],str2[62]);varcompare();strcpy(str2[82],str3[52]);
fread(&com.command,sizeof(com.command),1,fpt1); /* type */
strcpy(str2[63],com.command);
strcpy(str3[50],str2[63]);varcompare();strcpy(str2[83],str3[52]);
fread(&com.command,sizeof(com.command),1,fpt1); /* into */
fread(&com.command,sizeof(com.command),1,fpt1);
strcpy(str2[64],com.command);
/**/
strcpy(str2[71],str2[81]);
strcpy(str2[72],str2[82]);
if(strcmp(str2[83],"integer")==0){
if(str2[71][0]=='+'&&str2[72][0]=='+'){
if(strlen(str2[71])==strlen(str2[72])){
if(strcomp(str2[71],str2[72])>0)strcpy(str2[73],str2[72]);
}
else if(strlen(str2[71])<strlen(str2[72]))strcpy(str2[73],str2[71]);
else if(strlen(str2[71])>strlen(str2[72]))strcpy(str2[73],str2[72]);
}
else if(str2[71][0]=='-'&&str2[72][0]=='-'){
if(strlen(str2[71])==strlen(str2[72])){
if(strcomp(str2[71],str2[72])<0)strcpy(str2[73],str2[72]);
}
else if(strlen(str2[71])>strlen(str2[72]))strcpy(str2[73],str2[71]);
else if(strlen(str2[71])<strlen(str2[72]))strcpy(str2[73],str2[72]);
}
else if(str2[71][0]=='-'&&str2[72][0]=='+'){
strcpy(str2[73],str2[71]);
}
else if(str2[71][0]=='+'&&str2[72][0]=='-'){
strcpy(str2[73],str2[72]);
}
```

```c
}
else if(strcmp(str2[83],"string")==0){
if(strcomp(str2[71],str2[72])>0)strcpy(str2[73],str2[72]);
else strcpy(str2[73],str2[71]);
}
else if(strcmp(str2[83],"number")==0){
strcpy(str2[101],str2[71]);numlesstomore();strcpy(str2[1],str2[100]);
strcpy(str2[101],str2[72]);numlesstomore();strcpy(str2[2],str2[100]);
if(str2[1][0]=='+'&&str2[2][0]=='+'){
if(strcmp(str2[1],str2[2])<0)strcpy(str2[73],str2[72]);
else if(strcmp(str2[1],str2[2])>0)strcpy(str2[73],str2[71]);
else if(strcmp(str2[1],str2[2])==0)strcpy(str2[73],str2[72]);
}
else if(str2[1][0]=='-'&&str2[2][0]=='-'){
if(strcmp(str2[1],str2[2])>0)strcpy(str2[73],str2[72]);
else if(strcmp(str2[1],str2[2])<0)strcpy(str2[73],str2[71]);
else if(strcmp(str2[1],str2[2])==0)strcpy(str2[73],str2[72]);
}
else if(str2[1][0]=='-'&&str2[2][0]=='+')strcpy(str2[73],str2[72]);
else if(str2[1][0]=='+'&&str2[2][0]=='-')strcpy(str2[73],str2[71]);
}
else if(strcmp(str2[83],"date")==0){
strcpy(str2[11],substring(str2[71],0,1));
strcpy(str2[12],substring(str2[71],3,4));
strcpy(str2[13],substring(str2[71],6,9));
strcat(str2[13],str2[12]);
strcat(str2[13],str2[11]);
strcpy(str2[21],substring(str2[72],0,1));
strcpy(str2[22],substring(str2[72],3,4));
strcpy(str2[23],substring(str2[72],6,9));
strcat(str2[23],str2[22]);
strcat(str2[23],str2[21]);
if(strcmp(str2[13],str2[23])==0)strcpy(str2[73],str2[23]);
else if(strcmp(str2[13],str2[23])>0)strcpy(str2[73],str2[13]);
else if(strcmp(str2[13],str2[23])<0)strcpy(str2[73],str2[23]);
strcpy(str2[74],"\0");
strcpy(str2[74],substring(str2[73],6,7));
strcat(str2[74],"-");
strcat(str2[74],substring(str2[73],4,5));
strcat(str2[74],"-");
strcat(str2[74],substring(str2[73],0,3));
strcpy(str2[73],str2[74]);
}
else if(strcmp(str2[83],"time")==0){
strcpy(str2[11],substring(str2[71],0,1));
strcpy(str2[12],substring(str2[71],3,4));
strcpy(str2[13],substring(str2[71],6,7));
```

```
strcpy(str2[14],substring(str2[71],9,10));
strcat(str2[14],str2[11]);
strcat(str2[14],str2[12]);
strcat(str2[14],str2[13]);
strcpy(str2[21],substring(str2[72],0,1));
strcpy(str2[22],substring(str2[72],3,4));
strcpy(str2[23],substring(str2[72],6,7));
strcpy(str2[24],substring(str2[72],9,10));
strcat(str2[24],str2[21]);
strcat(str2[24],str2[22]);
strcat(str2[24],str2[23]);
if(strcmp(str2[14],str2[24])==0)strcpy(str2[73],str2[24]);
else if(strcmp(str2[14],str2[24])>0)strcpy(str2[73],str2[14]);
else if(strcmp(str2[14],str2[24])<0)strcpy(str2[73],str2[24]);
strcpy(str2[74],"\0");
strcpy(str2[74],substring(str2[73],2,3));
strcat(str2[74],":");
strcat(str2[74],substring(str2[73],4,5));
strcat(str2[74],":");
strcat(str2[74],substring(str2[73],6,7));
strcat(str2[74],":");
strcat(str2[74],substring(str2[73],0,1));
strcpy(str2[73],str2[74]);
}
strcpy(str2[71],str2[73]);
strcpy(str3[56],str2[64]);strcpy(str3[58],str2[73]);varappend();
fread(&com.command,sizeof(com.command),1,fpt1);
goto end;
}
/* ---------------------------------------------------------- */
else if(strcmp(com.command,"lefttrim")==0){
fread(&com.command,sizeof(com.command),1,fpt1); /* of */
fread(&com.command,sizeof(com.command),1,fpt1);
strcpy(str2[61],com.command);
strcpy(str3[50],str2[61]);varcompare();strcpy(str2[81],str3[52]);
fread(&com.command,sizeof(com.command),1,fpt1); /* upto */
fread(&com.command,sizeof(com.command),1,fpt1);
strcpy(str2[62],com.command);
strcpy(str3[50],str2[62]);varcompare();strcpy(str2[82],str3[52]);
fread(&com.command,sizeof(com.command),1,fpt1); /* into */
fread(&com.command,sizeof(com.command),1,fpt1);
strcpy(str2[63],com.command);
u=0;for(o=atoi(str2[82])-1;str2[81][o]!='\0';o++)str2[83][u++]=str2[81][o];
str2[83][u]='\0';
/*printf("%s ",str2[63]);printf("%s ",str2[83]);*/
strcpy(str3[56],str2[63]);strcpy(str3[58],str2[83]);varappend();
fread(&com.command,sizeof(com.command),1,fpt1);
```

```c
goto end;
}
/* ---------------------------------------------------------- */
else if(strcmp(com.command,"righttrim")==0){
fread(&com.command,sizeof(com.command),1,fpt1); /* of */
fread(&com.command,sizeof(com.command),1,fpt1);
strcpy(str2[61],com.command);
strcpy(str3[50],str2[61]);varcompare();strcpy(str2[81],str3[52]);
fread(&com.command,sizeof(com.command),1,fpt1); /* upto */
fread(&com.command,sizeof(com.command),1,fpt1);
strcpy(str2[62],com.command);
strcpy(str3[50],str2[62]);varcompare();strcpy(str2[82],str3[52]);
fread(&com.command,sizeof(com.command),1,fpt1); /* into */
fread(&com.command,sizeof(com.command),1,fpt1);
strcpy(str2[63],com.command);
u=0;
for(o=0;o<=strlen(str2[81])-atoi(str2[82])-1;o++)str2[83][u++]=str2[81][o];
str2[83][u]='\0';
/*printf("%s ",str2[63]);printf("%s ",str2[83]);*/
strcpy(str3[56],str2[63]);strcpy(str3[58],str2[83]);varappend();
fread(&com.command,sizeof(com.command),1,fpt1);
goto end;
}
/* ---------------------------------------------------------- */
else if(strcmp(com.command,"leftpad")==0){
fread(&com.command,sizeof(com.command),1,fpt1); /* of */
fread(&com.command,sizeof(com.command),1,fpt1);
strcpy(str2[61],com.command);
strcpy(str3[50],str2[61]);varcompare();strcpy(str2[81],str3[52]);
fread(&com.command,sizeof(com.command),1,fpt1); /* upto */
fread(&com.command,sizeof(com.command),1,fpt1);
strcpy(str2[62],com.command);
strcpy(str3[50],str2[62]);varcompare();strcpy(str2[82],str3[52]);
fread(&com.command,sizeof(com.command),1,fpt1); /* with */
fread(&com.command,sizeof(com.command),1,fpt1);
strcpy(str2[63],com.command);
strcpy(str3[50],str2[63]);varcompare();strcpy(str2[83],str3[52]);
fread(&com.command,sizeof(com.command),1,fpt1); /* into */
fread(&com.command,sizeof(com.command),1,fpt1);
strcpy(str2[64],com.command);
u=0;
for(o=0;o<atoi(str2[82]);o++)str2[84][u++]=str2[83][0];
for( ;o<=strlen(str2[81]);o++)str2[84][u++]=str2[81][o];
str2[84][u]='\0';
strcpy(str3[56],str2[64]);strcpy(str3[58],str2[84]);varappend();
fread(&com.command,sizeof(com.command),1,fpt1);
goto end;
```

```c
}
/* ----------------------------------------------------------- */
else if(strcmp(com.command,"rightpad")==0){
fread(&com.command,sizeof(com.command),1,fpt1); /* of */
fread(&com.command,sizeof(com.command),1,fpt1);
strcpy(str2[61],com.command);
strcpy(str3[50],str2[61]);varcompare();strcpy(str2[81],str3[52]);
fread(&com.command,sizeof(com.command),1,fpt1); /* from */
fread(&com.command,sizeof(com.command),1,fpt1);
strcpy(str2[62],com.command);
strcpy(str3[50],str2[62]);varcompare();strcpy(str2[82],str3[52]);
fread(&com.command,sizeof(com.command),1,fpt1); /* with */
fread(&com.command,sizeof(com.command),1,fpt1);
strcpy(str2[63],com.command);
strcpy(str3[50],str2[63]);varcompare();strcpy(str2[83],str3[52]);
fread(&com.command,sizeof(com.command),1,fpt1); /* into */
fread(&com.command,sizeof(com.command),1,fpt1);
strcpy(str2[64],com.command);
u=0;
for(o=0;o<atoi(str2[82]);o++)str2[84][u++]=str2[81][o];
for(o=atoi(str2[82]);o<=strlen(str2[81]);o++)str2[84][u++]=str2[83][o];
str2[84][u]='\0';
strcpy(str3[56],str2[64]);strcpy(str3[58],str2[84]);varappend();
fread(&com.command,sizeof(com.command),1,fpt1);
goto end;
}
/* ----------------------------------------------------------- */
else if(strcmp(com.command,"replace")==0){
fread(&com.command,sizeof(com.command),1,fpt1); /* somex */
strcpy(str2[61],com.command);
strcpy(str3[50],str2[61]);varcompare();strcpy(str2[81],str3[52]);
fread(&com.command,sizeof(com.command),1,fpt1); /* where */
fread(&com.command,sizeof(com.command),1,fpt1); /* somey */
strcpy(str2[62],com.command);
strcpy(str3[50],str2[62]);varcompare();strcpy(str2[82],str3[52]);
fread(&com.command,sizeof(com.command),1,fpt1); /* with */
fread(&com.command,sizeof(com.command),1,fpt1); /* somez */
strcpy(str2[63],com.command);
strcpy(str3[50],str2[63]);varcompare();strcpy(str2[83],str3[52]);
fread(&com.command,sizeof(com.command),1,fpt1); /* into */
fread(&com.command,sizeof(com.command),1,fpt1); /* somep */
strcpy(str2[64],com.command);
flag[0]=0;
j=strlen(str2[83]);
l=strlen(str2[82]);
o=0;
for( ; ; ){
```

```
for(o=0;str2[81][o]!='\0';o++){
q=o;
for(p=0;p<l;p++){
if(str2[81][o++]==str2[82][p])flag[o]=1;
else {flag[o]=2;break;}
}
o=q;
if(flag[o]==1){
for(r=0;r<q;r++)str2[74][r]=str2[81][r];
for(s=0;s<j;s++)str2[74][r+s]=str2[83][s];
u=0;
for(t=r+l;t<strlen(str2[81]);t++)str2[74][r+s+(u++)]=str2[81][t];
}
}
/* printf("%s ",str2[74]);getch(); */
strcpy(str2[81],str2[74]);
if(o==strlen(str2[81]))break;
}
strcpy(str3[56],str2[64]);strcpy(str3[58],str2[74]);varappend();
fread(&com.command,sizeof(com.command),1,fpt1);
goto end;
}
/* ---------------------------------------------------------- */
else if(strcmp(com.command,"character")==0){
fread(&com.command,sizeof(com.command),1,fpt1); /* of */
fread(&com.command,sizeof(com.command),1,fpt1); /* somex */
strcpy(str2[61],com.command);
strcpy(str3[50],str2[61]);varcompare();strcpy(str2[81],str3[52]);
fread(&com.command,sizeof(com.command),1,fpt1); /* at */
fread(&com.command,sizeof(com.command),1,fpt1); /* somey */
strcpy(str2[62],com.command);
strcpy(str3[50],str2[62]);varcompare();strcpy(str2[82],str3[52]);
fread(&com.command,sizeof(com.command),1,fpt1); /* into */
fread(&com.command,sizeof(com.command),1,fpt1); /* somez */
strcpy(str2[63],com.command);
sscanf(str2[82],"%i",&o);
str2[73][0]=str2[81][o];
strcpy(str2[74],str2[73]);
strcpy(str3[56],str2[63]);strcpy(str3[58],str2[74]);varappend();
fread(&com.command,sizeof(com.command),1,fpt1);
goto end;
}
/* ---------------------------------------------------------- */
else if(strcmp(com.command,"decode")==0){
fread(&com.command,sizeof(com.command),1,fpt1); /* somex */
strcpy(str2[61],com.command);
strcpy(str3[50],str2[61]);varcompare();strcpy(str2[81],str3[52]);
```

```
fread(&com.command,sizeof(com.command),1,fpt1); /* somey */
strcpy(str2[62],com.command);
strcpy(str3[50],str2[62]);varcompare();strcpy(str2[82],str3[52]);
fread(&com.command,sizeof(com.command),1,fpt1); /* into */
fread(&com.command,sizeof(com.command),1,fpt1); /* retval */
strcpy(str2[63],com.command);
if(strcmp(str2[81],str2[82])==0)strcpy(str2[73],"equal");
else strcpy(str2[73],"notequal");
strcpy(str3[56],str2[63]);strcpy(str3[58],str2[73]);varappend();
fread(&com.command,sizeof(com.command),1,fpt1);
goto end;
}
/* ---------------------------------------------------------- */
else if(strcmp(com.command,"absolute")==0){
fread(&com.command,sizeof(com.command),1,fpt1); /* of */
fread(&com.command,sizeof(com.command),1,fpt1); /* somex */
strcpy(str2[61],com.command);
strcpy(str3[50],str2[61]);varcompare();strcpy(str2[81],str3[52]);
fread(&com.command,sizeof(com.command),1,fpt1); /* into */
fread(&com.command,sizeof(com.command),1,fpt1); /* somey */
strcpy(str2[62],com.command);
if(str2[81][0]=='-')str2[81][0]='+';
/*printf("%s ",str2[81]);*/
strcpy(str3[56],str2[62]);strcpy(str3[58],str2[81]);varappend();
fread(&com.command,sizeof(com.command),1,fpt1);
goto end;
}
/* ---------------------------------------------------------- */
else if(strcmp(com.command,"polynomial")==0){
strcpy(str2[57],"+0.0");
fread(&com.command,sizeof(com.command),1,fpt1); /* somey */
strcpy(str2[0],com.command);
fread(&com.command,sizeof(com.command),1,fpt1); /* eq */
while(1){
fread(&com.command,sizeof(com.command),1,fpt1);
if(strcmp(com.command,"endst")==0)goto labvee1;
strcpy(str2[61],com.command);
strcpy(str3[50],str2[61]);varcompare();strcpy(str2[81],str3[52]);
fread(&com.command,sizeof(com.command),1,fpt1); /* somex */
strcpy(str2[60],com.command);
strcpy(str3[50],str2[60]);varcompare();strcpy(str2[80],str3[52]);
fread(&com.command,sizeof(com.command),1,fpt1);
strcpy(str2[63],com.command);
strcpy(str3[50],str2[63]);varcompare();strcpy(str2[83],str3[52]);
strcpy(str2[81],str2[80]);
strcpy(str2[82],str2[83]);
powerit();
```

```
/* x pow n */
strcpy(str3[1],str3[4]);
/*coeff*/
strcpy(str3[2],str2[81]);
mulnumit();
strcpy(str3[2],str2[11]); /* product */
strcpy(str3[1],str2[57]);
strcpy(str2[101],str3[1]);numlesstomore();strcpy(str2[1],str2[100]);
strcpy(str2[101],str3[2]);numlesstomore();strcpy(str2[2],str2[100]);
strcpy(str2[14],addnum(str2[1],str2[2]));
strcpy(str2[101],str2[14]);nummoretoless();strcpy(str2[99],str2[100]);
strcpy(str2[57],str2[99]);/* sum of terms */
}
labvee1:
strcpy(str3[56],str2[0]);strcpy(str3[58],str2[57]);varappend();
goto end;
}
/* --------------------------------------------------------- */
else if(strcmp(com.command,"administer")==0){
fread(&com.command,sizeof(com.command),1,fpt1);
if(strcmp(com.command,"let")==0){
fread(&com.command,sizeof(com.command),1,fpt1); /* system */
fread(&com.command,sizeof(com.command),1,fpt1); /* manager */
fread(&com.command,sizeof(com.command),1,fpt1); /* password1 */
strcpy(str2[31],com.command);
fread(&com.command,sizeof(com.command),1,fpt1); /* password2 */
strcpy(str2[32],com.command);
strcpy(str3[50],str2[31]);varcompare();strcpy(str2[41],str3[52]);
strcpy(str3[50],str2[32]);varcompare();strcpy(str2[42],str3[52]);
fpt2=fopen("sysdba.ini","r+");
myfgets(str3[31],fpt2);
myfgets(str3[32],fpt2);
fclose(fpt2);
if(strcmp(str2[41],str3[31])==0&&strcmp(str2[42],str3[32])==0){
fread(&com.command,sizeof(com.command),1,fpt1);
if(strcmp(com.command,"change")==0){
fread(&com.command,sizeof(com.command),1,fpt1);
if(strcmp(com.command,"passwords")==0){
fread(&com.command,sizeof(com.command),1,fpt1); /* to */
fread(&com.command,sizeof(com.command),1,fpt1);
strcpy(str2[33],com.command);
fread(&com.command,sizeof(com.command),1,fpt1);
strcpy(str2[34],com.command);
strcpy(str3[50],str2[33]);varcompare();strcpy(str2[43],str3[52]);
strcpy(str3[50],str2[34]);varcompare();strcpy(str2[44],str3[52]);
fpt2=fopen("sysdba.ini","w+");
myfputs(str2[43],fpt2);printf("%s ",str2[43]);
```

```c
myfputs(str2[44],fpt2);printf("%s ",str2[44]);
fclose(fpt2);
}
}
else if(strcmp(com.command,"drop")==0){
fread(&com.command,sizeof(com.command),1,fpt1);
if(strcmp(com.command,"username")==0){
fread(&com.command,sizeof(com.command),1,fpt1);
strcpy(str2[31],com.command);
strcpy(str3[50],str2[31]);varcompare();strcpy(str2[41],str3[52]);
fread(&com.command,sizeof(com.command),1,fpt1); /* with */
fread(&com.command,sizeof(com.command),1,fpt1);
if(strcmp(com.command,"password")==0){
fread(&com.command,sizeof(com.command),1,fpt1);
strcpy(str2[32],com.command);
strcpy(str3[50],str2[32]);varcompare();strcpy(str2[42],str3[52]);
fclose(fpt2);
fclose(fpt10);
fpt2=fopen("sysdba.rig","r+");
fpt10=fopen("temp.dat","w+");
while(1){
myfgets(str2[51],fpt2);if(feof(fpt2))break;
myfgets(str2[52],fpt2);if(feof(fpt2))break;
myfgets(str2[53],fpt2);if(feof(fpt2))break;
myfgets(str2[54],fpt2);if(feof(fpt2))break;
myfgets(str2[55],fpt2);if(feof(fpt2))break;
myfgets(str2[56],fpt2);if(feof(fpt2))break;
myfgets(str2[57],fpt2);if(feof(fpt2))break;
myfgets(str2[58],fpt2);if(feof(fpt2))break;
myfgets(str2[59],fpt2);if(feof(fpt2))break;
if(strcmp(str2[51],str2[41])==0&&strcmp(str2[52],str2[42])==0){}
else {
myfputs(str2[51],fpt10);
myfputs(str2[52],fpt10);
myfputs(str2[53],fpt10);
myfputs(str2[54],fpt10);
myfputs(str2[55],fpt10);
myfputs(str2[56],fpt10);
myfputs(str2[57],fpt10);
myfputs(str2[58],fpt10);
myfputs(str2[59],fpt10);
}
}
}
}
fclose(fpt2);
fclose(fpt10);
```

```
fpt2=fopen("sysdba.rig","w+");
fpt10=fopen("temp.dat","r+");
while((ch=getc(fpt10))!=EOF)putc(ch,fpt2);
fclose(fpt2);
fclose(fpt10);
}
else if(strcmp(com.command,"dropall")==0){
fread(&com.command,sizeof(com.command),1,fpt1);
if(strcmp(com.command,"usernames")==0){
fread(&com.command,sizeof(com.command),1,fpt1);
strcpy(str2[31],com.command);
strcpy(str3[50],str2[31]);varcompare();strcpy(str2[41],str3[52]);
fclose(fpt2);
fclose(fpt10);
fpt2=fopen("sysdba.rig","r+");
fpt10=fopen("temp.dat","w+");
while(1){
myfgets(str2[51],fpt2);if(feof(fpt2))break;
myfgets(str2[52],fpt2);if(feof(fpt2))break;
myfgets(str2[53],fpt2);if(feof(fpt2))break;
myfgets(str2[54],fpt2);if(feof(fpt2))break;
myfgets(str2[55],fpt2);if(feof(fpt2))break;
myfgets(str2[56],fpt2);if(feof(fpt2))break;
myfgets(str2[57],fpt2);if(feof(fpt2))break;
myfgets(str2[58],fpt2);if(feof(fpt2))break;
myfgets(str2[59],fpt2);if(feof(fpt2))break;
if(strcmp(str2[51],str2[41])==0){}
else {
myfputs(str2[51],fpt10);
myfputs(str2[52],fpt10);
myfputs(str2[53],fpt10);
myfputs(str2[54],fpt10);
myfputs(str2[55],fpt10);
myfputs(str2[56],fpt10);
myfputs(str2[57],fpt10);
myfputs(str2[58],fpt10);
myfputs(str2[59],fpt10);
}
}
fclose(fpt2);
fclose(fpt10);
fpt2=fopen("sysdba.rig","w+");
fpt10=fopen("temp.dat","r+");
while((ch=getc(fpt10))!=EOF)putc(ch,fpt2);
fclose(fpt2);
fclose(fpt10);
}
```

```c
}
else if(strcmp(com.command,"specify")==0){
fread(&com.command,sizeof(com.command),1,fpt1);
strcpy(str2[31],com.command);
fread(&com.command,sizeof(com.command),1,fpt1);
strcpy(str2[32],com.command);
fread(&com.command,sizeof(com.command),1,fpt1);
strcpy(str2[33],com.command);
fread(&com.command,sizeof(com.command),1,fpt1);
strcpy(str2[34],com.command);
fread(&com.command,sizeof(com.command),1,fpt1);
strcpy(str2[35],com.command);
fread(&com.command,sizeof(com.command),1,fpt1);
strcpy(str2[36],com.command);
fread(&com.command,sizeof(com.command),1,fpt1);
strcpy(str2[37],com.command);
fread(&com.command,sizeof(com.command),1,fpt1);
strcpy(str2[38],com.command);
strcpy(str3[50],str2[31]);varcompare();strcpy(str2[41],str3[52]);
strcpy(str3[50],str2[32]);varcompare();strcpy(str2[42],str3[52]);
strcpy(str3[50],str2[33]);varcompare();strcpy(str2[43],str3[52]);
strcpy(str3[50],str2[34]);varcompare();strcpy(str2[44],str3[52]);
strcpy(str3[50],str2[35]);varcompare();strcpy(str2[45],str3[52]);
strcpy(str3[50],str2[36]);varcompare();strcpy(str2[46],str3[52]);
strcpy(str3[50],str2[37]);varcompare();strcpy(str2[47],str3[52]);
strcpy(str3[50],str2[38]);varcompare();strcpy(str2[48],str3[52]);
fclose(fpt2);
fclose(fpt10);
fpt2=fopen("sysdba.rig","r+");
if(fpt2==NULL)fpt2=fopen("sysdba.rig","w+");
fpt10=fopen("temp.dat","w+");
flag[10]=0;
while(1){
myfgets(str2[51],fpt2);if(feof(fpt2))break;
myfgets(str2[52],fpt2);if(feof(fpt2))break;
myfgets(str2[53],fpt2);if(feof(fpt2))break;
myfgets(str2[54],fpt2);if(feof(fpt2))break;
myfgets(str2[55],fpt2);if(feof(fpt2))break;
myfgets(str2[56],fpt2);if(feof(fpt2))break;
myfgets(str2[57],fpt2);if(feof(fpt2))break;
myfgets(str2[58],fpt2);if(feof(fpt2))break;
myfgets(str2[59],fpt2);if(feof(fpt2))break;
if(strcmp(str2[41],str2[51])==0&&
  strcmp(str2[42],str2[52])==0&&
  strcmp(str2[43],str2[53])==0&&
  strcmp(str2[44],str2[54])==0&&
  strcmp(str2[45],str2[55])==0&&
```

```c
  strcmp(str2[46],str2[56])==0&&
  strcmp(str2[47],str2[57])==0&&
  strcmp(str2[48],str2[58])==0&&
  strcmp("~",str2[59])==0){}
else {
myfputs(str2[51],fpt10);
myfputs(str2[52],fpt10);
myfputs(str2[53],fpt10);
myfputs(str2[54],fpt10);
myfputs(str2[55],fpt10);
myfputs(str2[56],fpt10);
myfputs(str2[57],fpt10);
myfputs(str2[58],fpt10);
myfputs("~",fpt10);
}
}
myfputs(str2[41],fpt10);
myfputs(str2[42],fpt10);
myfputs(str2[43],fpt10);
myfputs(str2[44],fpt10);
myfputs(str2[45],fpt10);
myfputs(str2[46],fpt10);
myfputs(str2[47],fpt10);
myfputs(str2[48],fpt10);
myfputs("~",fpt10);
fclose(fpt2);
fclose(fpt10);
fpt10=fopen("temp.dat","r+");
fpt2=fopen("sysdba.rig","w+");
while((ch=getc(fpt10))!=EOF)putc(ch,fpt2);
fclose(fpt2);
fclose(fpt10);
}
}
}
fread(&com.command,sizeof(com.command),1,fpt1);
goto end;
}
/* ----------------------------------------------------- */
else if(strcmp(com.command,"endecrb")==0){
/* endecrb endst */
printf("Encrypt or Decrypt file(e/d)? ");
fflush(stdin);
ch=getchar();
if(ch=='e'){/*2*/
printf("Bucketed type or Non-bucketed type(b/n) ? ");
fflush(stdin);
```

```c
ch=getchar();
if(ch=='n'){/*3*/
printf("Enter the name of the file to be encrypted : ");
fflush(stdin);
gets(fname1);
fpt1=fopen(fname1,"r+");
if(fpt1==NULL){printf("File not opened.Exiting...");getch();exit(0);}
fpt2=fopen("temp.dat","w+");
while((ch=getc(fpt1))!=EOF){/*4*/
if(ch==EOF)ch=254;
else ch+=7;
putc(ch,fpt2);
}/*4*/
fclose(fpt1);
fclose(fpt2);
fpt1=fopen(fname1,"w+");
fpt2=fopen("temp.dat","r+");
while((ch=getc(fpt2))!=EOF)putc(ch,fpt1);
fclose(fpt1);
fclose(fpt2);
}/*3*/
else if(ch=='b'){/*5*/
printf("Enter the name of the file to be encrypted : ");
fflush(stdin);
gets(fname1);
while(1){/*6*/
fpt1=fopen(fname1,"r+");
if(fpt1==NULL){printf("File not opened.Exiting...");getch();exit(0);}
fpt2=fopen("temp.dat","w+");
while((ch=getc(fpt1))!=EOF){/*7*/
if(ch==EOF)ch=254;
else ch+=7;
putc(ch,fpt2);
}/*7*/
fclose(fpt1);
fclose(fpt2);
fpt1=fopen(fname1,"w+");
fpt2=fopen("temp.dat","r+");
while((ch=getc(fpt2))!=EOF)putc(ch,fpt1);
fclose(fpt1);
fclose(fpt2);
strcpy(number,substring(fname1,4,7));
sscanf(number,"%i",&num1);
++num1;
if(num1>9999)break;
else {/*8*/
    sprintf(namepart,"%i",num1);
```

```c
        strcpy(fnameprior,substring(fname1,0,3));
        strcat(fnameprior,namepart);
        strcat(fnameprior,".dat");
        strcpy(fname1,fnameprior);
        printf("%s ",fname1);
        }/*8*/
}/*6*/
}/*5*/
}/*2*/
else if(ch=='d'){/*9*/
printf("Bucketed type or Non-bucketed type(b/n) ? ");
fflush(stdin);
ch=getchar();
if(ch=='n'){/*10*/
printf("Enter the name of the file to be decrypted : ");
fflush(stdin);
gets(fname1);
fpt1=fopen(fname1,"r+");
if(fpt1==NULL){printf("File not opened.Exiting...");getch();exit(0);}
fpt2=fopen("temp.dat","w+");
while((ch=getc(fpt1))!=EOF){/*11*/
if(ch==254)ch=EOF;
else ch-=7;
putc(ch,fpt2);
}/*11*/
fclose(fpt1);
fclose(fpt2);
fpt1=fopen(fname1,"w+");
fpt2=fopen("temp.dat","r+");
while((ch=getc(fpt2))!=EOF)putc(ch,fpt1);
fclose(fpt1);
fclose(fpt2);
}/*10*/
else if(ch=='b'){/*12*/
printf("Enter the name of the file to be decrypted : ");
fflush(stdin);
gets(fname1);
while(1){
fpt1=fopen(fname1,"r+");
if(fpt1==NULL){printf("File not opened.Exiting...");getch();exit(0);}
fpt2=fopen("temp.dat","w+");
while((ch=getc(fpt1))!=EOF){/*11*/
if(ch==254)ch=EOF;
else ch-=7;
putc(ch,fpt2);
}/*11*/
fclose(fpt1);
```

```c
fclose(fpt2);
fpt1=fopen(fname1,"w+");
fpt2=fopen("temp.dat","r+");
while((ch=getc(fpt2))!=EOF)putc(ch,fpt1);
fclose(fpt1);
fclose(fpt2);
strcpy(number,substring(fname1,4,7));
sscanf(number,"%i",&num1);
++num1;
if(num1>9999)break;
else {/*13*/
    sprintf(namepart,"%i",num1);
    strcpy(fnameprior,substring(fname1,0,3));
    strcat(fnameprior,namepart);
    strcat(fnameprior,".dat");
    strcpy(fname1,fnameprior);
    printf("%s ",fname1);
    }/*13*/
}/*12*/
}/*1*/
}
fread(&com.command,sizeof(com.command),1,fpt1);
goto end;
}
/* ----------------------------------------------------- */
else if(strcmp(com.command,"decrec")==0){
fread(&com.command,sizeof(com.command),1,fpt1);
strcpy(str2[0],com.command);
strcpy(str3[50],str2[0]);varcompare();strcpy(str2[1],str3[52]);
strcpy(filename,str2[1]);
strcpy(filename2,"colnames.dat");
fclose(fpt7);
fpt7=fopen("colnames.dat","w+");
for(u=0; ;u++){
sprintf(str2[2],"%i",u);
fread(&com.command,sizeof(com.command),1,fpt1);
if(strcmp(com.command,"endst")==0)goto labeldec;
myfputs(str2[2],fpt7);
myfputs(com.command,fpt7);
}
labeldec:
fclose(fpt7);
goto end;
}
/* ----------------------------------------------------- */
else if(strcmp(com.command,"display")==0){
fread(&com.command,sizeof(com.command),1,fpt1);
```

```c
if(strcmp(com.command,"all")==0){
fread(&com.command,sizeof(com.command),1,fpt1);
if(strcmp(com.command,"of")==0){
fread(&com.command,sizeof(com.command),1,fpt1);
strcpy(str2[0],com.command);
strcpy(str3[50],str2[0]);varcompare();strcpy(str2[1],str3[52]);
fread(&com.command,sizeof(com.command),1,fpt1);
strcpy(str2[40],com.command);
strcpy(str3[50],str2[40]);varcompare();strcpy(str2[60],str3[52]);
li2=0;
fclose(fpt7);
fpt7=fopen("colnames.dat","r+");
while(1){
fseek(fpt7,0L,SEEK_SET);
while(1){
myfgets(str2[8],fpt7);if(feof(fpt7))break;
myfgets(str2[9],fpt7);
printf("%s ",str2[9]);
}
putchar('\n');
printf("-----------------------------------------------------------------\
------------\n");
getch();
u=0;
fclose(fpt3);
fpt3=fopen(str2[1],"r+");
fseek(fpt3,li2,SEEK_SET);
while(1){
myfgets(str2[2],fpt3);if(feof(fpt3))goto labeldisp;
if(strcmp(str2[2],"~")!=0)printf("%s ",str2[2]);
else {putchar('\n');++u;if(u>=atoi(str2[60]))goto labelu;}
}
labelu:
li2=ftell(fpt3);
}
}
}
labeldisp:
fclose(fpt7);
fclose(fpt3);
fread(&com.command,sizeof(com.command),1,fpt1);
goto end;
}
/* ------------------------------------------------------- */
else if(strcmp(com.command,"selectif")==0){
place=place2;
/*printf("place=%i ",place);getch();*/
```

```
fread(&com.command,sizeof(com.command),1,fpt1);
strcpy(str3[81],com.command);
fread(&com.command,sizeof(com.command),1,fpt1);
strcpy(str3[82],com.command);
fread(&com.command,sizeof(com.command),1,fpt1);
strcpy(str3[83],com.command);
/*printf("%s %s %s ",str3[81],str3[82],str3[83]);*/
fclose(fpt3);
fpt3=fopen(filename,"r+");
fseek(fpt3,place,SEEK_SET);
fclose(fpt7);
fpt7=fopen("colnames.dat","r+");
w=0;
while(1){
myfgets(str3[21],fpt7);if(feof(fpt7))break;
myfgets(str3[28],fpt7);if(feof(fpt7))break;
++w;
/*printf("%s %s ",str3[28],str3[81]);*/
if(strcmp(str3[28],str3[81])==0){break;}
}
/*printf("$%i ",w);*/
fseek(fpt7,0L,SEEK_SET);
v=0;
flag[57]=0;
while(1){
myfgets(str3[21],fpt7);
if(feof(fpt7)){
flag[57]=1;
strcpy(str3[50],str3[83]);varcompare();strcpy(str3[22],str3[52]);
goto labelselectif1;
}
myfgets(str3[27],fpt7);if(feof(fpt7))break;
if(strcmp(str3[27],str3[83])==0)break;
++v;
}
labelselectif1:
/*printf("%i %i ",v,flag[57]);*/
fclose(fpt3);
fpt3=fopen(filename,"r+");
if(flag[57]==0){
fseek(fpt3,place,SEEK_SET);
for(k=0;k<v;k++)myfgets(str3[22],fpt3);
}
fclose(fpt3);
fpt3=fopen(filename,"r+");
fseek(fpt3,place,SEEK_SET);
for(k=0;k<w;k++){myfgets(str3[23],fpt3);/*printf("0-%s ",str3[23]);*/}
```

```c
strcpy(str3[2],str3[23]);
strcpy(str2[1],str3[82]);
strcpy(str3[12],str3[22]);
/*printf("%s %s %s ",str3[2],str2[1],str3[12]);*/
fclose(fpt3);
fpt3=fopen(filename,"r+");
fseek(fpt3,place,SEEK_SET);
flag[0]=0;
if(strcmp(str2[1],"gt")==0){
if(str3[2][0]=='+'&&str3[12][0]=='+'){
flag[1]=0;
for(k=0;str3[2][k]!='\0';k++)if(str3[2][k]=='.'){flag[1]=1;break;}
flag[2]=0;
for(y=0;str3[12][y]!='\0';y++)if(str3[12][y]=='.'){flag[2]=1;break;}
if(flag[1]==1&&flag[2]==1){
if(k==y){if(strcmp(str3[2],str3[12])>0)flag[0]=1;}
else if(k>y)flag[0]=1;
else flag[0]=0;
}
else if(flag[1]==0&&flag[2]==0){
if(strcomp(str3[2],str3[12])==+1)flag[0]=1;
else flag[0]=0;
}
}
else if(str3[2][0]=='-'&&str3[12][0]=='-'){
flag[1]=0;
for(k=0;str3[2][k]!='\0';k++)if(str3[2][k]=='.'){flag[1]=1;break;}
flag[2]=0;
for(y=0;str3[12][y]!='\0';y++)if(str3[12][y]=='.'){flag[2]=1;break;}
if(flag[1]==1&&flag[2]==1){
if(k==y){if(strcmp(str3[2],str3[12])<0)flag[0]=1;}
else if(k<y)flag[0]=1;
else flag[0]=0;
}
else if(flag[1]==0&&flag[2]==0){
if(strcomp(str3[2],str3[12])==-1)flag[0]=1;
else flag[0]=0;
}
}
else if(str3[2][0]=='+'&&str3[12][0]=='-'){
flag[0]=1;
}
else if(str3[2][0]=='-'&&str3[12][0]=='+'){
flag[0]=0;
}
else if(strcmp(str3[2],str3[12])>0)flag[0]=1;
}
```

```c
else if(strcmp(str2[1],"lt")==0){
if(str3[2][0]=='+'&&str3[12][0]=='+'){
flag[1]=0;
for(k=0;str3[2][k]!='\0';k++)if(str3[2][k]=='.'){flag[1]=1;break;}
flag[2]=0;
for(y=0;str3[12][y]!='\0';y++)if(str3[12][y]=='.'){flag[2]=1;break;}
if(flag[1]==1&&flag[2]==1){
if(k==y){if(strcmp(str3[2],str3[12])<0)flag[0]=1;}
else if(k<y)flag[0]=1;
else flag[0]=0;
}
else if(flag[1]==0&&flag[2]==0){
if(strcomp(str3[2],str3[12])==-1)flag[0]=1;
else flag[0]=0;
}
}
else if(str3[2][0]=='-'&&str3[12][0]=='-'){
flag[1]=0;
for(k=0;str3[2][k]!='\0';k++)if(str3[2][k]=='.'){flag[1]=1;break;}
flag[2]=0;
for(y=0;str3[12][y]!='\0';y++)if(str3[12][y]=='.'){flag[2]=1;break;}
if(flag[1]==1&&flag[2]==1){
if(k==y){if(strcmp(str3[2],str3[12])>0)flag[0]=1;}
else if(k>y)flag[0]=1;
else flag[0]=0;
}
else if(flag[1]==0&&flag[2]==0){
if(strcomp(str3[2],str3[12])==+1)flag[0]=1;
else flag[0]=0;
}
}
else if(str3[2][0]=='+'&&str3[12][0]=='-'){
flag[0]=0;
}
else if(str3[2][0]=='-'&&str3[12][0]=='+'){
flag[0]=1;
}
else if(strcmp(str3[2],str3[12])<0)flag[0]=1;
}
else if(strcmp(str2[1],"eq")==0){
if(strcmp(str3[2],str3[12])==0)flag[0]=1;
}
else if(strcmp(str2[1],"ge")==0){
if(str3[2][0]=='+'&&str3[12][0]=='+'){
flag[1]=0;
for(k=0;str3[2][k]!='\0';k++)if(str3[2][k]=='.'){flag[1]=1;break;}
flag[2]=0;
```

```c
for(y=0;str3[12][y]!='\0';y++)if(str3[12][y]=='.'){flag[2]=1;break;}
if(flag[1]==1&&flag[2]==1){
if(k==y){if(strcmp(str3[2],str3[12])>=0)flag[0]=1;}
else if(k>y)flag[0]=1;
else flag[0]=0;
}
else if(flag[1]==0&&flag[2]==0){
if(strcomp(str3[2],str3[12])==1||strcomp(str3[2],str3[12])==0)flag[0]=1;
else flag[0]=0;
}
}
else if(str3[2][0]=='-'&&str3[12][0]=='-'){
flag[1]=0;
for(k=0;str3[2][k]!='\0';k++)if(str3[2][k]=='.'){flag[1]=1;break;}
flag[2]=0;
for(y=0;str3[12][y]!='\0';y++)if(str3[12][y]=='.'){flag[2]=1;break;}
if(flag[1]==1&&flag[2]==1){
if(k==y){if(strcmp(str3[2],str3[12])<=0)flag[0]=1;}
else if(k<y)flag[0]=1;
else flag[0]=0;
}
else if(flag[1]==0&&flag[2]==0){
if(strcomp(str3[2],str3[12])==-1||strcomp(str3[2],str3[12])==0)flag[0]=1;
else flag[0]=0;
}
}
else if(str3[2][0]=='+'&&str3[12][0]=='-'){
flag[0]=1;
}
else if(str3[2][0]=='-'&&str3[12][0]=='+'){
flag[0]=0;
}
else if(strcmp(str3[2],str3[12])>=0)flag[0]=1;
}
else if(strcmp(str2[1],"le")==0){
if(str3[2][0]=='+'&&str3[12][0]=='+'){
flag[1]=0;
for(k=0;str3[2][k]!='\0';k++)if(str3[2][k]=='.'){flag[1]=1;break;}
flag[2]=0;
for(y=0;str3[12][y]!='\0';y++)if(str3[12][y]=='.'){flag[2]=1;break;}
if(flag[1]==1&&flag[2]==1){
if(k==y){if(strcmp(str3[2],str3[12])<=0)flag[0]=1;}
else if(k<y)flag[0]=1;
else flag[0]=0;
}
else if(flag[1]==0&&flag[2]==0){
if(strcomp(str3[2],str3[12])==-1||strcomp(str3[2],str3[12])==0)flag[0]=1;
```

```c
else flag[0]=0;
}
}
else if(str3[2][0]=='-'&&str3[12][0]=='-'){
flag[1]=0;
for(k=0;str3[2][k]!='\0';k++)if(str3[2][k]=='.'){flag[1]=1;break;}
flag[2]=0;
for(y=0;str3[12][y]!='\0';y++)if(str3[12][y]=='.'){flag[2]=1;break;}
if(flag[1]==1&&flag[2]==1){
if(k==y){if(strcmp(str3[2],str3[12])>=0)flag[0]=1;}
else if(k>y)flag[0]=1;
else flag[0]=0;
}
else if(flag[1]==0&&flag[2]==0){
if(strcomp(str3[2],str3[12])==1||strcomp(str3[2],str3[12])==0)flag[0]=1;
else flag[0]=0;
}
}
else if(str3[2][0]=='+'&&str3[12][0]=='-'){
flag[0]=0;
}
else if(str3[2][0]=='-'&&str3[12][0]=='+'){
flag[0]=1;
}
else if(strcmp(str3[2],str3[12])<=0)flag[0]=1;
}
else if(strcmp(str2[1],"ne")==0){
if(strcmp(str3[2],str3[12])!=0)flag[0]=1;
}
if(flag[0]==1)strcat(logic[0],"1");
else if(flag[0]==0)strcat(logic[0],"0");
/*printf(">%s ",logic[0]);*/
fclose(fpt3);
fpt3=fopen(filename,"r+");
fseek(fpt3,place,SEEK_SET);
d=0;
while(1){myfgets(str3[97],fpt3);++d;if(strcmp(str3[97],"~")==0)break;}
fseek(fpt3,place,SEEK_SET);
fread(&com.command,sizeof(com.command),1,fpt1);
goto end;
}
/* -------------------------------------------------- */
else if(strcmp(com.command,"applylogic")==0){
u=0;
while(1){
fread(&com.command,sizeof(com.command),1,fpt1);
if(strcmp(com.command,"endst")!=0){
```

```
logic[1][u]=com.command[0];++u;
}
else {
logic[1][u]='\0';
/*puts(logic[1]);*/
u=0;
for(k=0;logic[0][u]!='\0';k++)
{logic[2][k]=logic[0][u];logic[2][++k]=logic[1][u];++u;}
logic[2][k]='\0';
/*puts(logic[2]);*/
for( ; ; ){
k=0;
if(logic[2][k+1]=='a'){
if(logic[2][k]=='0'||logic[2][k+2]=='0')ch='0';else ch='1';
}
else if(logic[2][k+1]=='o'){
if(logic[2][k]=='1'||logic[2][k+2]=='1')ch='1';else ch='0';
}
l=0;m=3;logic[1][l]=ch;
for(l==1; ;l++){if(logic[2][m]!='\0')logic[1][l]=logic[2][m];else break;m++;}
logic[1][l]='\0';
logic[2][0]=ch;logic[2][1]='\0';
strcat(logic[2],logic[1]);
/*puts(logic[2]);*/
if(logic[2][1]=='\0'){goto end;}
}
}
}
goto end;
}
/* ---------------------------------------------------- */
else if(strcmp(com.command,"electrec")==0){
fread(&com.command,sizeof(com.command),1,fpt1);
strcpy(str3[11],com.command);
fread(&com.command,sizeof(com.command),1,fpt1);
strcpy(str3[12],com.command);
fclose(fpt3);
fpt3=fopen(filename,"r+");
place=place2;
fseek(fpt3,place,SEEK_SET);
/*printf("-->?%li ",place);*/
if(logic[2][0]=='1'){
/*printf("entered 1");*/
fclose(fpt3);
fpt3=fopen(filename,"r+");
fseek(fpt3,place,SEEK_SET);
for(k=0;k<d-3;k++){
```

```c
myfgets(str3[34],fpt3);
/*printf("->%s ",str3[34]);*/
if(feof(fpt3))break;
}
strcpy(str3[13],substring(str3[12],0,1));
/*myfputs(str3[13],fpt3);*/
fclose(fpt10);
fpt10=fopen("temp.dat","r+");
if(fpt10==NULL)fpt10=fopen("temp.dat","w+");
fseek(fpt10,0L,SEEK_END);
fclose(fpt3);
fpt3=fopen(filename,"r+");
fseek(fpt3,place,SEEK_SET);
l=0;while(1){
++l;
myfgets(str3[77],fpt3);
if(l==d-2)myfputs(str3[13],fpt10);
else if(strcmp(str3[77],"~")==0)break;
else myfputs(str3[77],fpt10);
}
myfputs("~",fpt10);
}
else if(logic[2][0]=='0'){
/*printf("entered 0");*/
fclose(fpt3);
fpt3=fopen(filename,"r+");
fseek(fpt3,place,SEEK_SET);
fclose(fpt10);
fpt10=fopen("temp.dat","r+");
if(fpt10==NULL)fpt10=fopen("temp.dat","w+");
fseek(fpt10,0L,SEEK_END);
while(1){
myfgets(str3[16],fpt3);if(feof(fpt3))break;
myfputs(str3[16],fpt10);
if(strcmp(str3[16],"~")==0){/*printf("nextrec ");*/break;}
}
}
labelelectrec:
/*printf("labelelectrecif:");*/
myfgets(str3[23],fpt3);
li2=ftell(fpt3);
fseek(fpt3,0L,SEEK_END);
li=ftell(fpt3);
/*printf("@%li %li ",li,li2);getch();*/
if(li==li2){
fclose(fpt3);fclose(fpt10);
/*printf("eof eof eof eof ");getch();*/
```

```c
fread(&com.command,sizeof(com.command),1,fpt1);
if(strcmp(com.command,"oneofto")==0){
fread(&com.command,sizeof(com.command),1,fpt1);
strcpy(labelvar[var[4]],com.command);
rewind(fpt1);
for(i=0;!feof(fpt1);i++){
fread(&com.command,sizeof(com.command),1,fpt1);
if(strcmp(com.command,"labelit")==0){
fread(&com.command,sizeof(com.command),1,fpt1);
if(strcmp(com.command,labelvar[var[4]])==0){
fclose(fpt10);
fclose(fpt3);
fpt10=fopen("temp.dat","r+");
fpt3=fopen(filename,"w+");
while((ch=getc(fpt10))!=EOF){/*putchar(ch);*/putc(ch,fpt3);}
fclose(fpt3);
fclose(fpt10);
/*fpt10=fopen("temp.dat","w+");*/
/*printf("WAIT");getch();*/
goto end;
}
}
}
}
}
fclose(fpt3);
fpt3=fopen(filename,"r+");
fseek(fpt3,place,SEEK_SET);
/*printf("=>%li ",place);*/
while(1){
myfgets(str3[23],fpt3);
if(strcmp(str3[23],"~")==0)break;
}
place2=ftell(fpt3);
/*printf("--->%li ",place2);*/
strcpy(logic[0],"\0");
fread(&com.command,sizeof(com.command),1,fpt1);
goto end;
}
/* ---------------------------------------------------- */
else if(strcmp(com.command,"tonumber")==0){
fread(&com.command,sizeof(com.command),1,fpt1); /* of */
fread(&com.command,sizeof(com.command),1,fpt1);
strcpy(str2[0],com.command);
strcpy(str3[50],str2[0]);varcompare();strcpy(str2[1],str3[52]);
strcat(str2[1],".0");
fclose(fpt2);
```

```c
strcpy(str3[56],str2[0]);strcpy(str3[58],str2[1]);varappend();
fread(&com.command,sizeof(com.command),1,fpt1);
goto end;
}
/* ------------------------------------------------------------ */
else if(strcmp(com.command,"tointeger")==0){
fread(&com.command,sizeof(com.command),1,fpt1); /* of */
fread(&com.command,sizeof(com.command),1,fpt1);
strcpy(str2[4],com.command);
strcpy(str3[50],str2[4]);varcompare();strcpy(str2[1],str3[52]);
for(y=0;str2[1][y]!='.';y++)str2[11][y]=str2[1][y];str2[11][y]='\0';
strcpy(str3[56],str2[4]);strcpy(str3[58],str2[11]);varappend();
fread(&com.command,sizeof(com.command),1,fpt1);
goto end;
}
/* ------------------------------------------------------------ */
else if(strcmp(com.command,"recnums")==0){
fread(&com.command,sizeof(com.command),1,fpt1);
strcpy(str2[91],com.command);
strcpy(str3[50],str2[91]);varcompare();strcpy(str2[81],str3[52]);
strcpy(str3[1],"+0");
one=1;
str3[2][0]='+';
sprintf(str2[10],"%i",one);
strcat(str3[2],str2[10]);
fpt3=fopen(str2[81],"r+");
fpt10=fopen("temp.dat","w+");
fseek(fpt3,0L,SEEK_END);
li=ftell(fpt3);
fclose(fpt3);
fpt3=fopen(str2[81],"r+");
for(cnt=0; ;cnt++){
myfgets(str3[74],fpt3);if(feof(fpt3))goto labelendof;
if(strcmp(str3[74],"~")==0)goto labelendof;
}
labelendof:
fclose(fpt3);
fpt3=fopen(str2[81],"r+");
cnt2=0;
while(1){
li2=ftell(fpt3);
if(li2>=li)goto label1;
myfgets(str2[0],fpt3);
++cnt2;
if(cnt2>=cnt-1){
myfputs(str2[0],fpt10);
increment_recnum();
```

```
strcpy(str3[1],str2[0]);
myfputs(str2[0],fpt10);
myfputs("~",fpt10);
myfgets(str2[0],fpt3);
myfgets(str2[0],fpt3);
cnt2=0;
}
else {myfputs(str2[0],fpt10);}
}
label1:
fclose(fpt3);
fclose(fpt10);
fpt10=fopen("temp.dat","r+");
fpt3=fopen(str2[81],"w+");
while((ch=getc(fpt10))!=EOF)putc(ch,fpt3);
fclose(fpt3);
fclose(fpt10);
fread(&com.command,sizeof(com.command),1,fpt1);
goto end;
}
/* ------------------------------------------------------- */
else if(strcmp(com.command,"recstats")==0){
fread(&com.command,sizeof(com.command),1,fpt1);
strcpy(str3[10],com.command);
fread(&com.command,sizeof(com.command),1,fpt1);
strcpy(str3[11],com.command);
fread(&com.command,sizeof(com.command),1,fpt1);
strcpy(str3[12],com.command);
strcpy(str3[50],str3[10]);varcompare();strcpy(str3[80],str3[52]);
strcpy(str3[50],str3[11]);varcompare();strcpy(str3[81],str3[52]);
strcpy(str3[50],str3[12]);varcompare();strcpy(str3[82],str3[52]);
u=atoi(str3[82]);
fclose(fpt3);
fpt3=fopen(str3[80],"r+");
if(fpt3==NULL){printf("File not opened.Exiting...");getch();goto end2;}
fclose(fpt10);
fpt10=fopen("temp.dat","w+");
t=1;
for(s=1; ;s++){
myfgets(str2[79],fpt3);if(feof(fpt3))goto label1cop;
if(s!=((t*(u-3))+((t-1)*2)))myfputs(str2[79],fpt10);
else {myfputs(str3[81],fpt10);++t;}
}
label1cop:
fclose(fpt10);
fclose(fpt3);
fpt10=fopen("temp.dat","r+");
```

```c
fpt3=fopen(str3[80],"w+");
while((ch=getc(fpt10))!=EOF){putc(ch,fpt3);}
fclose(fpt3);
fclose(fpt10);
fread(&com.command,sizeof(com.command),1,fpt1);
goto end;
}
/* ------------------------------------------------------- */
else if(strcmp(com.command,"convertdate")==0){
fread(&com.command,sizeof(com.command),1,fpt1); /* of */
fread(&com.command,sizeof(com.command),1,fpt1);
strcpy(str2[70],com.command);
strcpy(str3[50],str2[70]);varcompare();strcpy(str2[71],str3[52]);
convert_date();
fread(&com.command,sizeof(com.command),1,fpt1); /* into */
fread(&com.command,sizeof(com.command),1,fpt1);
strcpy(str2[81],com.command);
strcpy(str3[56],str2[81]);strcpy(str3[58],str2[72]);varappend();
fread(&com.command,sizeof(com.command),1,fpt1);
goto end;
}
/* ------------------------------------------------------- */
else if(strcmp(com.command,"converttime")==0){
fread(&com.command,sizeof(com.command),1,fpt1); /* of */
fread(&com.command,sizeof(com.command),1,fpt1);
strcpy(str2[70],com.command);
strcpy(str3[50],str2[70]);varcompare();strcpy(str2[73],str3[52]);
convert_time();
fread(&com.command,sizeof(com.command),1,fpt1); /* into */
fread(&com.command,sizeof(com.command),1,fpt1);
strcpy(str2[81],com.command);
strcpy(str3[56],str2[81]);strcpy(str3[58],str2[74]);varappend();
fread(&com.command,sizeof(com.command),1,fpt1);
goto end;
}
/* ------------------------------------------------------- */
else if(strcmp(com.command,"endif")==0){
fread(&com.command,sizeof(com.command),1,fpt1);
strcpy(str2[4],com.command);
goto end;
}
else if(strcmp(com.command,"endst")==0){goto end;}
else if(strcmp(com.command,"end")==0){gotoxy(25,0);goto end2;}
/* ------------------------------------------------------- */
/*
else if(strcmp(com.command,"labelit")==0){
fread(&com.command,sizeof(com.command),1,fpt1);
```

```c
fread(&com.command,sizeof(com.command),1,fpt1);
goto end;
}
*/
else {
if(strcmp(com.command,"labelit")==0){
while(fread(&com.command,sizeof(com.command),1,fpt1)==1){
if(strcmp(com.command,"endst")==0){goto end;}
}
}
/*
else {
printf("Bad Command...?! => %s ",com.command);
goto end2;
}
*/
}
end:
fclose(fpt2);continue;
}
/* ---------------------------------------------------------- */
end2:
fcloseall();
flushall();
}
/*
==========================================================
*/
/* --------------------------------------------- */
int *fpt3myfputs(char st[81],FILE *fp)
{
char st2[81]="";
char ccc;
int yy;
ccc='.';
li3=ftell(fp);
for(yy=0;yy<=81;yy++)
{if(putc(ccc,fp)==EOF){fseek(fp,li3,SEEK_SET);putc(EOF,fp);return EOF;}
                      else {fseek(fp,li3,SEEK_SET);break;}}
for(yy=0;st[yy]!='\0';yy++){
putc(st[yy],fp);
}
ccc=',';
putc(ccc,fp);
return 0;
}
myfputs(char st[81],FILE *fp)
```

```c
{
char st2[81]="";
char ccc;
int yy;
for(yy=0;st[yy]!='\0';yy++){
putc(st[yy],fp);
}
ccc=',';
putc(ccc,fp);
return;
}
myfgets(char st[81],FILE *fp)
{
long int ii=0;
int yy;
while(1){
ch=getc(fp);
if(ch==','){st[ii]='\0';return;}
else if(ch!=','){
if(ch!=EOF){st[ii++]=ch;}
else if(ch==EOF){
if(feof(fp)){st[ii]='\0';return;}
else {st[ii]='\0';}
}
}
}
return;
}
/* ---------------------------------------- */
intof(char a)
{
switch(a)
{
case '0':io=0;break;
case '1':io=1;break;
case '2':io=2;break;
case '3':io=3;break;
case '4':io=4;break;
case '5':io=5;break;
case '6':io=6;break;
case '7':io=7;break;
case '8':io=8;break;
case '9':io=9;break;
default:io=0;break;
}
return io;
}
```

```c
charof(int ii)
{
switch(ii)
{
case 0:co='0';break;
case 1:co='1';break;
case 2:co='2';break;
case 3:co='3';break;
case 4:co='4';break;
case 5:co='5';break;
case 6:co='6';break;
case 7:co='7';break;
case 8:co='8';break;
case 9:co='9';break;
default:co='0';break;
}
return co;
}
char *complement(char n22[81])
{
int kk;
ch=n22[0];
for(kk=1;kk<=79;kk++)if(n22[kk]!='.')n22[kk]=charof(9-intof(n22[kk]));
n22[0]=ch;
n22[++kk]='\0';
return n22;
}
char *addint(char n1[81],char n2[81])
{
char num1[81]="\0",num2[81]="\0",
    x[81]="\0",x1[81]="\0",x2[81]="\0",temp[81]="\0";
int ix,j,k,l,c1,c2,ir,r,y,i1,i2,io,co,flag,ij;
ts=80;
if(n1[0]==n2[0]){
c1=0;
y=79;
intres3:
ir=intof(n1[y])+intof(n2[y])+c1;
c2=ir/10;
if(ir>9)r=ir-10;
else r=ir;
res[y]=charof(r);
y=y-1;
c1=c2;
if(y>=2)goto intres3;
/*res[y]=charof(c1);*/res[1]='0';
res[0]=n1[0];
```

```
return res;
}
else {
flag=2;
for(ij=1;ij<=ts-1;ij++){
if(n1[ij]>n2[ij]){flag=1;break;}
else if(n1[ij]<n2[ij]){flag=0;break;}
else {flag=2;}
}
if(n1[0]<n2[0])
{if(flag==2){for(ij=1;ij<=ts-1;ij++)res[ij]='0';res[0]='+';goto print;}
else if(flag==1){res[0]=n1[0];strcpy(n2,complement(n2));}
else if(flag==0){res[0]=n2[0];strcpy(n1,complement(n1));}}
else if(n2[0]<n1[0])
{if(flag==2){for(ij=1;ij<=ts-1;ij++)res[ij]='0';res[0]='-';goto print;}
else if(flag==0){res[0]=n2[0];strcpy(n1,complement(n1));}
else if(flag==1){res[0]=n1[0];strcpy(n2,complement(n2));}}
c1=0;
y=79;
intres4:
ir=intof(n1[y])+intof(n2[y])+c1;
c2=ir/10;
if(ir>9)r=ir-10;
else r=ir;
res[y]=charof(r);
y=y-1;
c1=c2;
if(y>=2)goto intres4;
res[1]='0';
strcpy(str2[101],"+1");intlesstomore();strcpy(str3[11],str2[100]);
strcpy(str2[101],"-1");intlesstomore();strcpy(str3[12],str2[100]);
if(res[0]=='+')strcpy(res,addint(res,str3[11]));
else if(res[0]=='-')strcpy(res,addint(res,str3[12]));
print:
return res;
}
}
char *addnum(char n1[81],char n2[81])
{
char num1[81]="\0",num2[81]="\0",
    x[81]="\0",x1[81]="\0",x2[81]="\0",temp[81]="\0";
int ix,j,k,l,c1,c2,ir,r,y,i1,i2,io,co,flag,ij;
ip=67;
ts=80;
if(n1[0]==n2[0]){
c1=0;
y=ts-1;
```

```
intres3:
if(y!=67)ir=intof(n1[y])+intof(n2[y])+c1;
c2=ir/10;
if(ir>9)r=ir-10;
else r=ir;
if(y!=67)res[y]=charof(r);else res[y]='.';
y=y-1;
c1=c2;
if(y>=2)goto intres3;
/*res[y]=charof(c1);*/res[1]='0';
res[0]=n1[0];
return res;
}
else {
flag=2;
for(ij=1;ij<=ts-1;ij++){
if(n1[ij]>n2[ij]){flag=1;break;}
else if(n1[ij]<n2[ij]){flag=0;break;}
else {flag=2;}
}
if(n1[0]<n2[0])
{if(flag==2){for(ij=1;ij<=ts-1;ij++)if(ij!=67)res[ij]='0';
else res[ij]='.';res[0]='+';goto print;}
else if(flag==1){res[0]=n1[0];strcpy(n2,complement(n2));}
else if(flag==0){res[0]=n2[0];strcpy(n1,complement(n1));}}
else if(n2[0]<n1[0])
{if(flag==2){for(ij=1;ij<=ts-1;ij++)if(ij!=67)res[ij]='0';
else res[ij]='.';res[0]='-';goto print;}
else if(flag==0){res[0]=n2[0];strcpy(n1,complement(n1));}
else if(flag==1){res[0]=n1[0];strcpy(n2,complement(n2));}}
c1=0;
y=ts-1;
intres4:
if(y!=67)ir=intof(n1[y])+intof(n2[y])+c1;
c2=ir/10;
if(ir>9)r=ir-10;
else r=ir;
if(y!=67)res[y]=charof(r);else res[y]='.';
y=y-1;
c1=c2;
if(y>=2)goto intres4;
if(flag==1)res[1]='0';else if(flag==0)res[1]='0';
strcpy(str2[101],"+0.000001");numlesstomore();strcpy(str3[11],str2[100]);
strcpy(str2[101],"-0.000001");numlesstomore();strcpy(str3[12],str2[100]);
if(res[0]=='+')strcpy(res,addnum(res,str3[11]));
else if(res[0]=='-')strcpy(res,addnum(res,str3[12]));
print:
```

```
return res;
}
}
char *subint(char n1[81],char n2[81])
{
char num1[81]="\0",num2[81]="\0",
    x[81]="\0",x1[81]="\0",x2[81]="\0",temp[81]="\0";
int ix,j,k,l,c1,c2,ir,r,y,i1,i2,io,co,flag,ij;
ip=80;
ts=ip;
if(n2[0]=='+')n2[0]='-';else if(n2[0]=='-')n2[0]='+';
if(n1[0]==n2[0]){
c1=0;
y=ts-1;
intres5:
ir=intof(n1[y])+intof(n2[y])+c1;
c2=ir/10;
if(ir>9)r=ir-10;
else r=ir;
res[y]=charof(r);
y=y-1;
c1=c2;
if(y>=2)goto intres5;
/*res[y]=charof(c1);*/res[1]='0';
res[0]=n1[0];
return res;
}
else {
flag=2;
for(ij=1;ij<=ts-1;ij++){
if(n1[ij]>n2[ij]){flag=1;break;}
else if(n1[ij]<n2[ij]){flag=0;break;}
else {flag=2;}
}
if(n1[0]<n2[0])
{if(flag==2){for(ij=1;ij<=ts-1;ij++)res[ij]='0';res[0]='+';goto print;}
else if(flag==1){res[0]=n1[0];strcpy(n2,complement(n2));}
else if(flag==0){res[0]=n2[0];strcpy(n1,complement(n1));}}
else if(n2[0]<n1[0])
{if(flag==2){for(ij=1;ij<=ts-1;ij++)res[ij]='0';res[0]='-';goto print;}
else if(flag==0){res[0]=n2[0];strcpy(n1,complement(n1));}
else if(flag==1){res[0]=n1[0];strcpy(n2,complement(n2));}}
c1=0;
y=ts-1;
intres6:
ir=intof(n1[y])+intof(n2[y])+c1;
c2=ir/10;
```

```
if(ir>9)r=ir-10;
else r=ir;
res[y]=charof(r);
y=y-1;
c1=c2;
if(y>=2)goto intres6;
if(flag==1)res[1]='0';else if(flag==0)res[1]='0';
strcpy(str2[101],"+1");intlesstomore();strcpy(str3[11],str2[100]);
strcpy(str2[101],"-1");intlesstomore();strcpy(str3[12],str2[100]);
if(res[0]=='+')strcpy(res,addint(res,str3[11]));
else if(res[0]=='-')strcpy(res,addint(res,str3[12]));
print:
return res;
}
}
char *subnum(char n1[81],char n2[81])
{
char num1[81]="\0",num2[81]="\0",
    x[81]="\0",x1[81]="\0",x2[81]="\0",temp[81]="\0";
int ix,j,k,l,c1,c2,ir,r,y,i1,i2,io,co,flag,ij;
ip=67;
ts=80;
if(n2[0]=='+')n2[0]='-';else if(n2[0]=='-')n2[0]='+';
if(n1[0]==n2[0]){
c1=0;
y=ts-1;
intres3:
if(y!=67)ir=intof(n1[y])+intof(n2[y])+c1;
c2=ir/10;
if(ir>9)r=ir-10;
else r=ir;
if(y!=67)res[y]=charof(r);else res[y]='.';
y=y-1;
c1=c2;
if(y>=2)goto intres3;
/*res[y]=charof(c1);*/res[1]='0';
res[0]=n1[0];
return res;
}
else {
flag=2;
for(ij=1;ij<=ts-1;ij++){
if(n1[ij]>n2[ij]){flag=1;break;}
else if(n1[ij]<n2[ij]){flag=0;break;}
else {flag=2;}
}
if(n1[0]<n2[0])
```

```
{if(flag==2){
for(ij=1;ij<=ts-1;ij++)
if(ij!=73)res[ij]='0';else res[ij]='.';res[0]='+';goto print;}
else if(flag==1){res[0]=n1[0];strcpy(n2,complement(n2));}
else if(flag==0){res[0]=n2[0];strcpy(n1,complement(n1));}}
else if(n2[0]<n1[0]){if(flag==2)
{for(ij=1;ij<=ts-1;ij++)
if(ij!=67)res[ij]='0';else res[ij]='.';res[0]='-';goto print;}
else if(flag==0){res[0]=n2[0];strcpy(n1,complement(n1));}
else if(flag==1){res[0]=n1[0];strcpy(n2,complement(n2));}}
c1=0;
y=ts-1;
intres4:
if(y!=67)ir=intof(n1[y])+intof(n2[y])+c1;
c2=ir/10;
if(ir>9)r=ir-10;
else r=ir;
if(y!=67)res[y]=charof(r);else res[y]='.';
y=y-1;
c1=c2;
if(y>=2)goto intres4;
if(flag==1)res[1]='0';else if(flag==0)res[1]='0';
strcpy(str2[101],"+1");numlesstomore();strcpy(str3[11],str2[100]);
strcpy(str2[101],"-1");numlesstomore();strcpy(str3[12],str2[100]);
if(res[0]=='+')strcpy(res,addnum(res,str3[11]));
else if(res[0]=='-')strcpy(res,addnum(res,str3[12]));
print:
return res;
}
}
intlesstomore()
{
int ix,iy;
for(ix=0;str2[101][ix]!='\0';ix++);--ix;
for(iy=79;iy>=1;iy--)if(ix!=0){str2[100][iy]=str2[101][ix--];}
                          else {str2[100][iy]='0';}
str2[100][0]=str2[101][0];
str2[100][80]='\0';
}
intmoretoless()
{
int ix,iy;
str2[100][0]=str2[101][0];
for(ix=1;str2[101][ix]=='0';ix++);iy=0;
if(str2[101][ix]=='\0'){str2[100][1]='0';str2[100][2]='\0';return;}
for( ;str2[101][ix]!='\0';ix++)str2[100][++iy]=str2[101][ix];
str2[100][++iy]='\0';
```

```c
return;
}
numlesstomore()
{
int ix,iy,iz;
for(ix=0;str2[101][ix]!='\0';ix++);
for(iz=0;str2[101][iz]!='.';iz++);
for(iy=79;iy>=67+(ix-iz);iy--)str2[100][iy]='0';
for( ;iy>67;iy--)str2[100][iy]=str2[101][--ix];
str2[100][67]='.';
ix-=2;
for(iy=66;str2[101][ix]!='+'&&str2[101][ix]!='-';iy--)
{str2[100][iy]=str2[101][ix--];}
for( ;iy>=1;iy--)str2[100][iy]='0';
str2[100][0]=str2[101][0];
str2[100][80]='\0';
}
nummoretoless()
{
int ix,iy,iz;
str2[101][80]='\0';
iz=1;
for(ix=1;ix<=79;ix++)
if(str2[101][ix]=='0'&&str2[101][ix+1]=='.')
{
for( ;ix<=79;ix++)str2[100][iz++]=str2[101][ix];
str2[100][iz]='\0';str2[100][0]=str2[101][0];
return;
}
else if(str2[101][ix]=='0'&&str2[101][ix+1]!='0'){++ix;break;}
else if(str2[101][ix]=='0'&&str2[101][ix+1]=='0')continue;
iy=1;for( ;ix<=79;ix++)str2[100][iy++]=str2[101][ix];
str2[100][iy]='\0';
str2[100][0]=str2[101][0];
return;
}
char *substring(char st[81],int iii,int jjj)
{
int lll;
char st9[81];
for(lll=0;lll<=(jjj-iii);lll++)st9[lll]=st[iii+lll];
st9[lll++]='\0';
return st9;
}
int *strcomp(char s1[81],char s2[81])
{
int ij;
```

```c
flag[55]=0;
if(strlen(s1)==strlen(s2)){
for(ij=1;s1[ij]!='\0'&&s2[ij]!='\0';ij++){
if(s1[ij]==s2[ij]){flag[55]=0;}
else if(s1[ij]>s2[ij]){flag[55]=1;break;}
else if(s1[ij]<s2[ij]){flag[55]=-1;break;}
}
}
else if(strlen(s1)<strlen(s2)){flag[55]=-1;}
else if(strlen(s1)>strlen(s2)){flag[55]=1;}
return flag[55];
}
nullify(char st[81])
{
int ii;
for(ii=0;ii<=80;ii++)st[ii]='\0';
}
nullifyvars()
{
int ii,jj;
for(ii=0;ii<=100;ii++)for(jj=0;jj<=80;jj++)vars1[ii][jj]='\0';
for(ii=0;ii<=100;ii++)for(jj=0;jj<=80;jj++)vars2[ii][jj]='\0';
}
char *varcompare()
{
for(j=0;strcmp(vars1[j],str3[50])!=0;j++)
if(strcmp(vars1[j],"\0")==0)goto lab123;
strcpy(str3[52],vars2[j]);
lab123:
return;
}
char *varappend()
{
fclose(fpt14);
fpt14=fopen("constrai.var","r+");
if((ch=getc(fpt14))==EOF){fclose(fpt14);goto labelvar1;}
fseek(fpt14,0L,SEEK_SET);
while(!feof(fpt14)){/*20*/
myfgets(str2[41],fpt14);
if(strcmp(str2[41],str3[56])==0){/*21*/
myfgets(str2[42],fpt14);
if(strcmp(str2[42],"default")==0){/*22*/
myfgets(str2[43],fpt14);
for(f=0;str2[43][f]!='\0';f++){/*23*/
if(str2[43][f]!='#')str2[49][f]=str2[43][f];
else str2[49][f]=' ';
}/*23*/
```

```c
str2[49][f]='\0';
strcpy(str3[58],str2[49]);
myfgets(str2[44],fpt14);
goto labelvar1;
}/*22*/
else if(strcmp(str2[42],"notnull")==0){
myfgets(str2[43],fpt14);
if(strcmp(str3[58],"NIL")==0){
printf("\nNotNull Constraint violated...");getch();
myfgets(str2[44],fpt14);
goto labelvar2;
}
myfgets(str2[44],fpt14);
goto labelvar1;
}
else if(strcmp(str2[42],"check")==0){
myfgets(str2[43],fpt14);
g=0;
h=0;
for(f=0;str2[43][f]!='\0';f++)
{
if(str2[43][f]!='&'&&str2[43][f]!='#'){checkarr[g][h++]=str2[43][f];}
else if(str2[43][f]=='&'){checkarr[g][h]='\0';h=0;++g;}
else if(str2[43][f]=='#')checkarr[g][h++]=' ';
}
checkarr[g][h]='\0';
flag[9]=0;
for(g=0;strcmp(checkarr[g],"\0")!=0;g++){
if(strcmp(checkarr[g],str3[58])==0)
{flag[9]=1;myfgets(str2[44],fpt14);goto labelvar1;}
}
labelvar3:
printf("\nCheck Constraint violated...");getch();
myfgets(str2[44],fpt14);
goto labelvar2;
}
else if(strcmp(str2[42],"maybe")==0){/*9*/
myfgets(str2[43],fpt14);
i=0;j=0;
labelvar4:
switch(str2[43][i])
{
case '_':
switch(str3[58][j])
{
case '\0':
printf("Maybe Constraint violated...");getch();goto labelvar2;
```

```c
break;
default:
++i;++j;
goto labelvar4;
break;
}
break;
case '%':
switch(str3[58][j])
{
case '\0':
printf("Maybe Constraint violated...");getch();goto labelvar2;
break;
default:
++j;
labelR1:
switch(str2[43][i])
{
case '\0':
goto labelvar1;
break;
default:
++i;
goto labelR1;
break;
}
}
break;
case '\0':
goto labelvar1;
break;
default:
if(str2[43][i]==str3[58][j]){
++i;++j;
goto labelvar4;
}
else {
printf("Maybe Constraint violated...");getch();goto labelvar2;
}
}/* end of main switch */
}
}
myfgets(str2[42],fpt14);myfgets(str2[43],fpt14);myfgets(str2[44],fpt14);
}/*20*/
/**/
labelvar1:
for(j=0;strcomp(vars1[j],"\0")!=0;j++){
```

```c
if(strcomp(vars1[j],str3[56])==0){strcpy(vars2[j],str3[58]);goto labelvar2;}
}
if(strcomp(vars1[j],"\0")==0)
{
strcpy(vars1[j],str3[56]);
strcpy(vars2[j],str3[58]);
}
labelvar2:
fclose(fpt14);
return;
}
/* ----------------------------------------------------------------- */
char *divint2()
{
flag[11]=0;
h=0;
str3[0][h]='+';
str2[1][0]=str2[2][0]='+';
strcpy(str2[91],str2[1]);strcpy(str2[92],str2[2]);
strcpy(str2[101],str2[1]);intmoretoless();strcpy(str2[31],str2[100]);
strcpy(str2[101],str2[2]);intmoretoless();strcpy(str2[32],str2[100]);
/*printf("a.%s %s ",str2[31],str2[32]);getch();*/
strcpy(str3[40],"+1");
strcpy(str2[101],str3[40]);intlesstomore();strcpy(str3[50],str2[100]);
strcpy(str2[101],str3[40]);intlesstomore();strcpy(str3[51],str2[100]);
a=strlen(str2[31]);
b=strlen(str2[32]);
strcpy(str2[33],substring(str2[31],0,b-1));
strcpy(str2[34],substring(str2[32],0,b-1));
/*printf("b.%s %s ",str2[33],str2[34]);getch();*/
if(strcmp(str2[33],str2[34])<0){
if(a<=b){/*str3[0][1]='0';*/strcat(str3[0],"0");goto pras4;}
strcpy(str2[35],substring(str2[31],b,b));
strcat(str2[33],str2[35]);
flag[11]=1;
++b;
}
/*printf("c.%s %s ",str2[33],str2[34]);getch();*/
strcpy(str2[101],str2[33]);intlesstomore();strcpy(str3[54],str2[100]);
strcpy(str2[101],str2[34]);intlesstomore();strcpy(str3[55],str2[100]);
pras1:
strcpy(str2[1],str3[40]);
strcpy(str2[2],str2[34]);
/*printf("1.%s %s ",str2[1],str2[2]);getch();*/
mulint2();
str2[22][0]='+';
strcpy(str2[101],str2[22]);intlesstomore();strcpy(str3[52],str2[100]);
```

```c
strcpy(str2[101],str2[22]);intlesstomore();strcpy(str2[37],str2[100]);
strcpy(str2[101],str2[33]);intlesstomore();strcpy(str3[53],str2[100]);
/*printf("2.%s ",str2[22]);getch();*/
if(strcmp(str3[52],str3[53])<0){    /* str2[91] */
/*printf("#.%s %s ",str3[50],str3[51]);getch();*/
strcpy(str3[50],addint(str3[50],str3[51]));
strcpy(str2[101],str3[50]);intmoretoless();strcpy(str3[40],str2[100]);
strcpy(str2[101],str3[52]);intlesstomore();strcpy(str3[61],str2[100]);
/*printf(">%s ",str3[40]);*/
goto pras1;
}
else if(strcmp(str3[52],str3[53])==0){
strcpy(str2[101],str3[40]);intlesstomore();strcpy(str2[77],str2[100]);
strcpy(str2[101],str3[52]);intlesstomore();strcpy(str3[61],str2[100]);
goto pras5;
}
strcpy(str2[77],subint(str3[50],str3[51]));
complement(str3[51]);
str3[51][0]='+';
pras5:
strcpy(str2[101],str2[77]);intmoretoless();strcpy(str2[22],str2[100]);
/*printf("3.%s ",str2[22]);getch();*/
str3[0][++h]=str2[22][1];
/*printf("-%c-",str3[0][h]);getch();*/
/*printf("4.%s %s ",str3[54],str3[61]);getch();*/
strcpy(str3[66],subint(str3[54],str3[61]));
complement(str3[61]);
str3[61][0]='+';
/*printf("5.%s ",str3[66]);getch();*/
strcpy(str2[101],str3[66]);intmoretoless();strcpy(str3[77],str2[100]);
/*printf("6.%s ",str3[77]);getch();*/
pras2:
++b;
strcpy(str2[35],substring(str2[31],b-1,b-1));
if(b>strlen(str2[31]))goto pras3;
strcat(str3[77],str2[35]);
/*printf("*.%s ",str3[77]);getch();*/
strcpy(str2[101],str3[77]);intlesstomore();strcpy(str3[57],str2[100]);
strcpy(str2[101],str2[34]);intlesstomore();strcpy(str3[58],str2[100]);
if(strcmp(str3[57],str3[58])<0){str3[0][++h]='0';goto pras2;}
strcpy(str2[33],str3[77]);
strcpy(str2[101],str2[33]);intlesstomore();strcpy(str3[54],str2[100]);
strcpy(str3[40],"+1");
/*printf("7.%s %s ",str3[40],str2[34]);getch();*/
strcpy(str3[50],"+1");
strcpy(str2[101],str3[50]);intlesstomore();strcpy(str3[59],str2[100]);
strcpy(str3[50],str3[59]);
```

```c
goto pras1;
pras3:
str3[0][++h]='\0';
/*printf("*>%s ",str3[0]);getch();*/
/*printf(">>>>>%s ",str2[22]);getch();*/
/* ------------------------------------------------------------ */
pras4:
strcpy(str2[32],str3[0]);
str2[32][0]=sign;
/*printf("*****>>>>>%s ",str2[32]);getch();*/
/*
for(k=1;k<=80;k++){if(str2[32][k]=='+'||str2[32][k]=='-')
                        {str2[32][k]='\0';break;}
                        }
*/
}
/* ------------------------------------------------------------ */
char *mulint2()
{
str2[1][0]=str2[2][0]='+';
if(strcmp(str2[1],"+0")==0||
   strcmp(str2[2],"+0")==0||
   strcmp(str2[1],"-0")==0||
   strcmp(str2[2],"-0")==0){str3[7][1]='0';str3[7][2]='\0';goto nagara1;}
/* ------------- */
strcpy(str3[24],"+0");
strcpy(str2[101],str3[24]);intlesstomore();strcpy(str3[14],str2[100]);
/* ------------- */
strcpy(str2[101],str2[1]);intmoretoless();strcpy(str3[1],str2[100]);
strcpy(str2[101],str2[2]);intmoretoless();strcpy(str3[2],str2[100]);
/*printf("%s %s ",str3[1],str3[2]);*/
/* reverse the strings */
t=0;for(s=strlen(str3[1])-1;s>=0;s--)str3[31][t++]=str3[1][s];
str3[31][--t]='\0';
t=0;for(s=strlen(str3[2])-1;s>=0;s--)str3[32][t++]=str3[2][s];
str3[32][--t]='\0';
/*printf("%s %s ",str3[31],str3[32]);*/
/* ------------- */
/* when both the strings are single digited */
l=0;m=0;
if(strlen(str3[31])==1&&strlen(str3[32])==1){
o=(int)(str3[31][l])-48;n=(int)(str3[32][m])-48;
p=n*o;
sprintf(str3[17],"%i",p);
strcpy(str3[7],"+");strcat(str3[7],str3[17]);
goto nagara1;
}
```

```c
/* ------------- */
/* when the second is single digited and the first is not so */
c=0;
if(strlen(str3[31])>1&&strlen(str3[32])==1){
for(m=0;str3[31][m]!='\0';m++){
o=(int)(str3[31][m])-48;n=(int)(str3[32][0])-48;
/*printf("%i %i ",o,n);*/
p=n*o+c;
/*printf("%i ",p);*/
sprintf(str3[17],"%i",p);
if(strlen(str3[17])==2){
a=(int)(str3[17][1])-48;
sprintf(str3[59],"%i",a);
str3[18][m]=str3[59][0];
c=(int)(str3[17][0])-48;
}
else if(strlen(str3[17])==1){
a=(int)(str3[17][0])-48;
sprintf(str3[59],"%i",a);
str3[18][m]=str3[59][0];
c=0;
}
}
if(c!=0)
{a=(int)(str3[17][0])-48;sprintf(str3[59],"%i",a);str3[18][m]=str3[59][0];}
str3[18][++m]='\0';
/*printf("=>%s ",str3[18]);*/
/* now reverse the string */
t=0;for(s=strlen(str3[18])-1;s>=0;s--)str3[17][t++]=str3[18][s];
str3[17][t]='\0';
strcpy(str3[7],"+");strcat(str3[7],str3[17]);
goto nagara1;
}
/* if both the strings are multi digited */
strcpy(str3[1],"+");strcpy(str3[2],"+");
strcat(str3[1],str3[31]);strcat(str3[2],str3[32]);
/*printf("%s %s ",str3[1],str3[2]);*/
y=0;x=0;
for(l=1;str3[2][l]!='\0';l++){
c=0;s=0;p=0;
for(m=1;str3[1][m]!='\0';m++){ /* no zeros inside ex 709 */
o=(int)(str3[2][l])-48;n=(int)(str3[1][m])-48;
/*printf("#.%i %i ",n,o);*/
if(n==0){p=c;c=0;}
else {p=n*o;p+=c;}
sprintf(str3[71],"%i",p);
/*printf(">>>%s ",str3[71]);*/
```

```c
if(str3[71][1]=='\0'){
if(str3[71][1]=='0'){r=0;q=p;c=0;}
else {r=(int)(str3[71][0])-48;q=r;c=0;}
}
else {r=(int)(str3[71][0])-48;q=(int)(str3[71][1])-48;c=r;}
/*printf("$.%i %i ",q,r);*/
/*c=r;*/
str3[3][s]=(char)q+48;
++s;
}
str3[3][s]='\0';
/*printf("here...%s ",str3[3]);*/
str3[4][0]=(char)c+48;
t=1;for(s=strlen(str3[3])-1;s>=0;s--)str3[4][t++]=str3[3][s];
str3[4][t]='\0';
/*printf(">*>*>%s ",str3[4]);*/
for(z=0;z<y;z++)str3[5][z]=(char)x+48;
for(f=t-1;f>=0;f--)str3[5][z++]=str3[4][f];
str3[5][z++]='+';
str3[5][z]='\0';
/*printf("here2...%s ",str3[5]);*/
++y;
for(a=0;str3[5][a]!='\0';a++)str3[6][strlen(str3[5])-1-a]=str3[5][a];
str3[6][strlen(str3[5])-1+1]='\0';
/*printf("here3...%s ",str3[6]);*/
strcpy(str2[101],str3[6]);intlesstomore();strcpy(str3[16],str2[100]);
strcpy(str3[14],addint(str3[16],str3[14]));
/*printf("here4...%s ",str3[14]);*/
}
strcpy(str2[101],str3[14]);intmoretoless();strcpy(str3[7],str2[100]);
nagara1:
strcpy(str2[22],str3[7]);
str2[22][0]=sign;
/*printf("***>>>%s ",str2[22]);*/
}
/* ------------------------------------------------------------------ */
mountall()
{
/*system("cls");*/
system("mount c: c:\\ > mount.inf");
system("mount d: d:\\ > mount.inf");
system("mount e: e:\\ > mount.inf");
system("mount f: f:\\ > mount.inf");
system("mount g: g:\\ > mount.inf");
system("mount h: h:\\ > mount.inf");
system("mount i: i:\\ > mount.inf");
system("mount j: j:\\ > mount.inf");
```

```c
system("mount k: k:\\ > mount.inf");
system("mount l: l:\\ > mount.inf");
system("mount m: m:\\ > mount.inf");
system("mount n: n:\\ > mount.inf");
system("mount o: o:\\ > mount.inf");
system("mount p: p:\\ > mount.inf");
system("mount q: q:\\ > mount.inf");
system("mount r: r:\\ > mount.inf");
system("mount s: s:\\ > mount.inf");
system("mount t: t:\\ > mount.inf");
system("mount u: u:\\ > mount.inf");
system("mount v: v:\\ > mount.inf");
system("mount w: w:\\ > mount.inf");
system("mount x: x:\\ > mount.inf");
system("mount y: y:\\ > mount.inf");
system("mount z: z:\\ > mount.inf");
/*system("cls");*/
}
char *increment_bucket()
{
strcpy(str2[1],curr_bucket);
strcpy(str2[2],substring(str2[1],4,7));
sscanf(str2[2],"%i",&v);
++v;
sprintf(str2[3],"%i",v);
if(v<=9999){curr_bucket[4]=str2[3][0];curr_bucket[5]=str2[3][1];
            curr_bucket[6]=str2[3][2];curr_bucket[7]=str2[3][3];}
return curr_bucket;
}
char *decrement_bucket()
{
strcpy(str2[1],curr_bucket);
strcpy(str2[2],substring(str2[1],4,7));
sscanf(str2[2],"%i",&v);
--v;
sprintf(str2[3],"%i",v);
if(v>=1111){curr_bucket[4]=str2[3][0];curr_bucket[5]=str2[3][1];
            curr_bucket[6]=str2[3][2];curr_bucket[7]=str2[3][3];}
return curr_bucket;
}
revseek(FILE *fp)
{
while(1){
fseek(fp,-2L,SEEK_CUR);
if((ch=getc(fp))==',')return;
}
}
```

```c
char *timeit(char ts[81])
{
char ts1[3],ts2[3],ts3[3],ts4[3],ts5[8];
int cc,dd;
strcpy(ts1,substring(ts,0,1));
strcpy(ts2,substring(ts,3,4));
strcpy(ts3,substring(ts,6,7));
strcpy(ts4,substring(ts,9,10));
if(strcmp(ts4,"am")==0)strcpy(ts5,"a");
else if(strcmp(ts4,"md")==0)strcpy(ts5,"b");
else if(strcmp(ts4,"pm")==0)strcpy(ts5,"c");
else if(strcmp(ts4,"mn")==0)strcpy(ts5,"d");
strcat(ts5,ts1);
strcat(ts5,ts2);
strcat(ts5,ts3);
return ts5;
}
/* ------------------------------------ */
decimate(char st[81],int ii)
{
char st2[81];
int jj,kk;
for(jj=0;st[jj]!='.';jj++)st2[jj]=st[jj];
st2[jj]='.';
kk=0;
++jj;
for( ;st[jj]!='\0';jj++,kk++)if(kk<ii)st2[jj]=st[jj];
st2[jj]='\0';
strcpy(st,st2);
}
/* ------------------------------------ */
increment_recnum()
{
strcpy(str2[101],str3[1]);intlesstomore();strcpy(str2[1],str2[100]);
strcpy(str2[101],str3[2]);intlesstomore();strcpy(str2[2],str2[100]);
strcpy(str2[14],addint(str2[1],str2[2]));
strcpy(str2[101],str2[14]);intmoretoless();strcpy(str2[24],str2[100]);
strcpy(str2[0],str2[24]);
}
convert_date()
{
strcpy(str2[72],substring(str2[71],6,9));
strcat(str2[72],substring(str2[71],3,4));
strcat(str2[72],substring(str2[71],0,1));
}
convert_time()
{
```

```
strcpy(str2[74],substring(str2[73],9,10));
strcat(str2[74],substring(str2[73],6,7));
strcat(str2[74],substring(str2[73],3,4));
strcat(str2[74],substring(str2[73],0,1));
}
/* =================== The End ====================== */
```

*

testof12.cvb
begin
storeval somex eq +123456789.987654321234 endst
storeval somey eq +987654321234.432123456789 endst
storeval somep eq +4 endst
storeval someq eq +9 endst
storeval somet eq +11 endst
dump somez eq addnum of somex somey ofend endst
message anyvar somez endst
message line endst
dump somez eq subnum of somex somey ofend endst
message anyvar somez endst
message line endst
dump somez eq mulnum of somex somey ofend endst
message anyvar somez endst
message line endst
round of somez to somet into somer endst
message anyvar somer endst
message line endst
dump somez eq divnum of somex somey ofend endst
message anyvar somez endst
message line endst
power of somex to somep into somez endst
message anyvar somez endst
message line endst
round of somez to someq into somer endst
message anyvar somer endst
end

*

genmaths.cvb
begin
storeval somex eq +798643234566778889999087654337654456789 endst
storeval somey eq +98765412889887608706441243748569474 endst
dump somez eq addint of somex somey ofend endst
message anyvar somez endst
get someq endst
storeval somex eq +98743456789977665543212556667778998776666309.17 endst
storeval somey eq +70036787768970909873214457899909877666660898987.123
```
```

```
endst
dump somez eq addnum of somex somey ofend endst
message anyvar somez endst
get someq endst
storeval somex eq +897645689987900988776654321245567888899700367 endst
storeval somey eq +123465859857646636620090098726235525367409 endst
dump somez eq subint of somex somey ofend endst
message anyvar somez endst
get someq endst
storeval somex eq +987652134568900990098877665554443333321344567.178
endst
storeval somey eq +700367987653234567889900999887654433321234.123 endst
dump somez eq subnum of somex somey ofend endst
message anyvar somez endst
get someq endst
storeval somex eq +8976543245678899988877665544321234466789 endst
storeval somey eq +7865321234098098876555543224556667876 endst
dump somez eq mulint of somex somey ofend endst
message anyvar somez endst
get someq endst
storeval somex eq +309989654321234566778889008765 44.1723 endst
storeval somey eq +98765432123466778899999090965 5700367.127 endst
dump somez eq mulnum of somex somey ofend endst
message anyvar somez endst
get someq endst
storeval somex eq +908345600987665554443332112445677899999888700367
endst
storeval somey eq +30987657 endst
dump somez eq divint of somex somey ofend endst
message anyvar somez endst
get someq endst
storeval somex eq +56789765432124556678890999887766554321223.87679
endst
storeval somey eq +9876.567 endst
dump somez eq divnum of somex somey ofend endst
message anyvar somez endst
get someq endst
end

*

buctesto.cvb
begin
storeval bucname eq char abcd1111.dat endchar endst
increment bucname endst
message anyvar bucname endst
decrement bucname endst
message anyvar bucname endst
```

end

*

buctest1.cvb
begin
storeval bucname eq char abcd4329.dat endchar endst
storeval somechar eq char x endchar endst
storeval numbucs eq +0 endst
storeval count eq +1 endst
storeval one eq +1 endst
storeval buccount eq +3 endst
comment Bucket limit may be fixed or variable endst
storeval buclim eq +512 endst
labelit label2 endst
dump numbucs eq addint of numbucs one ofend endst
if numbucs le buccount then 2
fileopen bucname endst
labelit label1 endst
writefile somechar into bucname endst
message anyvar count endst
dump count eq addint of count one ofend endst
if count le buclim then 1
goto label1 endst
endif 1
fileclose bucname endst
increment bucname endst
storeval count eq +1 endst
goto label2 endst
endif 2
end

*

buctest2.cvb
begin
storeval bucname eq char abcd4329.dat endchar endst
storeval somechar eq char x endchar endst
storeval numbucs eq +0 endst
storeval count eq +1 endst
storeval one eq +1 endst
storeval buccount eq +3 endst
comment Bucket limit may be fixed or variable endst
storeval buclim eq +128 endst
storeval status_ eq char notopened endchar endst
labelit label2 endst
dump numbucs eq addint of numbucs one ofend endst
if numbucs le buccount then 2
labelit label3 endst

```
fileopen bucname curdri drivenum status endst
message cat Drive : endcat endst
message anyvar drivenum endst
if status eq status_ then 3
dump drivenum eq addint of drivenum one ofend endst
setdisk drivenum endst
message cat INC endcat endst
goto label3 endst
endif 3
labelit label1 endst
writefile somechar into bucname endst
message anyvar count endst
dump count eq addint of count one ofend endst
if count le buclim then 1
goto label1 endst
endif 1
fileclose bucname endst
increment bucname endst
storeval count eq +1 endst
message cat Drive Number : endcat endst
message anyvar drivenum endst
dump drivenum eq addint of drivenum one ofend endst
setdisk drivenum endst
message cat Drive Number : endcat endst
message anyvar drivenum endst
goto label2 endst
endif 2
end

*
buctestx.cvb
begin
storeval bucname eq char abcd4329.dat endchar endst
storeval somecol eq char xyz endchar endst
storeval numbucs eq +0 endst
storeval count eq +1 endst
storeval one eq +1 endst
storeval buccount eq +3 endst
storeval curdri eq +2 endst
comment Bucket limit may be fixed or variable endst
storeval buclim eq +128 endst
storeval status_ eq char notopened endchar endst
labelit label2 endst
dump numbucs eq addint of numbucs one ofend endst
if numbucs le buccount then 2
open bucname for fresh curdri drivenum status endst
message anyvar curdri endst
```

```
message anyvar drivenum endst
message anyvar status endst
labelit label3 endst
insert somecol endst
message anyvar count endst
dump count eq addint of count one ofend endst
if count gt buclim then 1
increment bucname endst
storeval count eq +1 endst
goto label2 endst
endif 1
goto label3 endst
endif 2
end

*

buctesty.cvb
begin
storeval bucname eq char abcd4329.dat endchar endst
storeval somecol eq char xyz endchar endst
storeval numbucs eq +0 endst
storeval count eq +1 endst
storeval one eq +1 endst
storeval buccount eq +3 endst
storeval curdri eq +2 endst
storeval drive eq +2 endst
comment Bucket limit may be fixed or variable endst
storeval buclim eq +128 endst
storeval status_ eq char notopened endchar endst
labelit label2 endst
dump numbucs eq addint of numbucs one ofend endst
if numbucs le buccount then 2
open bucname for fresh curdri drivenum status endst
message anyvar curdri endst
message anyvar drivenum endst
message anyvar status endst
if status eq status_ then 3
dump drive eq addint of drive one ofend endst
setdisk drive endst
endif 3
labelit label3 endst
insert somecol endst
message anyvar count endst
dump count eq addint of count one ofend endst
if count gt buclim then 1
increment bucname endst
dump drive eq addint of drive one ofend endst
```

```
setdisk drive endst
storeval count eq +1 endst
goto label2 endst
endif 1
goto label3 endst
endif 2
end

*

addintq.rmf
declare somex somey somez endst
begin
storeval somex eq +987654321 endst
storeval somey eq +123456789 endst
dump somez eq addint of somex somey ofend endst
message anyvar somez endst
storeval somex eq +987654321 endst
storeval somey eq -123456789 endst
dump somez eq addint of somex somey ofend endst
message anyvar somez endst
storeval somex eq -987654321 endst
storeval somey eq +123456789 endst
dump somez eq addint of somex somey ofend endst
message anyvar somez endst
storeval somex eq -987654321 endst
storeval somey eq -123456789 endst
dump somez eq addint of somex somey ofend endst
message anyvar somez endst
end

*

addnumq.rmf
declare somex somey somez endst
begin
storeval somex eq +987654.321 endst
storeval somey eq +12345.6789 endst
dump somez eq addnum of somex somey ofend endst
message anyvar somez endst
storeval somex eq +987654.321 endst
storeval somey eq -12345.6789 endst
dump somez eq addnum of somex somey ofend endst
message anyvar somez endst
storeval somex eq -987654.321 endst
storeval somey eq +12345.6789 endst
dump somez eq addnum of somex somey ofend endst
message anyvar somez endst
storeval somex eq -987654.321 endst
```

storeval somey eq -12345.6789 endst
dump somez eq addnum of somex somey ofend endst
message anyvar somez endst
end

*

subintq.rmf
declare somex somey somez endst
begin
storeval somex eq +987654321 endst
storeval somey eq +123456789 endst
dump somez eq subint of somex somey ofend endst
message anyvar somez endst
storeval somex eq +987654321 endst
storeval somey eq -123456789 endst
dump somez eq subint of somex somey ofend endst
message anyvar somez endst
storeval somex eq -987654321 endst
storeval somey eq +123456789 endst
dump somez eq subint of somex somey ofend endst
message anyvar somez endst
storeval somex eq -987654321 endst
storeval somey eq -123456789 endst
dump somez eq subint of somex somey ofend endst
message anyvar somez endst
end

*

subnumq.rmf
declare somex somey somez endst
begin
storeval somex eq +987654.321 endst
storeval somey eq +12345.6789 endst
dump somez eq subnum of somex somey ofend endst
message anyvar somez endst
storeval somex eq +987654.321 endst
storeval somey eq -12345.6789 endst
dump somez eq subnum of somex somey ofend endst
message anyvar somez endst
storeval somex eq -987654.321 endst
storeval somey eq +12345.6789 endst
dump somez eq subnum of somex somey ofend endst
message anyvar somez endst
storeval somex eq -987654.321 endst
storeval somey eq -12345.6789 endst
dump somez eq subnum of somex somey ofend endst

```
message anyvar somez endst
end

*

mulintq.rmf
declare somex somey somez endst
begin
storeval somex eq +987654 endst
storeval somey eq +12345 endst
dump somez eq mulint of somex somey ofend endst
message anyvar somez endst
storeval somex eq +987654 endst
storeval somey eq -12345 endst
dump somez eq mulint of somex somey ofend endst
message anyvar somez endst
storeval somex eq -987654 endst
storeval somey eq +12345 endst
dump somez eq mulint of somex somey ofend endst
message anyvar somez endst
storeval somex eq -987654 endst
storeval somey eq -12345 endst
dump somez eq mulint of somex somey ofend endst
message anyvar somez endst
end

*

mulnumq.rmf
declare somex somey somez endst
begin
storeval somex eq +9876.67 endst
storeval somey eq +123.345 endst
dump somez eq mulnum of somex somey ofend endst
message anyvar somez endst
storeval somex eq +9876.67 endst
storeval somey eq -123.345 endst
dump somez eq mulnum of somex somey ofend endst
message anyvar somez endst
storeval somex eq -9876.67 endst
storeval somey eq +123.345 endst
dump somez eq mulnum of somex somey ofend endst
message anyvar somez endst
storeval somex eq -9876.67 endst
storeval somey eq -123.345 endst
dump somez eq mulnum of somex somey ofend endst
message anyvar somez endst
end
```

```
*
divintq.rmf
declare somex somey somez endst
begin
storeval somex eq +987654 endst
storeval somey eq +123 endst
dump somez eq divint of somex somey ofend endst
message anyvar somez endst
storeval somex eq +987654 endst
storeval somey eq -123 endst
dump somez eq divint of somex somey ofend endst
message anyvar somez endst
storeval somex eq -987654 endst
storeval somey eq +123 endst
dump somez eq divint of somex somey ofend endst
message anyvar somez endst
storeval somex eq -987654 endst
storeval somey eq -123 endst
dump somez eq divint of somex somey ofend endst
message anyvar somez endst
end

*
divnumq.rmf
declare somex somey somez endst
begin
storeval somex eq +987654.765 endst
storeval somey eq +123.53 endst
dump somez eq divnum of somex somey ofend endst
message anyvar somez endst
storeval somex eq +987654.765 endst
storeval somey eq -123.53 endst
dump somez eq divnum of somex somey ofend endst
message anyvar somez endst
storeval somex eq -987654.765 endst
storeval somey eq +123.53 endst
dump somez eq divnum of somex somey ofend endst
message anyvar somez endst
storeval somex eq -987654.765 endst
storeval somey eq -123.53 endst
dump somez eq divnum of somex somey ofend endst
message anyvar somez endst
end

*
badcomm.sbl
declare somex endst
```

```
begin
storeval somex eq +100 endst
message anyvar somex endst
write somex endst
end


*

bucket.cvb
begin
comment You can maintain buckets of datafiles. endst
comment The first bucket may be aaaaaaaa.dat. endst
comment The last bucket may be z9999999.dat. endst
comment Each bucket may be limited by maximum filesize. endst
comment Use the 'filesize' command to
                limit the filesize to below maximum. endst
comment You can increment the bucket name by programming automatically.
endst
end



*

cascade.sbl
declare somex somey somes somet somea someb endst
begin
storeval somex eq char Naga Raja endchar endst
storeval somey eq char Mani Deep endchar endst
storeval somes eq +32 endst
charofint of somes into somet endst
cascade somex and somet into somea endst
cascade somea and somey into someb endst
message anyvar someb endst
end

*

cascade2.sbl
declare somex somey somes somet somea someb endst
begin
comment This programme gives errors endst
storeval somex eq char Naga Raja endchar endst
storeval somey eq char Mani Deep endchar endst
storeval somes eq +0 endst
charofint of somes into somet endst
cascade somex and somet into somea endst
cascade somea and somey into someb endst
message anyvar someb endst
message cat Somet : endcat endst
message anyvar somet endst
```

```
end

*

cascade3.sbl
declare somex somey somez endst
begin
storeval somex eq char Naga Raja endchar endst
storeval somey eq char Mani Deep endchar endst
cascade somex and somey into somez endst
message anyvar somez endst
end

*

charofin.rmf
declare somex somey endst
begin
storeval somex eq +120 endst
charofint of somex into somey endst
message anyvar somey endst
end

*

intofcha.rmf
declare somex somey endst
begin
storeval somex eq char x endchar endst
intofchar of somex into somey endst
message anyvar somey endst
end

*

colprn.sbl
declare col1 col2 somex somey x1 y1 x2 y2 somea someb endst
begin
storeval color1 eq +70 endst
storeval color2 eq +74 endst
storeval somex eq +42 endst
storeval somey eq +52 endst
storeval row1 eq +10 endst
storeval col1 eq +20 endst
storeval row2 eq +15 endst
storeval col2 eq +22 endst
setvideomode text endst
gotorowcol row1 col1 endst
printchar somex color1 endst
get somea endst
gotorowcol row2 col2 endst
```

```
printchar somey color2 endst
get someb endst
end


*

combihar.cvb
Don't run these programs as they may cause
problems to the Hardware Ports by doing I/O.
Note,the code is commentated.
begin
comment For_hardware_port_inport endst
comment storeval  portnum eq +3 endst
comment direct inport portnum into somex endst
comment message anyvar somex endst
end
begin
comment For_hardware_port_outport endst
comment storeval somey eq +123 endst
comment storeval portnum eq +1 endst
comment direct outport somey to portnum endst
comment message anyvar portnum endst
end


*

combisof.cvb
Don't run these programs as any networks
may be present.
Just study them,they are for Software Port I/O.
If you run them they may cause problem
to the networks like.
Note,the code is commentated.
begin
comment For_software_port_inport endst
comment storeval  portnum eq +5555 endst
comment indirect inport portnum into somex endst
comment message anyvar somex endst
end
begin
comment For_software_port_outport endst
comment storeval somey eq +123 endst
comment storeval portnum eq +6666 endst
comment indirect outport somey to portnum endst
comment message anyvar portnum endst
end


*

comment.cbl
```

```
begin
comment This is Prasanna Kumar endst
message cat Develop Your Own DBMApps... endcat endst
comment This_is_Naga_Raju_too endst
end


*

compare.sbl
declare somex somey somez endst
begin
storeval somex eq char nagaraju endchar endst
storeval somey eq char nagarjuna endchar endst endst
if somex gt somey then 1
message cat Okay endcat endst
endif 1
get somez endst
end


*

curdri2.sbl
begin
storeval filename eq char invoice.dat endchar endst
storeval curdri eq +2 endst
fileopen filename curdri drivenum status endst
message anyvar curdri endst
message anyvar drivenum endst
message anyvar status endst
fileclose filename endst
open filename curdri drivenum status endst
message anyvar curdri endst
message anyvar drivenum endst
message anyvar status endst
fileclose filename endst
end

*

data.cbl
begin
storeval file eq char data.cbx endchar endst
storeval somez1 eq +999 endst
storeval somez2 eq +888 endst
storeval somez3 eq +777 endst
storeval somez4 eq +666 endst
storeval somez5 eq +555 endst
storeval somez6 eq +444 endst
storeval somez7 eq +333 endst
```

```
storeval somez8 eq +222 endst
storeval somez9 eq +111 endst
open file for fresh curdri drivenum status endst
insert somez9 endst
insert somez8 endst
insert somez7 endst
insert somez6 endst
insert somez5 endst
insert somez4 endst
insert somez3 endst
insert somez2 endst
insert somez1 endst
end

*

data.cbx
+111,+222,+333,+444,+555,+666,+777,+888,+999,
*

data.dat

*

dir.sbl
declare somex endst
begin
storeval somex eq char dir/p endchar endst
system somex endst
end

*

elemdbms.dbm
declare endst
begin
comment An elementary database management application endst
comment Create employee.dat with a hash followed by a comma endst
storeval one eq +1 endst
storeval two eq +2 endst
storeval three eq +3 endst
storeval four eq +4 endst
storeval five eq +5 endst
storeval six eq +6 endst
storeval unlock eq char un endchar endst
storeval recnum eq +1 endst
storeval datafile eq char employee.dat endchar endst
storeval tempfile eq char temp.dat endchar endst
storeval offset eq +0 endst
storeval hash eq char # endchar endst
storeval star eq char * endchar endst
```

```
open tempfile for fresh curdri drivenum status endst
insert star endst
open datafile for writeread curdri drivenum status endst
longseek offset endst
labelit label3 endst
get someo endst
setvideomode text endst
message cat --------------------------------------------------- endcat endst
message line endst
message cat *********** XYZ Production Company *************** endcat endst
message line endst
message cat --------------------------------------------------- endcat endst
message line endst
message cat *********** 1.Insert Records ******************* endcat endst
message line endst
message cat *********** 2.Select Records ******************* endcat endst
message line endst
message cat *********** 3.Update Records ******************** endcat endst
message line endst
message cat *********** 4.Delete Records ******************** endcat endst
message line endst
message cat *********** 5.Report Records ******************* endcat endst
message line endst
message cat *********** 6.Quit **************************** endcat endst
message line endst
message cat --------------------------------------------------- endcat endst
message line endst
message cat Enter Your Choice... endcat endst
get someq endst
storeval somep eq char + endchar endst
cascade somep and someq into somer endst
if somer eq one then 1
call insertion endst
endif 1
if somer eq two then 2
call selection endst
endif 2
if somer eq three then 3
call updation endst
endif 3
if somer eq four then 4
call deletion endst
endif 4
if somer eq five then 5
call reporting endst
endif 5
if somer eq six then 6
```

```
goto label2 endst
endif 6
goto label3 endst
labelit label2 endst
end
function insertion is
message cat Enter empno : endcat endst
get empno endst
message cat Enter ename : endcat endst
get ename endst
message cat Enter wages : endcat endst
get wages endst
insert empno endst
insert ename endst
insert wages endst
insert unlock endst
insert recnum endst
dump recnum eq addint of recnum one ofend endst
endcall
function selection is
storeval offset eq +0 endst
labelit label5 endst
open datafile for writeread curdri drivenum status endst
longseek offset endst
read empno oneofto label3 endst
read ename oneofto label3 endst
read wages oneofto label3 endst
read status2 oneofto label3 endst
read recnum oneofto label3 endst
longtell offset endst
message anyvar empno endst
message anyvar ename endst
message anyvar wages endst
message anyvar status2 endst
message anyvar recnum endst
message line endst
goto label5 endst
endcall
function updation is
storeval offset eq +0 endst
message cat Enter old wage : endcat endst
get oldwage endst
message cat Enter new wage : endcat endst
get newwage endst
open tempfile for fresh curdri drivenum status endst
insert star endst
labelit label109 endst
```

```
open datafile for writeread curdri drivenum status endst
longseek offset endst
read empno oneofto label7 endst
read ename oneofto label7 endst
read wages oneofto label7 endst
read status2 oneofto label7 endst
read recnum oneofto label7 endst
filetell offset endst
if wages eq oldwage then 3
open tempfile for writeread curdri drivenum status endst
insert empno endst
insert ename endst
insert newwage endst
insert status2 endst
insert recnum endst
endif 3
if wages ne oldwage then 4
open tempfile for writeread curdri drivenum status endst
insert empno endst
insert ename endst
insert wages endst
insert status2 endst
insert recnum endst
endif 4
goto label109 endst
labelit label7 endst
storeval offset eq +0 endst
open datafile for fresh curdri drivenum status endst
insert hash endst
labelit label111 endst
open tempfile for writeread curdri drivenum status endst
longseek offset endst
read empno oneofto label112 endst
read ename oneofto label112 endst
read wages oneofto label112 endst
read status2 oneofto label112 endst
read recnum oneofto label112 endst
longtell offset endst
open datafile for writeread curdri drivenum status endst
insert empno endst
insert ename endst
insert wages endst
insert status2 endst
insert recnum endst
goto label111 endst
labelit label112 endst
endcall
```

```
function deletion is
storeval offset eq +0 endst
message cat Enter employee name : endcat endst
get empname endst
open tempfile for fresh curdri drivenum status endst
insert star endst
labelit label102 endst
open datafile for writeread curdri drivenum status endst
longseek offset endst
read empno oneofto label101 endst
read ename oneofto label101 endst
read wages oneofto label101 endst
read status2 oneofto label101 endst
read recnum oneofto label101 endst
filetell offset endst
open tempfile for writeread curdri drivenum status endst
if empname ne ename then 1
insert empno endst
insert ename endst
insert wages endst
insert status2 endst
insert recnum endst
endif 1
goto label102 endst
labelit label101 endst
storeval offset eq +0 endst
open datafile for fresh curdri drivenum status endst
insert hash endst
labelit label105 endst
open tempfile for writeread curdri drivenum status endst
longseek offset endst
read empno oneofto label104 endst
read ename oneofto label104 endst
read wages oneofto label104 endst
read status2 oneofto label104 endst
read recnum oneofto label104 endst
longtell offset endst
open datafile for writeread curdri drivenum status endst
insert empno endst
insert ename endst
insert wages endst
insert status2 endst
insert recnum endst
goto label105 endst
labelit label104 endst
endcall
function reporting is
```

```
storeval offset eq +0 endst
labelit label16 endst
open datafile for writeread curdri drivenum status endst
longseek offset endst
read empno oneofto label17 endst
read ename oneofto label17 endst
read wages oneofto label17 endst
read status2 oneofto label17 endst
read recnum oneofto label17 endst
longtell offset endst
webrep cat <html> endcat endst
webrep line endst
webrep cat <body> endcat endst
webrep line endst
webrep cat <table border="1" bgcolor="lightgreen" align="center"
width="350"> endcat endst
webrep line endst
webrep cat <caption align="top"><h2>Employee Wages</h2></caption> endcat
endst
webrep line endst
webrep cat <width="180" height="180" align="right" /> endcat endst
webrep line endst
webrep cat <tr><th>Employee Number </th><td> endcat endst
webrep anyvar empno endst
webrep line endst
webrep cat </td></tr> endcat endst
webrep cat <tr><th>Employee Name </th><td> endcat endst
webrep anyvar ename endst
webrep line endst
webrep cat </td></tr> endcat endst
webrep cat <tr><th>Employee Wages </th><td> endcat endst
webrep anyvar wages endst
webrep line endst
webrep cat </td></tr></table> endcat endst
webrep line endst
webrep cat </body> endcat endst
webrep line endst
webrep cat </html> endcat endst
webrep line endst
goto label16 endst
labelit label17 endst
endcall

*

employee.dat

*
```

```
equal.cbl
declare somex somey endst
begin
storeval somex eq char * endchar endst
storeval somey eq char * endchar endst
if somex eq somey then 1
message cat Okay1 endcat endst
endif 1
if somex eq somey then 2
message cat Okay2 endcat endst
endif 2
end

*

example.cbl
declare somex somey endst
begin
storeval somex eq char Naga Raju endchar endst
storeval somey eq +999 endst
message anyvar somex endst
message anyvar somey endst
end

*

example2.cbl
declare somex somey somez endst
begin
storeval somex eq +777777 endst
storeval somey eq +888888 endst
storeval somez eq +999999 endst
message anyvar somex endst
message anyvar somey endst
message anyvar somez endst
end

*

exampro2.sbl
begin
storeval filename eq char exampro.dat endchar endst
open filename curdri drivenum status endst
call insert_somex endst
call insert_somex endst
call insert_somex endst
open filename curdri drivenum status endst
call read_somey endst
call read_somey endst
message anyvar somey endst
```

```
end
function insert_somex is
storeval somex eq char Nagaraju endchar endst
storeval comma eq char , endchar endst
storeval somep eq +0 endst
storeval someq eq +1 endst
fileopen filename curdri drivenum status endst
substring somex length into somel endst
storevar somer eq somep endst
storevar somes eq someq endst
labelit label1 endst
substring somex from somer to somes into somez endst
writefile somez into filename endst
dump somei eq addint of somer someq ofend endst
dump somej eq addint of somes someq ofend endst
storevar somer eq somei endst
storevar somes eq somej endst
if somer lt somel then 1
goto label1 endst
endif 1
writefile comma into filename endst
fileclose filename endst
endcall
function read_somey is
storeval somex eq char endchar endst
storeval comma eq char , endchar endst
storeval three eq +3 endst
fileopen filename curdri drivenum status endst
labelit label11 endst
readfile somechar from filename endst
if somechar ne comma then 1
cascade somex and somechar into somey endst
storevar somex eq somey endst
goto label11 endst
endif 1
fileclose filename endst
substring somey length into somel endst
substring somey from three to somel into somez endst
message anyvar somez endst
endcall

*

examprog.cbl
begin
storeval filename eq char examprog.dat endchar endst
storeval somex eq +999 endst
open filename for fresh curdri drivenum status endst
```

```
insert somex endst
insert somex endst
insert somex endst
open filename for writeread curdri drivenum status endst
read somey oneofto label1 endst
read somey oneofto label1 endst
message anyvar somey endst
labelit label1 endst
end


*

factoria.sbl
declare somex somey somez somea someb somec endst
begin
comment Find_the_factorials_of_integers endst
storeval somex eq +0 endst
storeval somea eq +1 endst
storeval someb eq +5 endst
factorial of somex into somey endst
factorial of somea into somez endst
factorial of someb into somec endst
message anyvar somey endst
message anyvar somez endst
message anyvar somec endst
end


*

factorq.sbl
declare somex somey endst
begin
storeval somex eq +9 endst
factorial of somex into somey endst
message anyvar somey endst
end


*

fileex0.cbl
begin
storeval somex1 eq +111 endst
storeval somex2 eq +222 endst
storeval somex3 eq +333 endst
storeval file1 eq char input.cbx endchar endst
storeval file2 eq char output.cbx endchar endst
open file1 for fresh curdri drivenum status endst
insert somex1 endst
insert somex2 endst
```

```
insert somex3 endst
open file2 for fresh curdri drivenum status endst
insert somex3 endst
insert somex2 endst
insert somex1 endst
open file1 for writeread curdri drivenum status endst
read somey1 oneofto label2 endst
read somey2 oneofto label2 endst
read somey3 oneofto label2 endst
open file2 for writeread curdri drivenum status endst
read somez1 oneofto label2 endst
read somez2 oneofto label2 endst
read somez3 oneofto label2 endst
message anyvar somey1 endst
message anyvar somey2 endst
message anyvar somey3 endst
message anyvar somez1 endst
message anyvar somez2 endst
message anyvar somez3 endst
labelit label2 endst
end

*

fileex1.cbl
begin
storeval offset1 eq +3 endst
storeval file1 eq char data.cbx endchar endst
open file1 for writeread curdri drivenum status endst
forward offset1 endst
read somex1 oneofto label2 endst
message anyvar somex1 endst
gofor begining endst
storeval offset2 eq +2 endst
longseek offset2 endst
read somex2 oneofto label2 endst
message anyvar somex2 endst
longtell offset3 endst
message anyvar offset3 endst
labelit label2 endst
end

*

filesize.cvb
begin
storeval filename eq char rajadata.dat endchar endst
filesize of filename into somefs endst
message anyvar somefs endst
```

end

filetest.sbl
begin
storeval filename eq char file.dat endchar endst
fileopen filename curdri drivenum status endst
storeval somex eq char q endchar endst
writefile somex into filename endst
writefile somex into filename endst
writefile somex into filename endst
writefile somex into filename endst
writefile somex into filename endst
fileseek filename for begining endst
filetell filename into somelong endst
message anyvar somelong endst
fileseek filename for ending endst
filetell filename into somelong endst
message anyvar somelong endst
fileseek filename for back endst
filetell filename into somelong endst
message anyvar somelong endst
fileseek filename for forth endst
filetell filename into somelong endst
message anyvar somelong endst
fileseek filename for begining endst
readfile somestr from filename endst
message anyvar somestr endst
fileclose filename endst
end

function.cbl
declare somex somey somez somer somes somet sum diff endst
begin
storeval somex eq +100 endst
storeval somey eq +200 endst
call sum endst
message cat function completed... endcat endst
message cat returned endcat endst
message anyvar somes endst
message line endst
call diff endst
message cat function completed... endcat endst
message cat returned endcat endst
message anyvar somet endst
end

function diff is
dump somer eq subint of somex somey ofend endst
storevar somet eq somer endst
endcall
function sum is
dump somez eq addint of somex somey ofend endst
storevar somes eq somez endst
endcall

*
funfun.sbl
declare somea someb somex somey somez fun0 fun1 fun2 fun3 fun4 endst
begin
message cat You need not necessarily have nested functions... endcat endst
message line endst
message cat You may have sequential function calls instead... endcat endst
message line endst
storeval somea eq char Venkata endchar endst
storeval somex eq char Naga endchar endst
storeval somey eq char Raju endchar endst
storeval somez eq char Rani endchar endst
storeval someb eq char Prasanna endchar endst
call fun0 endst
call fun1 endst
call fun2 endst
call fun3 endst
call fun4 endst
end
function fun4 is
message anyvar someb endst
message line endst
endcall
function fun1 is
message anyvar somex endst
message line endst
endcall
function fun2 is
message anyvar somey endst
message line endst
endcall
function fun3 is
message anyvar somez endst
message line endst
endcall
function fun0 is
message anyvar somea endst
message line endst

```
endcall

*

get.cbl
declare somex somey somez endst
begin
message cat Enter some value: endcat endst
get somex endst
message anyvar somex endst
message cat Enter some value: endcat endst
get somey endst
message anyvar somey endst
message cat Enter some value: endcat endst
get somez endst
message anyvar somez endst
end

*

getkey.cbl
declare scancode asciicode endst
begin
getkey scancode asciicode endst
message anyvar scancode endst
message anyvar asciicode endst
end

*

getrc.cbl
declare row col somex somey endst
begin
storeval row eq +10 endst
storeval col eq +20 endst
gotorowcol row col endst
getrowcol somex somey endst
message anyvar somex endst
message anyvar somey endst
end

*

getroco.sbl
declare x1 y1 somex somey endst
begin
storeval x1 eq +10 endst
storeval y1 eq +20 endst
gotorowcol x1 y1 endst
message cat Nagaraju endcat endst
getrowcol somex somey endst
```

```
message anyvar somex endst
message anyvar somey endst
end

*

getup.cbl
declare username password endst
begin
message cat Enter username : endcat endst
get username endst
message cat Enter password : endcat endst
getpassword password endst
message anyvar username endst
message anyvar password endst
end


*

goto.cbl
begin
labelit label1 endst
message cat Srinivasa Computers,Darsi endcat endst
message line endst
goto label1 endst
end

*

gotorc.cbl
declare row col somex endst
begin
storeval row eq +10 endst
storeval col eq +15 endst
gotorowcol row col endst
get somex endst
message anyvar somex endst
end

*

if.cbl
declare somex somey endst
begin
storeval somex eq -62.437 endchar endst
storeval somey eq +624.37 endchar endst
message anyvar somex endst
message anyvar somey endst
message line endst
if somex lt somey then 1
```

```
message cat lt Okay endcat endst
endif 1
if somex gt somey then 1
message cat gt Okay endcat endst
endif 1
if somex le somey then 1
message cat le Okay endcat endst
endif 1
if somex ge somey then 1
message cat ge Okay endcat endst
endif 1
if somex eq somey then 1
message cat eq Okay endcat endst
endif 1
if somex ne somey then 1
message cat ne Okay endcat endst
endif 1
end

*

ifcom.cbl
begin
storeval somex eq +9999 endst
storeval somey eq naga endst
if somex lt somey then 1
message anyvar somex endst
message anyvar somey endst
endif 1
end

*

infind.cbl
begin
storeval somex eq char In case of infinities and indeterminate forms algebra
          we do not at all care endchar endst
message anyvar somex endst
end

*

input

*

input.cbx
+111,+222,+333,
*

input1.dat
```

```
*
input2.dat

*
instring.cbl
declare somex somey somez somea someb somez endst
begin
storeval somex eq char ABCDABCDABCDABCDABCDABCDABCD endchar endst
storeval somey eq char D endchar endst
storeval somea eq +5 endst
storeval someb eq +4 endst
instring of somey from somea occurence someb in somex into somez endst
message anyvar somez endst
end

*
instrin2.cbl
declare somea somem somej somek somel endst
begin
storeval somea eq +2.7 endst
storeval somem eq char . endchar endst
storeval somej eq +0 endst
storeval somek eq +1 endst
instring of somem from somej occurence somek in somea into somel endst
message anyvar somel endst
end

*
intofcha.cbl
declare somex somey endst
begin
storeval somex eq char x endchar endst
intofchar of somex into somey endst
message anyvar somey endst
end

*
intofile.sbl
begin
storeval filename eq char intofile.dat endchar endst
storeval somex eq char Nagaraju endchar endst
storeval comma eq char , endchar endst
storeval somep eq +0 endst
storeval someq eq +1 endst
fileopen filename curdri drivenum status endst
substring somex length into somel endst
storevar somer eq somep endst
```

```
storevar somes eq someq endst
labelit label1 endst
substring somex from somer to somes into somez endst
writefile somez into filename endst
dump somei eq addint of somer someq ofend endst
dump somej eq addint of somes someq ofend endst
storevar somer eq somei endst
storevar somes eq somej endst
if somer lt somel then 1
goto label1 endst
endif 1
writefile comma into filename endst
fileclose filename endst
end
```

*

```
jsconn.sbl
begin
comment BRADI1 is a software that runs on Windows Operating System. endst
comment Comma Seperated Values(CSVs) may be the File contents. endst
comment There is a facillity in JavaScript for text file I/O. endst
comment HTML,CSS & JS may be the Frontend. endst
comment With the webrep command,you can create *.js files. endst
comment The *.js files may be checked in a Web Browser like Opera. endst
comment With the system command of BRADI1,Web Browsers may be run.
endst
comment Text file I/O for all the data entered may be done in CSV form. endst
comment Photo comparisons and other graphics may be done in *.js. endst
comment The default report.htm may be copied to report.js and run. endst
comment So with this Frontend,Middleware and Backend you can do all. endst
end
```

*

```
longst.cbl
begin
storeval tabname eq char student.dat endchar endst
storeval cols eq +5 endst
storeval count eq +0 endst
storeval one eq +1 endst
storeval maxcnt eq +50 endst
storeval seven eq +7 endst
open tabname for fresh curdri drivenum status endst
labelit label1 endst
dump count eq addint of count one ofend endst
insert count endst
if count le maxcnt then 1
goto label1 endst
```

```
endif 1
gofor begining endst
forward cols endst
longtell longfptt endst
message anyvar longfptt endst
gofor begining endst
dump longfpt eq addint of longfptt seven ofend endst
longseek longfpt endst
read somex oneofto label3 endst
message anyvar somex endst
labelit label3 endst
end


*

matrices.dat

*

matrix.cvb
begin
storeval matrfile eq char matr1111.dat endchar endst
storeval somex eq +999 endst
storeval somey eq +9999 endst
storeval somez eq +99 endst
storeval matname1 eq char mat1 endchar endst
storeval matname2 eq char mat2 endchar endst
storeval matname3 eq char mat3 endchar endst
storeval dims1 eq +5 endst
storeval dims2 eq +4 endst
storeval dims3 eq +3 endst
storeval dim1 eq +3 endst
storeval dim2 eq +1 endst
storeval dim3 eq +4 endst
storeval dim4 eq +5 endst
storeval dim5 eq +2 endst
putmat matrfile matname1 dims2 dim4 dim3 dim2 dim1 somey endst
putmat matrfile matname2 dims1 dim5 dim4 dim3 dim2 dim1 somex endst
putmat matrfile matname3 dims3 dim4 dim3 dim2 somez endst
putmat matrfile matname1 dims2 dim2 dim3 dim2 dim1 somex endst
putmat matrfile matname2 dims1 dim4 dim3 dim5 dim2 dim1 somey endst
putmat matrfile matname3 dims3 dim4 dim5 dim3 somey endst
getmat matrfile matname3 dims3 dim4 dim3 dim2 someq endst
message anyvar someq endst
delmat matrfile matname3 dims3 dim4 dim3 dim2 endst
end


*
```

```
maxfisi.cvb
begin
storeval somex eq char Maximum filesize is less than 4GB endchar endst
message anyvar somex endst
end


*

memdeal.fis
begin
storeval segaddr eq +0 endst
storeval string eq char Venkata Naga Raja Prasanna Kumar... endchar endst
putmem segaddr string endst
getmem segaddr string output endst
message anyvar output endst
end


*

menu.cvb
begin
storeval somestring1 eq char *Education Management System* endchar endst
storeval somestring0 eq char ---------------------------- endchar endst
storeval somestring2 eq char *Data Entry Screens********** endchar endst
storeval somestring3 eq char *Select Records************* endchar endst
storeval somestring4 eq char *Update Records************* endchar endst
storeval somestring5 eq char *Delete Records************* endchar endst
storeval somestring6 eq char *Web Reports**************** endchar endst
storeval somestring7 eq char *Web Communications********* endchar endst
storeval somestring8 eq char *Web Transactions*********** endchar endst
storeval color eq +75 endst
storeval highlight eq +27 endst
storeval row eq +5 endst
storeval col eq +20 endst
storeval row2 eq +24 endst
storeval col2 eq +40 endst
storeval row3 eq +7 endst
storeval one eq +1 endst
setvideomode text endst
gotorowcol row col endst
printit somestring1 and color endst
dump row eq addint of row one ofend endst
gotorowcol row col endst
printit somestring0 and color endst
dump row eq addint of row one ofend endst
gotorowcol row col endst
printit somestring2 and color endst
dump row eq addint of row one ofend endst
gotorowcol row col endst
```

```
printit somestring3 and color endst
dump row eq addint of row one ofend endst
gotorowcol row col endst
printit somestring4 and color endst
dump row eq addint of row one ofend endst
gotorowcol row col endst
printit somestring5 and color endst
dump row eq addint of row one ofend endst
gotorowcol row col endst
printit somestring6 and color endst
dump row eq addint of row one ofend endst
gotorowcol row col endst
printit somestring7 and color endst
dump row eq addint of row one ofend endst
gotorowcol row col endst
printit somestring8 and color endst
gotorowcol row3 col endst
printit somestring2 and highlight endst
gotorowcol row2 col2 endst
get stay endst
setvideomode text endst
end

*

message.sbl
declare somex somey endst
begin
storeval somex eq +99.99 endst
storevar somey eq somex endst
message cat Naga Raju endcat endst
message anyval +33.33 endst
message space 10 endst
message anyvar somey endst
message line endst
comment This is a documentation endst
end

*

modifydb.cvb
begin
comment Maintain a status column in the data file. endst
comment Maintain a record number at the end. endst
comment The status may be 'un' for unlock,'lo' for lock,
           'de' for delete,'up' for update. endst
comment At last,you can remove the 'de' records by a programme. endst
comment At last,you can remove the 'up' records by a programme. endst
comment Insertion takes place at the end. endst
```

```
comment This improves the speed of deal. endst
comment The record number may be added or subtracted
          by dump' addint or subint commands. endst
end


*
newfact.cbl
begin
storeval somex eq +55 endst
factorial of somex into somey endst
message anyvar somey endst
end


*
null.sbl
declare somex somea someb somep someq endst
begin
storeval somex eq char endchar endst
message cat M endcat endst
message anyvar somex endst
message cat N endcat endst
message line endst
storeval somea eq char X endchar endst
storeval someb eq char Y endchar endst
cascade somea and somex into somep endst
cascade somep and someb into someq endst
message anyvar someq endst
end


*
null2.sbl
declare somex somey endst
begin
storeval somex eq char NULL endchar endst
message cat Enter somey : endcat endst
get somey endst
if somex eq somey then 1
message cat You entered 'NULL' endcat endst
endif
end


*
outofile.sbl
begin
storeval filename eq char intofile.dat endchar endst
storeval somex eq char endchar endst
storeval comma eq char , endchar endst
```

storeval three eq +3 endst
fileopen filename curdri drivenum status endst
labelit label1 endst
readfile somechar from filename endst
if somechar ne comma then 1
cascade somex and somechar into somey endst
storevar somex eq somey endst
goto label1 endst
endif 1
fileclose filename endst
substring somey length into somel endst
substring somey from three to somel into somez endst
message anyvar somey endst
message anyvar somez endst
end

*

intofile.sbl
begin
storeval filename eq char intofile.dat endchar endst
storeval somex eq char Nagaraju endchar endst
storeval comma eq char , endchar endst
storeval somep eq +0 endst
storeval someq eq +1 endst
fileopen filename curdri drivenum status endst
substring somex length into somel endst
storevar somer eq somep endst
storevar somes eq someq endst
labelit label1 endst
substring somex from somer to somes into somez endst
writefile somez into filename endst
dump somei eq addint of somer someq ofend endst
dump somej eq addint of somes someq ofend endst
storevar somer eq somei endst
storevar somes eq somej endst
if somer lt somel then 1
goto label1 endst
endif 1
writefile comma into filename endst
fileclose filename endst
end

*

output

*

output.cbl

```
begin
storeval file eq char input2.dat endchar endst
storeval output eq char output.dat endchar endst
storeval square eq char square endchar endst
storeval two eq +2 endst
storeval appendix eq char .o endchar endst
storeval offset1 eq +0 endst
open output for fresh curdri drivenum status endst
labelit label1 endst
open file for writeread curdri drivenum status endst
longseek offset1 endst
read varname oneofto label2 endst
read varval oneofto label2 endst
dump offset1 eq addint of offset1 two ofend endst
cascade varval and appendix into varval2 endst
power of varval2 to two into square2 endst
open output for writeread curdri drivenum status endst
insert square endst
insert square2 endst
goto label1 endst
labelit label2 endst
end

*

output.cbx
+333,+222,+111,
*

output.dat

*

power.sbl
declare somex somey somez endst
begin
comment Power_of_a_number_to_an_integer endst
storeval somex eq +9.963 endst
storeval somey eq +4 endst
power of somex to somey into somez endst
message anyvar somez endst
end

*

power2.sbl
declare somex somey somez somep somer endst
begin
comment Power_of_+2.5_to_-2 endst
storeval somex eq +2.5 endst
storeval somey eq +2 endst
```

```
storeval somer eq +1.0 endst
power of somex to somey into somez endst
dump somep eq divnum of somer somez ofend endst
message anyvar somep endst
end


*

powerq.sbl
declare somex somey somez endst
begin
storeval somex eq -54.23 endst
storeval somey eq +7 endst
power of somex to somey into somez endst
message anyvar somez endst
end



*

powtest.sbl
begin
storeval somex eq +3.0 endst
storeval somey eq -2 endst
power of somex to somey into somez endst
message anyvar somez endst
end

*

printit.cvb
begin
storeval somestring1 eq char *Data Entry** endchar endst
storeval somestring2 eq char *Data Manage* endchar endst
storeval color eq +100 endst
storeval highlight eq +50 endst
storeval row eq +10 endst
storeval col eq +15 endst
storeval row2 eq +0 endst
storeval col2 eq +0 endst
storeval one eq +1 endst
storeval noofsps eq +10 endst
setvideomode text endst
gotorowcol row col endst
printit somestring1 and color endst
dump row eq addint of row one ofend endst
gotorowcol row col endst
printit somestring2 and color endst
dump row eq subint of row one ofend endst
gotorowcol row col endst
```

```
printit somestring1 and highlight endst
gotorowcol row col endst
getkey scancode asciicode endst
spaceit noofsps and color endst
gotorowcol row2 col2 endst
message anyvar data endst
getrowcol row3 col3 endst
message anyvar row3 endst
message anyvar col3 endst
end

*

rajadata.dat

*

raju.dat

*

read.sbl
declare filename endoffile somestr somex endst
begin
storeval filename eq char write.dat endchar endst
storeval endoffile eq char EOF endchar endst
readfile somestr from filename endst
message anyvar somestr endst
readfile somestr from filename endst
message anyvar somestr endst
labelit label1 endst
readfile somestr from filename endst
message anyvar somestr endst
get somex endst
if somestr eq endoffile then 1
goto label2 endst
endif 1
goto label1 endst
labelit label2 endst
end

*

report.htm

*

round.sbl
declare somea someb somec somed somex somey somez someq endst
begin
storeval somea eq +999999.99995 endst
storeval someb eq -12345.67885 endst
```

storeval somec eq +12345.67894 endst
storeval somed eq -999999.99994 endst
storeval somex eq +4 endst
storeval somey eq +1 endst
storeval somez eq +0 endst
round of somea to somex into someq endst
message anyval +1 endst
message anyvar someq endst
round of someb to somex into someq endst
message anyval +2 endst
message anyvar someq endst
round of somec to somex into someq endst
message anyval +3 endst
message anyvar someq endst
round of somed to somex into someq endst
message anyval +4 endst
message anyvar someq endst
round of somea to somey into someq endst
message anyval +5 endst
message anyvar someq endst
round of someb to somey into someq endst
message anyval +6 endst
message anyvar someq endst
round of somec to somey into someq endst
message anyval +7 endst
message anyvar someq endst
round of somed to somey into someq endst
message anyval +8 endst
message anyvar someq endst
round of somea to somez into someq endst
message anyval +9 endst
message anyvar someq endst
round of someb to somez into someq endst
message anyval +10 endst
message anyvar someq endst
round of somec to somez into someq endst
message anyval +11 endst
message anyvar someq endst
round of somed to somez into someq endst
message anyval +12 endst
message anyvar someq endst
end

*

segaddr.fis
begin
storeval segaddr eq +0 endst

```
storeval string1 eq char Venkata endchar endst
storeval string2 eq char Nagaraja endchar endst
storeval string3 eq char Prasanna endchar endst
storeval string4 eq char Kumar endchar endst
putmem segaddr string1 endst
putmem segaddr string2 endst
putmem segaddr string3 endst
putmem segaddr string4 endst
getmem segaddr string1 output endst
message anyvar output endst
getmem segaddr string2 output endst
message anyvar output endst
getmem segaddr string3 output endst
message anyvar output endst
getmem segaddr string4 output endst
message anyvar output endst
end

*

seqfuns.cvb
begin
comment You need not necessarily have nested functions endst
comment You may have sequential function calls instead endst
comment int s; endst
comment main() endst
comment { endst
comment int p=100; endst
comment int a=2; endst
comment multiply(p,a) endst
comment print s; endst
comment } endst
comment multiply(p,a) endst
comment { endst
comment int q=p*a; endst
comment int b=3; endst
comment multiply2(q,b) endst
comment } endst
comment multiply2(q,b) endst
comment { endst
comment int r=q*b; endst
comment int c=4; endst
comment multiply3(r,c) endst
comment } endst
comment multiply3(r,c) endst
comment { endst
comment s=r*c; endst
comment } endst
```

```
storeval somep eq +999 endst
storeval somea eq +2 endst
storeval someb eq +3 endst
storeval somec eq +4 endst
call multiply endst
message anyvar someq endst
message line endst
call multiply2 endst
message anyvar somer endst
message line endst
call multiply3 endst
message anyvar somes endst
message line endst
end
function multiply is
message anyvar somep endst
message anyvar somea endst
dump someq eq mulint of somep somea ofend endst
message anyvar someq endst
endcall
function multiply2 is
message anyvar someq endst
message anyvar someb endst
dump somer eq mulint of someq someb ofend endst
message anyvar somer endst
endcall
function multiply3 is
message anyvar somer endst
message anyvar somec endst
dump somes eq mulint of somer somec ofend endst
message anyvar somes endst
endcall

*

setdisk.cbl
begin
storeval drivenumber eq +3 endst
setdisk drivenumber endst
end

*

setvid.cbl
declare r c somex endst
begin
storeval r eq +10 endst
storeval c eq +15 endst
setvideomode text endst
```

```
gotorowcol r c endst
get somex endst
end

*

signone.sbl
declare somex somey somez someq endst
begin
storeval somex eq char +1 endchar endst
storeval somey eq +0 endst
storeval somez eq +1 endst
substring somex from somey to somez into someq endst
message anyvar someq endst
end

*

signzero.sbl
declare somea someb somec somed endst
begin
storeval somea eq char -0 endchar endst
storeval someb eq +0 endst
storeval somec eq +0 endst
substring somea from someb to somec into somed endst
message anyvar somed endst
end

*

sinx.cvb
begin
comment App that calculates sinx... endst
comment Sine of +3.3 endst
storeval somex eq +3.3 endst
call Sine_Find endst
message cat Sine of +3.3 is endcat endst
message anyvar result endst
end
function Sine_Find is
storevar term1 eq somex endst
storeval three eq +3 endst
storeval fact3 eq +6.0 endst
storeval somen eq +1 endst
power of somex to three into term2 endst
dump term2 eq divnum of term2 fact3 ofend endst
storeval five eq +5 endst
storeval fact5 eq +120.0 endst
power of somex to five into term3 endst
dump term3 eq divnum of term3 fact5 ofend endst
```

```
dump result eq subnum of term1 term2 ofend endst
dump result eq addnum of result term3 ofend endst
round of result to somen into result endst
endcall

*

splittim.cbl
begin
storeval timestamp eq char Mon Aug 07 17:33:05 2023 endchar endst
splittimestamp timestamp into day mon date hr min sec year endst
message anyvar day endst
message anyvar mon endst
message anyvar date endst
message anyvar hr endst
message anyvar min endst
message anyvar sec endst
message anyvar year endst
end

*

storeva2.sbl
declare somex somey endst
begin
storeval somex eq char endchar endst
storevar somey eq somex endst
message anyvar somex endst
message anyvar somey endst
end

*

storeva3.sbl
declare somex somey endst
begin
storeval somex eq char Nagaraju endchar endst
storevar somey eq somex endst
message anyvar somex endst
message anyvar somey endst
end

*

storeval.sbl
declare somex somey endst
begin
storeval somex eq +100 endst
storevar somey eq somex endst
message anyvar somex endst
message anyvar somey endst
```

end

*

stvalvar.sbl
declare somex somey endst
begin
storeval somex eq +1 endst
storevar somey eq somex endst
message anyvar somex endst
storeval somex eq +2 endst
storevar somey eq somex endst
message anyvar somey endst
end

*

subprog1.cbl
declare somex val1 somey val2 somez val3 inpfile outfile
    count count2 one endst
begin
comment This is how to get the variables of a loop endst
storeval somex eq char var1 endchar endst
storeval somey eq char var2 endchar endst
storeval val1 eq +0 endst
storeval val2 eq +0 endst
storeval count eq +0 endst
storeval count2 eq +9 endst
storeval one eq +1 endst
storeval somez eq char var3 endchar endst
storeval inpfile eq char input1.dat endchar endst
storeval outfile eq char input2.dat endchar endst
open inpfile for fresh curdri drivenum status endst
open outfile for fresh curdri drivenum status endst
labelit label1 endst
open inpfile for writeread curdri drivenum status endst
insert somex endst
insert val1 endst
insert somey endst
insert val2 endst
dump val3 eq addint of val1 val2 ofend endst
open outfile for writeread curdri drivenum status endst
insert somez endst
insert val3 endst
dump count eq addint of count one ofend endst
if count le count2 then 1
dump val1 eq addint of val1 one ofend endst
dump val2 eq addint of val2 one ofend endst
goto label1 endst

```
endif 1
end

*

subprog2.cbl
declare inpfile outfile offset two result res val3 val4 somez endst
begin
comment This program finds the squares in a loop endst
storeval inpfile eq char input2.dat endchar endst
storeval outfile eq char output.dat endchar endst
storeval offset eq +0 endst
storeval two eq +2 endst
storeval result eq char square endchar endst
open outfile for fresh curdri drivenum status endst
open inpfile for writeread curdri drivenum status endst
labelit label1 endst
read somez oneofto label2 endst
message anyvar somez endst
read val3 oneofto label2 endst
comment message anyvar val3 endst
tonumber of val3 endst
message anyvar val3 endst
power of val3 to two into res endst
message anyvar res endst
open outfile for writeread curdri drivenum status endst
insert result endst
insert res endst
open inpfile for writeread curdri drivenum status endst
dump offset eq addint of offset two ofend endst
forward offset endst
comment read somez oneofto label2 endst
goto label1 endst
labelit label2 endst
end

*

subsign.cbl
declare somex somey somez someq endst
begin
storeval somex eq -100 endst
storeval somey eq +0 endst
storeval somez eq +1 endst
substring somex from somey to somez into someq endst
message anyvar someq endst
end

*
```

```
substr.cbl
declare somex somey somez somel endst
begin
storeval somex eq char Nagarajaprasannakumar endchar endst
storeval somey eq +5 endst
storeval somez eq +8 endst
substring somex from somey to somez into somel endst
message anyvar somel endst
end

*

substr2.cbl
declare somex somey somez somep somel somem endst
begin
storeval somex eq char Nagarajaprasannakumar endchar endst
storeval somey eq +5 endst
storeval somez eq +5 endst
storeval somep eq +6 endst
substring somex from somey to somez into somel endst
message anyvar somel endst
substring somex from somey to somep into somem endst
message anyvar somem endst
end

*

substr3.cbl
declare somex somey somep somel endst
begin
storeval somex eq char endchar endst
storeval somey eq +5 endst
storeval somep eq +8 endst
substring somex from somey to somep into somel endst
message anyvar somel endst
end

*

substri.cbl
declare somex somey somez somea endst
begin
storeval somex eq char Gosukonda Venkata Naga Raja endchar endst
storeval somey eq +10 endst
storeval somez eq +17 endst
substring somex from somey to somez into somea endst
message anyvar somea endst
end

*
```

```
substri2.cbl
declare somea someb endst
begin
storeval somea eq char endchar endst
substring somea length into someb endst
message anyvar someb endst
end

*

substrin.cbl
declare somea someb endst
begin
storeval somea eq char Gosukonda Venkata Naga Raja endchar endst
substring somea length into someb endst
message anyvar someb endst
end

*

sysdba.rig
Prasanna,Sannidhanam,noread,nowrite,noadmin,nousername,nopassword,nof
ile,~,Nagaraju,Gosukonda,read,nowrite,admin,Neeraja,Velamakanni,allfiles,~,
Sreenu,Geethanjali,noread,nowrite,admin,Prasanna,allpasswords,allfiles,~,Pra
sanna,Sannidhanam,read,write,admin,Nagaraju,Gosukonda,nofile,~,Nagaraju,
Gosukonda,read,write,admin,allusernames,allpasswords,allfiles,~,Neeraja,Vela
makanni,noread,nowrite,admin,Prasanna,Sannidhanam,nofile,~,Nagaraju,CDB
Developer,read,nowrite,noadmin,allusernames,Kumar,allfiles,~,Neeraja,Velam
akanni,read,nowrite,admin,Sreenu,allpasswords,bank.dat,~,
*

system.cbl
declare somex endst
begin
storeval somex eq char type if.dbm endchar endst
system somex endst
end

*

temp.dat

*

test1.cbl
begin
comment If_there_are_any_other_commands/variables_DBMAT_neglects
endst
comment Run this DBM program without compilation directly endst
declare somex endst
declare somey endst
declare somez endst
```

```
storeval somex eq +100 endst
storeval somey eq +200 endst
storeval soemz eq +300 endst
message anyvar somex endst
message anyvar someq endst
end


*

test2.cbl
declare somex somey endst
begin
storeval somex eq char Nagaraju endchar endst
storeval somey eq char Amrutha endchar endst
message anyvar somex endst
message anyvar somey endst
end


*

testit.cvb
begin
storeval integer1 eq +987654321 endst
storeval integer2 eq -987654321 endst
storeval integer3 eq char 987654321 endchar endst
storeval integer4 eq +A987654321 endst
storeval integer5 eq -9876A54321 endst
storeval integer6 eq +9876.54321 endst
testit integer integer1 into retval endst
message anyvar retval endst
testit integer integer2 into retval endst
message anyvar retval endst
testit integer integer3 into retval endst
message anyvar retval endst
testit integer integer4 into retval endst
message anyvar retval endst
testit integer integer5 into retval endst
message anyvar retval endst
testit integer integer6 into retval endst
message anyvar retval endst
storeval number1 eq +98765.4321 endst
storeval number2 eq -98765.4321 endst
storeval number3 eq char 98765.4321 endchar endst
storeval number4 eq +A98765.4321 endst
storeval number5 eq -9876A5.4321 endst
storeval number6 eq +987654321 endst
testit number number1 into retval endst
message anyvar retval endst
testit number number2 into retval endst
```

```
message anyvar retval endst
testit number number3 into retval endst
message anyvar retval endst
testit number number4 into retval endst
message anyvar retval endst
testit number number5 into retval endst
message anyvar retval endst
testit number number6 into retval endst
message anyvar retval endst
storeval string1 eq char Nagaraju endchar endst
storeval string2 eq char +98654321 endchar endst
storeval string3 eq char -98654321 endchar endst
storeval string4 eq char 987654321 endchar endst
storeval string5 eq char +98765.4321 endchar endst
storeval string6 eq char -98765.4321 endchar endst
storeval string7 eq char 9Nagaraju endchar endst
storeval string8 eq char Naga9raju endchar endst
testit string string1 into retval endst
message anyvar retval endst
testit string string2 into retval endst
message anyvar retval endst
testit string string3 into retval endst
message anyvar retval endst
testit string string4 into retval endst
message anyvar retval endst
testit string string5 into retval endst
message anyvar retval endst
testit string string6 into retval endst
message anyvar retval endst
testit string string7 into retval endst
message anyvar retval endst
testit string string8 into retval endst
message anyvar retval endst
comment No testit for date and time data types endst
end

*

toint.rmf
declare num1 endst
begin
storeval num1 eq +321.123 endst
tointeger of num1 endst
message anyvar num1 endst
end

*

tonum.rmf
```

```
declare somex endst
begin
storeval somex eq +123 endst
tonumber of somex endst
message anyvar somex endst
end

*

tonumb.rmf
declare somex endst
begin
storeval somex eq +1.23 endst
tonumber of somex endst
message anyvar somex endst
end

*

trigger2.cvb
declare file1 file2 somex somey somez endst
begin
storeval file1 eq char naga.dat endchar endst
storeval file2 eq char raju.dat endchar endst
storeval somex eq +111 endst
storeval somey eq +222 endst
open file1 for fresh curdri drivenum status endst
insert somex endst
open file2 for fresh curdri drivenum status endst
insert somey endst
call Trigger_Function endst
end
function Trigger_Function is
open file1 for writeread curdri drivenum status endst
storeval somez eq +9999 endst
insert somez endst
endcall

*

validate.cvb
begin
storeval beg eq +0 endst
storeval one eq +1 endst
storeval next eq +2 endst
storeval plus eq char + endchar endst
storeval minus eq char - endchar endst
storeval zero eq +0 endchar endst
storeval nine eq +9 endchar endst
message cat Enter field : endcat endst
```

```
get field endst
call validation endst
end
function validation is
substring field from beg to one into somech endst
if somech eq plus then 2
goto label2 endst
endif 2
if somech eq minus then 3
goto label2 endst
endif 3
message cat Not an integer field.Exiting... endcat endst
goto label4 endst
labelit label2 endst
substring field length into len endst
dump len eq subint of len one ofend endst
message anyvar len endst
labelit label1 endst
storeval flag2 eq +0 endst
dump beg eq addint of beg one ofend endst
substring field from beg to next into somech endst
message anyvar somech endst
cascade plus and somech into somech2 endst
message anyvar somech2 endst
storeval flag1 eq +0 endst
if somech2 ge zero then 4
if somech2 le nine then 5
storeval flag1 eq +1 endst
dump next eq addint of next one ofend endst
if beg lt len then 1
goto label1 endst
endif 1
if beg ge len then 7
storeval flag2 eq +1 endst
goto label7 endst
endif 7
endif 5
endif 4
labelit label7 endst
message cat ... endcat endst
message anyvar flag1 endst
message anyvar flag2 endst
if flag1 eq zero then 6
if flag2 eq zero then 7
message cat Not an integer field.Exiting... endcat endst
goto label4 endst
endif 7
```

```
endif 6
message cat Yes an integer field.Exiting... endcat endst
labelit label4 endst
endcall

*

webrep.cbl
declare stdphoto stdno stdname endst
begin
storeval stdphoto eq char d:\img100.jpg endchar endst
storeval stdno eq char 86EC252 endchar endst
storeval stdname eq char Nagaraju endchar endst
webrep cat <html> endcat endst
webrep line endst
webrep cat <body> endcat endst
webrep line endst
webrep cat <table border="1" bgcolor="lightgreen" align="center"
width="350"> endcat endst
webrep line endst
webrep cat <caption align="top"><h2>SSC Marks List</h2></caption> endcat
endst
webrep line endst
webrep cat <tr><th>Student Identification</th><td><img src= endcat endst
webrep line endst
webrep anyvar stdphoto endst
webrep space 1 endst
webrep cat  width="180" height="180" align="right" /> endcat endst
webrep line endst
webrep cat </td></tr> endcat endst
webrep line endst
webrep cat <tr><th>Student Number </th><td> endcat endst
webrep anyvar stdno endst
webrep anyval 1 endst
webrep line endst
webrep cat </td></tr> endcat endst
webrep cat <tr><th>Student Name </th><td> endcat endst
webrep anyvar stdname endst
webrep line endst
webrep cat </td></tr></table> endcat endst
webrep line endst
webrep cat </body> endcat endst
webrep line endst
webrep cat </html> endcat endst
webrep line endst
end

*
```

```
write.sbl
declare filename somestr somestr3 somestr5 endst
begin
storeval filename eq char write.dat endchar endst
storeval somestr eq char x endchar endst
storeval line eq #10 endst
storeval somestr3 eq char y endchar endst
storeval space eq #32 endst
storeval somestr5 eq char z endchar endst
writefile somestr into filename endst
writefile line into filename endst
writefile somestr3 into filename endst
writefile space into filename endst
writefile somestr5 into filename endst
end

*

testit.cvb
begin
storeval integer1 eq +987654321 endst
storeval integer2 eq -987654321 endst
storeval integer3 eq char 987654321 endchar endst
storeval integer4 eq +A987654321 endst
storeval integer5 eq -9876A54321 endst
storeval integer6 eq +9876.54321 endst
testit integer integer1 into retval endst
message anyvar retval endst
testit integer integer2 into retval endst
message anyvar retval endst
testit integer integer3 into retval endst
message anyvar retval endst
testit integer integer4 into retval endst
message anyvar retval endst
testit integer integer5 into retval endst
message anyvar retval endst
testit integer integer6 into retval endst
message anyvar retval endst
storeval number1 eq +98765.4321 endst
storeval number2 eq -98765.4321 endst
storeval number3 eq char 98765.4321 endchar endst
storeval number4 eq +A98765.4321 endst
storeval number5 eq -9876A5.4321 endst
storeval number6 eq +987654321 endst
testit number number1 into retval endst
message anyvar retval endst
testit number number2 into retval endst
message anyvar retval endst
```

testit number number3 into retval endst
message anyvar retval endst
testit number number4 into retval endst
message anyvar retval endst
testit number number5 into retval endst
message anyvar retval endst
testit number number6 into retval endst
message anyvar retval endst
storeval string1 eq char Nagaraju endchar endst
storeval string2 eq char +98654321 endchar endst
storeval string3 eq char -98654321 endchar endst
storeval string4 eq char 987654321 endchar endst
storeval string5 eq char +98765.4321 endchar endst
storeval string6 eq char -98765.4321 endchar endst
storeval string7 eq char 9Nagaraju endchar endst
storeval string8 eq char Naga9raju endchar endst
testit string string1 into retval endst
message anyvar retval endst
testit string string2 into retval endst
message anyvar retval endst
testit string string3 into retval endst
message anyvar retval endst
testit string string4 into retval endst
message anyvar retval endst
testit string string5 into retval endst
message anyvar retval endst
testit string string6 into retval endst
message anyvar retval endst
testit string string7 into retval endst
message anyvar retval endst
testit string string8 into retval endst
message anyvar retval endst
comment No testit for date and time data types endst
end

*

printit.cvb
begin
storeval somestring1 eq char *Data Entry** endchar endst
storeval somestring2 eq char *Data Manage* endchar endst
storeval color eq +100 endst
storeval highlight eq +50 endst
storeval row eq +10 endst
storeval col eq +15 endst
storeval row2 eq +0 endst
storeval col2 eq +0 endst
storeval one eq +1 endst

```
storeval noofsps eq +10 endst
setvideomode text endst
gotorowcol row col endst
printit somestring1 and color endst
dump row eq addint of row one ofend endst
gotorowcol row col endst
printit somestring2 and color endst
dump row eq subint of row one ofend endst
gotorowcol row col endst
printit somestring1 and highlight endst
gotorowcol row col endst
getkey scancode asciicode endst
spaceit noofsps and color endst
gotorowcol row2 col2 endst
message anyvar data endst
getrowcol row3 col3 endst
message anyvar row3 endst
message anyvar col3 endst
end

*

spaceit.cvb

*

unique.ext
begin
storeval someh eq +4000.00 endst
storeval somei eq +7000.00 endst
storeval filename eq char bank.dat endchar endst
storeval colname eq char amount endchar endst
storeval type eq char number endchar endst
storeval offset eq +3 endst
storeval reclen eq +8 endst
unique of someh filename colname type offset reclen into someg endst
message anyvar someg endst
unique of somei filename colname type offset reclen into someg endst
message anyvar someg endst
end

*

del.ext
begin
storeval filename eq char bank.dat endchar endst
storeval colname eq char amount endchar endst
storeval offset eq +3 endst
storeval reclen eq +8 endst
del of filename colname offset reclen endst
```

end

*
gencos.dat
all
open
for
fresh
writeread
insert
read
oneofto
gofor
begining
fileseek
filetell
forward
filesize
increment
decrement
system
begin
endst
end
if
then
endif
goto
labelit
comment
message
anyval
anyvar
line
space
cat
endcat
storeval
char
endchar
storevar
lt
gt
eq
ne
le
ge

dump
addint
addnum
subint
subnum
mulint
mulnum
divint
divnum
power
factorial
of
ofend
substring
from
to
into
length
instring
occurence
in
charofint
intofchar
tointeger
tonumber
round
webrep
direct
inport
outport
indirect
call
function
endcall
getkey
getrowcol
get
getpassword
cascade
declare
and
setvideomode
text
graph
gotorowcol
is
drop

absolute
addconst
default
notnull
check
maybe
apowerx
avg
character
cnt
directly
convertcase
copyfile
decode
del
deletefile
dropconst
unique
emptyfile
greater
initcap
leftpad
upto
with
lefttrim
lesser
max
min
polynomial
power
replace
rightpad
righttrim
sum
tolower
toupper
varsize
rightpad
righttrim
at
putmat
getmat
delmat
filesize
toascii
tovalue
testit

convert
command.dbm
source.tmp
datafile.dat
csv
wsv
administer
let
system
manager
username
password
change
passwords
to
specify
drop
dropall
increment
decrement
fileopen
curdri
status
setdisk
decrec
selectall
display
selectif
applylogic
electrec
recnums
recstats
daysbet
dateat
dayat
dateform
timesbet
timestamp
splittimestamp
initcap
convertcase
toupper
tolower
varsize
lefttrim
righttrim
leftpad

rightpad
replace
character
decode
absolute
min
max
cnt
unique
del
recnums
recstats
convertdate
converttime

*

dateat.gen
begin
storeval date1 eq char 01-01-2000 endchar endst
storeval sign eq char - endchar endst
storeval days eq +1000 endst
dateat date1 sign days into date2 endst
message anyvar date2 endst
end

*

dateform.gen
begin
storeval date1 eq char 01-01-2000 endchar endst
storeval form1 eq char dd-mm-yyyy endchar endst
storeval centuary eq +21 endst
storeval form2 eq char dd-mon-yy endchar endst
storeval form3 eq char dd-mm-yyyy endchar endst
storeval form4 eq char dd-mon-yyyy endchar endst
dateform date1 form1 centuary form2 into date2 endst
message anyvar date2 endst
message line endst
dateform date1 form1 centuary form3 into date3 endst
message anyvar date3 endst
message line endst
dateform date1 form1 centuary form4 into date4 endst
message anyvar date4 endst
message line endst
end

*

dayat.gen

```
begin
storeval date1 eq char 01-01-2000 endchar endst
dayat date1 into day endst
message anyvar day endst
end
```

*

```
daysbet.gen
begin
storeval date1 eq char 01-01-2000 endchar endst
storeval date2 eq char 01-01-2020 endchar endst
daysbet date1 date2 into sign days endst
message anyvar sign endst
message anyvar days endst
end
```

*

```
splittim.gen
begin
storeval timestamp eq char Mon Aug 07 17:33:05 2023 endchar endst
splittimestamp timestamp into day mon date hr min sec year endst
message anyvar day endst
message anyvar mon endst
message anyvar date endst
message anyvar hr endst
message anyvar min endst
message anyvar sec endst
message anyvar year endst
end
```

*

```
sysdate.gen
begin
storeval command eq char gencsl daysbet.gen endchar endst
system command endst
end
```

*

```
timestam.sbl
declare somex endst
begin
timestamp to somex endst
message anyvar somex endst
end
```

```
*
timesbet.gen
begin
storeval date eq char 15-07-2004 endchar endst
storeval time1 eq char 07:27:34:am endchar endst
storeval time2 eq char 12:00:00:md endchar endst
storeval time3 eq char 06:12:57:pm endchar endst
storeval time4 eq char 12:00:00:mn endchar endst
timesbet time1 time2 into sign seconds endst
message anyvar sign endst
message anyvar seconds endst
timesbet time2 time3 into sign seconds endst
message anyvar sign endst
message anyvar seconds endst
timesbet time3 time4 into sign seconds endst
message anyvar sign endst
message anyvar seconds endst
timesbet time4 time1 into sign seconds endst
message anyvar sign endst
message anyvar seconds endst
end

*

absolute.bui
begin
storeval somex eq +3.3 endst
storeval somey eq -7.7 endst
absolute of somex into somez endst
message anyvar somez endst
absolute of somey into somez endst
message anyvar somez endst
end

*

characte.bui
begin
storeval somex eq char NagaRaju endchar endst
storeval somey eq +4 endst
character of somex at somey into somez endst
message anyvar somez endst
end

*

cnt.bui
begin
storeval filename eq char bank.dat endchar endst
storeval colname eq char amount endchar endst
```

```
storeval offset eq +3 endst
storeval reclen eq +8 endst
cnt of filename colname offset reclen into somey endst
directly message anyvar somey endst
end


*

convertc.bui
begin
storeval somex eq char NaGaRaJu endchar endst
convertcase of somex into somey endst
message anyvar somey endst
end


*

decode.bui
begin
storeval somex eq char Kumar endchar endst
storeval somey eq char Kumar endchar endst
storeval somez eq char kumar endchar endst
decode somex somey into retval endst
message anyvar retval endst
decode somex somez into retval endst
message anyvar retval endst
end


*

initcap.bui
begin
storeval somex eq char nagaraju endchar endst
initcap of somex into somey endst
message anyvar somey endst
end


*

leftpad.bui
begin
storeval somex eq char Naga Raja Prasanna Kumar endchar endst
storeval somey eq char . endchar endst
storeval somez eq +10 endst
leftpad of somex upto somez with somey into somep endst
message anyvar somep endst
end


*

lefttrim.bui
```

```
begin
storeval somex eq char Naga Raja Prasanna Kumar endchar endst
storeval somey eq +10 endst
lefttrim of somex upto somey into somez endst
message anyvar somez endst
end
```

*

```
max1.bui
begin
storeval filename eq char bank.dat endchar endst
storeval colname eq char accno endchar endst
storeval type eq char integer endchar endst
storeval offset eq +1 endst
storeval reclen eq +8 endst
max of filename colname type offset reclen into somey endst
message anyvar somey endst
end
```

*

```
min1.bui
begin
storeval filename eq char bank.dat endchar endst
storeval colname eq char accno endchar endst
storeval type eq char integer endchar endst
storeval offset eq +1 endst
storeval reclen eq +8 endst
min of filename colname type offset reclen into somey endst
message anyvar somey endst
end
```

*

```
sum.bui
begin
storeval filename eq char bank.dat endchar endst
storeval colname eq char accno endchar endst
storeval type eq char integer endchar endst
storeval offset eq +1 endst
storeval reclen eq +8 endst
sum of filename colname type offset reclen into somey endst
message anyvar somey endst
end
```

*

```
replace.bui
begin
storeval somex eq char Naga Raja Naga jaRa endchar endst
```

```
storeval somey eq char ja endchar endst
storeval somez eq char sri endchar endst
replace somex where somey with somez into somep endst
message anyvar somep endst
end


*

rightpad.bui
begin
storeval somex eq char Naga Raja Prasanna Kumar endchar endst
storeval somey eq char . endchar endst
storeval somez eq +10 endst
rightpad of somex from somez with somey into somep endst
message anyvar somep endst
end


*

righttri.bui
begin
storeval somex eq char Naga Raja Prasanna Kumar endchar endst
storeval somey eq +10 endst
righttrim of somex upto somey into somez endst
message anyvar somez endst
end

*

tolower.bui
begin
storeval somex eq char nAgArAjU endchar endst
tolower of somex into somey endst
message anyvar somey endst
end

*

toupper.bui
begin
storeval somex eq char nAgArAjU endchar endst
toupper of somex into somey endst
message anyvar somey endst
end

*

varsize.bui
begin
storeval somex eq char +98754321 endchar endst
```

```
varsize of somex into somey endst
message anyvar somey endst
end


*

bank.dat

*

addconst.ext
begin
addconst default +100 to somea endst
addconst default Naga#Raju to someb endst
addconst default +9999.999 to somec endst
addconst notnull xxxxxx to somed endst
addconst check Bombay&New#Delhi&Kolkata&Old#Madras to somee endst
addconst maybe na___ra% to somef endst
end


*

const1.ext
begin
storeval somea eq +200 endst
message anyvar somea endst
end

*

const2.ext
begin
storeval someb eq char Naga#Raju endchar endst
message anyvar someb endst
end

*

const3.ext
begin
storeval somec eq +9999999 endst
message anyvar somec endst
end

*

const4.ext
begin
storeval somed eq char NIL endchar endst
message anyvar somed endst
end
```

```
*
const5.ext
begin
storeval somed eq +1000 endst
message anyvar somed endst
end

*
const6.ext
begin
storeval somee eq char New Delhi endchar endst
message anyvar somee endst
end

*
const7.ext
begin
storeval somee eq char Old#Darsi endchar endst
message anyvar somee endst
end

*
const8.ext
begin
storeval somef eq char nagaraju endchar endst
message anyvar somef endst
end

*
const9.ext
begin
storeval somef eq char manideep endchar endst
message anyvar somef endst
end

*
const10.ext
begin
storeval someg eq +3000.00 endst
message anyvar someg endst
end

*
dropcons.ext
begin
dropconst check Bombay&New#Delhi&Kolkata&Old#Madras from somee endst
dropconst unique xxxxxx from someg endst
```

end

*

unique.ext
begin
storeval someh eq +4000.00 endst
storeval somei eq +7000.00 endst
storeval filename eq char bank.dat endchar endst
storeval colname eq char amount endchar endst
storeval type eq char number endchar endst
storeval offset eq +3 endst
storeval reclen eq +8 endst
unique of someh filename colname type offset reclen into someg endst
message anyvar someg endst
unique of somei filename colname type offset reclen into someg endst
message anyvar someg endst
end

*

convdate.cvb
begin
storeval date1 eq char 25-12-2025 endchar endst
storeval date2 eq char 15-07-2024 endchar endst
convertdate of date1 into data1 endst
message anyvar data1 endst
convertdate of date2 into data2 endst
message anyvar data2 endst
if data2 lt data1 then 10
message cat Correct! endcat endst
get somez endst
endif 10
end

*

convtime.cvb
begin
storeval time1 eq char 03:32:27:pm endchar endst
storeval time2 eq char 02:27:32:am endchar endst
converttime of time1 into data1 endst
message anyvar data1 endst
converttime of time2 into data2 endst
message anyvar data2 endst
if data2 lt data1 then 10
message cat Correct! endcat endst
get somez endst
endif 10
end

```
*
recnums.cvb
begin
storeval filename eq char admi1111.dat endchar endst
recnums filename endst
message cat Record numbers of the file modified... endcat endst
end


*
recstats.cvb
begin
storeval filename eq char admi1111.dat endchar endst
storeval reclen eq char 21 endchar endst
storeval status_ eq char de endchar endst
recstats filename status_ reclen endst
message cat Record statuses of the file modified... endcat endst
end


*
decrec.sud
begin
storeval filename eq char admisson.dat endchar endst
decrec filename admnno stdname admndate admntime fees attendence
    marks1 marks2 marks3 marks4 marks5 marks6 total testtot testattend
    dateoftest result endst
end


*
dispall.sud
begin
storeval filename eq char admisson.dat endchar endst
storeval numrows eq +4 endst
decrec filename admnno stdname admndate admntime fees attendence
    marks1 marks2 marks3 marks4 marks5 marks6 total testtot testattend
    dateoftest result endst
display all of filename numrows endst
end



*
electrec.sud
begin
comment select all columns for select/update/delete/lock/unlock/... endst
storeval filename eq char admisson.dat endchar endst
storeval fullattend eq char +75 endchar endst
storeval testmarks eq char +72 endchar endst
```

```
storeval threesixty eq char +360 endchar endst
storeval donation eq char +80000 endchar endst
storeval indiday eq char 15-08-2024 endchar endst
storeval distinction eq char +70 endchar endst
decrec filename admnno stdname admndate admntime fees attendence
    marks1 marks2 marks3 marks4 marks5 marks6 total testtot testattend
    dateoftest result endst
open filename for writeread curdri drivenum status endst
labelit label1 endst
selectif attendence ge fullattend endst
selectif marks4 le testmarks endst
selectif total le threesixty endst
selectif fees le donation endst
selectif admndate ge indiday endst
selectif result le distinction endst
applylogic or and or or and endst
electrec for update oneofto label2 endst
goto label1 endst
labelit label2 endst
end

*

selectif.sud
begin
comment select all columns for select/update/delete/lock/unlock/... endst
storeval filename eq char admisson.dat endchar endst
storeval fullattend eq char +75 endchar endst
storeval testmarks eq char +72 endchar endst
storeval threesixty eq char +360 endchar endst
storeval donation eq char +80000 endchar endst
storeval indiday eq char 15-08-2024 endchar endst
storeval distinction eq char +70 endchar endst
storeval status eq char un endchar endst
decrec filename admnno stdname admndate admntime fees attendence
    marks1 marks2 marks3 marks4 marks5 marks6 total testtot testattend
    dateoftest result endst
open filename for writeread curdri drivenum status endst
labelit label1 endst
selectif attendence lt fullattend endst
selectif marks4 gt testmarks endst
selectif total gt threesixty endst
selectif fees gt donation endst
selectif admndate lt indiday endst
selectif result gt distinction endst
applylogic and or and and or endst
electrec for delete oneofto label2 endst
goto label1 endst
```

labelit label2 endst
end

*

selall.sud
begin
comment selectall columns for select/update/delete/lock/unlock/... endst
storeval filename eq char admisson.dat endchar endst
decrec filename admnno stdname admndate admntime fees attendence
    marks1 marks2 marks3 marks4 marks5 marks6 total testtot testattend
    dateoftest result endst
selectall columns from filename for select endst
end

*

admisson.dat
xy0001,aaaaaa,01-06-2024,01:00:00:pm,+100000,+76,+75,+82,+92,+79,+87,+7
1,+486,12:00:00:md,+4,07-04-2025,+81,un,+1,~,xy0002,bbbbbb,02-06-2024,10
:20:30:am,+75000,+81,+67,+62,+57,+68,+97,+75,+406,12:00:00:md,+4,08-04-2
025,+67,un,+2,~,xy0003,cccccc,03-06-2024,02:50:45:pm,+85000,+87,+83,+91,
+77,+68,+90,+87,+496,12:00:00:md,+4,08-04-2025,+82,un,+3,~,xy0004,ddddd
d,04-06-2024,09:25:20:am,+95000,+89,+77,+67,+58,+78,+62,+47,+389,12:00:0
0:md,+4,09-04-2025,+64,un,+4,~,xy0005,eeeeee,05-06-2024,05:27:22:pm,+10
0000,+85,+67,+77,+82,+93,+57,+68,+444,12:00:00:md,+4,09-04-2025,+74,un,
+5,~,xy0006,ffffff,06-06-2024,03:26:09:pm,+90000,+79,+68,+53,+73,+72,+77,
+63,+406,12:00:00:md,+4,09-04-2025,+67,un,+6,~,xy0007,gggggg,07-06-2024,
01:27:23:pm,+87000,+77,+70,+77,+63,+71,+75,+82,+438,12:00:00:md,+4,10-04-
2025,+73,un,+7,~,xy0008,hhhhhh,07-06-2024,11:30:30:am,+77000,+65,+77,+6
3,+72,+83,+82,+77,+454,12:00:00:md,+4,10-04-2025,+75,un,+8,~,xy0009,iiiiii,
08-06-2024,10:11:15:am,+78000,+79,+71,+87,+63,+72,+63,+91,+447,12:00:00:
md,+4,10-04-2025,+74,un,+9,~,xy0010,jjjjjj,09-06-2024,10:27:23:am,+95000,+
75,+67,+83,+72,+77,+65,+90,+454,12:00:00:md,+4,11-04-2025,+75,un,+10,~,
*

drop.dba
begin
storeval password1 eq char Lilly endchar endst
storeval password2 eq char Berry endchar endst
storeval username3 eq char Nagaraju endchar endst
storeval password3 eq char Gosukonda endchar endst
administer let system manager password1 password2
        drop username username3 with password password3 endst
end

*

```
dropall.dba
begin
storeval password1 eq char Lilly endchar endst
storeval password2 eq char Berry endchar endst
storeval username1 eq char Nagaraju endchar endst
administer let system manager password1 password2
            dropall usernames username1 endst
end


*

sysman.dba
begin
storeval password1 eq char Lotus endchar endst
storeval password2 eq char Apple endchar endst
storeval newpassword1 eq char Lilly endchar endst
storeval newpassword2 eq char Berry endchar endst
administer let system manager password1 password2 change passwords to
            newpassword1 newpassword2 endst
end


*

sysrig.dba
begin
comment There are totally 9 columns in a record of sysdba.rig endst
comment Username1 is the first endst
comment Password1 or allpasswords is the second endst
comment Read or noread is the third endst
comment Write or nowrite is the fourth endst
comment Admin or noadmin is the fifth endst
comment Username2 or nousername or allusernames is the sixth endst
comment Password2 or nopassword or allpasswords is the seventh endst
comment Filename or nofile or allfiles is the eigth endst
comment A tide mark is automatically put as record terminus endst
storeval password11 eq char Lilly endchar endst
storeval password12 eq char Berry endchar endst
storeval username1 eq char Prasanna endchar endst
storeval password1 eq char Sannidhanam endchar endst
storeval readright eq char noread endchar endst
storeval writeright eq char nowrite endchar endst
storeval adminright eq char noadmin endchar endst
storeval username2 eq char nousername endchar endst
storeval password2 eq char nopassword endchar endst
storeval filename eq char nofile endchar endst
administer let system manager password11 password12 specify
```

username1 password1 readright writeright adminright
username2 password2 filename endst
storeval username1 eq char Nagaraju endchar endst
storeval password1 eq char Gosukonda endchar endst
storeval readright eq char read endchar endst
storeval writeright eq char nowrite endchar endst
storeval adminright eq char admin endchar endst
storeval username2 eq char Neeraja endchar endst
storeval password2 eq char Velamakanni endchar endst
storeval filename eq char allfiles endchar endst
administer let system manager password11 password12 specify
username1 password1 readright writeright adminright
username2 password2 filename endst
storeval username1 eq char Sreenu endchar endst
storeval password1 eq char Geethanjali endchar endst
storeval readright eq char noread endchar endst
storeval writeright eq char nowrite endchar endst
storeval adminright eq char admin endchar endst
storeval username2 eq char Prasanna endchar endst
storeval password2 eq char allpasswords endchar endst
storeval filename eq char allfiles endchar endst
administer let system manager password11 password12 specify
username1 password1 readright writeright adminright
username2 password2 filename endst
storeval username1 eq char Prasanna endchar endst
storeval password1 eq char Sannidhanam endchar endst
storeval readright eq char read endchar endst
storeval writeright eq char write endchar endst
storeval adminright eq char admin endchar endst
storeval username2 eq char Nagaraju endchar endst
storeval password2 eq char Gosukonda endchar endst
storeval filename eq char nofile endchar endst
administer let system manager password11 password12 specify
username1 password1 readright writeright adminright
username2 password2 filename endst
storeval username1 eq char Neeraja endchar endst
storeval password1 eq char Velamakanni endchar endst
storeval readright eq char read endchar endst
storeval writeright eq char nowrite endchar endst
storeval adminright eq char admin endchar endst
storeval username2 eq char Sreenu endchar endst
storeval password2 eq char allpasswords endchar endst
storeval filename eq char bank.dat endchar endst
administer let system manager password11 password12 specify
username1 password1 readright writeright adminright
username2 password2 filename endst
storeval username1 eq char Nagaraju endchar endst

storeval password1 eq char Gosukonda endchar endst
storeval readright eq char read endchar endst
storeval writeright eq char write endchar endst
storeval adminright eq char admin endchar endst
storeval username2 eq char allusernames endchar endst
storeval password2 eq char allpasswords endchar endst
storeval filename eq char allfiles endchar endst
administer let system manager password11 password12 specify
username1 password1 readright writeright adminright
username2 password2 filename endst
storeval username1 eq char Neeraja endchar endst
storeval password1 eq char Velamakanni endchar endst
storeval readright eq char noread endchar endst
storeval writeright eq char nowrite endchar endst
storeval adminright eq char admin endchar endst
storeval username2 eq char Prasanna endchar endst
storeval password2 eq char Sannidhanam endchar endst
storeval filename eq char nofile endchar endst
administer let system manager password11 password12 specify
username1 password1 readright writeright adminright
username2 password2 filename endst
storeval username1 eq char Nagaraju endchar endst
storeval password1 eq char CDBDeveloper endchar endst
storeval readright eq char read endchar endst
storeval writeright eq char nowrite endchar endst
storeval adminright eq char noadmin endchar endst
storeval username2 eq char allusernames endchar endst
storeval password2 eq char Kumar endchar endst
storeval filename eq char allfiles endchar endst
administer let system manager password11 password12 specify
username1 password1 readright writeright adminright
username2 password2 filename endst
storeval username1 eq char Neeraja endchar endst
storeval password1 eq char Velamakanni endchar endst
storeval readright eq char read endchar endst
storeval writeright eq char nowrite endchar endst
storeval adminright eq char admin endchar endst
storeval username2 eq char Sreenu endchar endst
storeval password2 eq char allpasswords endchar endst
storeval filename eq char bank.dat endchar endst
administer let system manager password11 password12 specify
username1 password1 readright writeright adminright
username2 password2 filename endst
end

*

sysdba.rig

Prasanna,Sannidhanam,noread,nowrite,noadmin,nousername,nopassword,nofile,~,Nagaraju,Gosukonda,read,nowrite,admin,Neeraja,Velamakanni,allfiles,~,Sreenu,Geethanjali,noread,nowrite,admin,Prasanna,allpasswords,allfiles,~,Prasanna,Sannidhanam,read,write,admin,Nagaraju,Gosukonda,nofile,~,Nagaraju,Gosukonda,read,write,admin,allusernames,allpasswords,allfiles,~,Neeraja,Velamakanni,noread,nowrite,admin,Prasanna,Sannidhanam,nofile,~,Nagaraju,CDB Developer,read,nowrite,noadmin,allusernames,Kumar,allfiles,~,Neeraja,Velamakanni,read,nowrite,admin,Sreenu,allpasswords,bank.dat,~,
*

sysdba.ini
Lilly,Berry,
*

sysman.ini
Lotus,Apple,
*

sysdat.cvb
begin
storeval date1 eq char 25-10-1992 endchar endst
storeval date2 eq char 15-07-1969 endchar endst
storeval datefile eq char datef.dat endchar endst
open datefile for fresh curdri drivenum status endst
insert date1 endst
insert date2 endst
end

*

sysdat2.cvb
begin
storeval datefile eq char datef.dat endchar endst
open datefile for writeread curdri drivenum status endst
read date1 oneofto label1 endst
read date2 oneofto label1 endst
daysbet date1 date2 into sign days endst
message anyvar sign endst
message anyvar days endst
storeval storfile eq char outcome.dat endchar endst
open storfile for fresh curdri drivenum status endst
insert sign endst
insert days endst
labelit label1 endst
end

*

flagapp.cbl
begin
storeval date_ eq char 17-12-1997 endchar endst
call convert_date endst

```
goto labelend endst
storeval filename eq char flaggui.dat endchar endst
storeval file1 eq char jfile1.dat endchar endst
storeval file2 eq char jfile2.dat endchar endst
storeval dummyfil eq char dummyfil.dat endchar endst
storeval flagdata eq char flagdata.dat endchar endst
storeval tide eq char ~ endchar endst
storeval comp1 eq char lt endchar endst
storeval comp2 eq char gt endchar endst
storeval comp3 eq char eq endchar endst
storeval comp4 eq char ne endchar endst
storeval comp5 eq char le endchar endst
storeval comp6 eq char ge endchar endst
storeval oper1 eq char and endchar endst
storeval oper2 eq char or endchar endst
storeval offset eq +0 endst
storeval six eq +6 endst
storeval yes eq char yes endchar endst
storeval no eq char no endchar endst
open flagdata for fresh curdri drivenum status endst
open filename for fresh curdri drivenum status endst
labelit label1234 endst
message cat Terminate with tide... endcat endst
message line endst
message cat Enter file name : endcat endst
get filex1 endst
message cat Enter column name : endcat endst
get colx1 endst
message cat Enter comparision : endcat endst
get compx1 endst
message cat Enter file name : endcat endst
get filex2 endst
message cat Enter column name : endcat endst
get colx2 endst
message cat Enter operator : endcat endst
get operx1 endst
open filename for writeread curdri drivenum status endst
fileseek offset endst
insert filex1 endst
insert colx1 endst
insert compx1 endst
insert filex2 endst
insert colx2 endst
insert operx1 endst
message cat Enter more(yes/no)? endcat endst
get option endst
if option eq yes then 1
```

```
dump offset eq addint of offset six ofend endst
fileseek offset endst
goto label1234 endst
endif 1
message cat To flag_function... endcat endst
message line endst
call flag_function endst
comment ----------------------------- endst
labelit labelend endst
end
function flag_function is
storeval flag1 eq +0 endst
storeval flag2 eq +0 endst
storeval flag3 eq +0 endst
storeval falg4 eq +0 endst
storeval flag5 eq +0 endst
storeval netflag eq +0 endst
storeval count1 eq +1 endst
storeval count2 eq +1 endst
storeval count3 eq +1 endst
storeval zero eq +0 endst
storeval one eq +1 endst
storeval two eq +2 endst
storeval three eq +3 endst
storeval five eq +5 endst
storeval six eq +6 endst
storeval somei eq +0 endst
storeval place eq +0 endst
storeval place1 eq +0 endst
storeval place2 eq +0 endst
storeval place3 eq +0 endst
storeval place4 eq +0 endst
storeval reclen1 eq + endst
storeval reclen1 eq +11 endst
storeval reclen2 eq +9 endst
storeval somei eq +0 endst
open flagdata for fresh curdri drivenum status endst
open filename for writeread curdri drivenum status endst
labelit label1 endst
comment message cat Count2 : endcat endst
comment message anyvar count2 endst
read somea oneofto label2 endst
comment message anyvar somea endst
if somea eq tide then 1
goto label3 endst
endif 1
read someb oneofto label2 endst
```

```
read somec oneofto label2 endst
read somed oneofto label2 endst
read somee oneofto label2 endst
read someo oneofto label2 endst
if someo eq tide then 1
storeval flag5 eq +1 endst
endif 1
filetell somei endst
if somea eq file1 then 3
open file1 for writeread curdri drivenum status endst
dump place1 eq addint of place1 someb ofend endst
dump place1 eq subint of place1 one ofend endst
comment message cat Place1 : endcat endst
comment message anyvar place1 endst
fileseek place1 endst
goto label4 endst
endif 3
if somea eq file2 then 4
open file2 for writeread curdri drivenum status endst
dump place2 eq addint of place2 someb ofend endst
dump place2 eq subint of place2 one ofend endst
comment message cat Place2 : endcat endst
comment message anyvar place2 endst
fileseek place2 endst
goto label4 endst
endif 4
labelit label4 endst
comment message cat FileOpened...1 endcat endst
comment get somez endst
read someg oneofto label200 endst
comment message anyvar someg endst
comment get somez endst
if somed ne dummyfil then 2
if somed eq file1 then 3
open file1 for writeread curdri drivenum status endst
dump place1 eq addint of place1 somee ofend endst
dump place1 eq subint of place1 one ofend endst
comment message cat Place1... endcat endst
comment message anyvar place1 endst
fileseek place1 endst
goto label4_ endst
endif 3
if somed eq file2 then 4
open file2 for writeread curdri drivenum status endst
dump place2 eq addint of place2 somee ofend endst
dump place2 eq subint of place2 one ofend endst
comment message cat Place2... endcat endst
```

```
comment message anyvar place2 endst
fileseek place2 endst
goto label4_ endst
endif 4
endif 2
if somed eq dummyfil then 5
storevar someh eq somee endst
goto label5 endst
endif 5
labelit label4_ endst
comment message cat FileOpened...2 endcat endst
read someh oneofto label500 endst
comment message anyvar someh endst
comment get somez endst
labelit label5 endst
comment message cat ........... endcat endst
comment message anyvar someg endst
comment message anyvar someh endst
comment message cat ----------- endcat endst
comment get somez endst
comment message cat Somec : endcat endst
comment message anyvar somec endst
if somec eq comp1 then 1
if someg lt someh then 2
storeval flag1 eq +1 endst
goto label6 endst
endif 2
endif 1
if somec eq comp2 then 1
if someg gt someh then 2
storeval flag1 eq +1 endst
goto label6 endst
endif 2
endif 1
if somec eq comp3 then 1
if someg eq someh then 2
storeval flag1 eq +1 endst
goto label6 endst
endif 2
endif 1
if somec eq comp4 then 1
if someg ne someh then 2
storeval flag1 eq +1 endst
goto label6 endst
endif 2
endif 1
if somec eq comp5 then 1
```

if someg le someh then 2
storeval flag1 eq +1 endst
goto label6 endst
endif 2
endif 1
if somec eq comp6 then 1
if someg ge someh then 2
storeval flag1 eq +1 endst
goto label6 endst
endif 2
endif 1
labelit label6 endst
comment message cat Flag1 : endcat endst
comment message anyvar flag1 endst
comment get somez endst
open filename for writeread curdri drivenum status endst
fileseek somei endst
storevar place1 eq place3 endst
storevar place2 eq place4 endst
dump count1 eq addint of count1 one ofend endst
if count1 eq two then 9
storevar flag2 eq flag1 endst
storeval flag1 eq +0 endst
goto label1 endst
endif 9
if count1 eq three then 11
storevar flag3 eq flag1 endst
if someo eq oper1 then 1
if flag3 eq one then 2
if flag1 eq one then 3
storevar netflag eq one endst
goto label11 endst
endif 3
endif 2
storevar netflag eq zero endst
goto label11 endst
endif 1
if someo eq oper2 then 1
if flag3 eq zero then 2
if flag1 eq zero then 3
storevar netflag eq zero endst
goto label11 endst
endif 3
endif 2
storevar netflag eq one endst
goto label11 endst
endif 1

endif 11
if count1 eq four then 9
storevar flag4 eq flag1 endst
if someo eq oper1 then 1
if flag4 eq one then 2
if flag1 eq one then 3
storevar netflag eq one endst
goto label11 endst
endif 3
endif 2
storevar netflag eq zero endst
goto label11 endst
endif 1
if someo eq oper2 then 1
if flag4 eq zero then 2
if flag1 eq zero then 3
storevar netflag eq zero endst
goto label11 endst
endif 3
endif 2
storevar netflag eq one endst
goto label11 endst
endif 1
labelit label11 endst
comment message cat Count1 : endcat endst
comment message anyvar count1 endst
comment message cat NetFlag : endcat endst
comment message anyvar netflag endst
comment ------------------------------------- endst
storeval flag1 eq +0 endst
if count1 eq five then 22
goto label11_ endst
endif 22
goto label1 endst
labelit label11_ endst
message cat Final NetFlag : endcat endst
message anyvar netflag endst
open flagdata for writeread curdri drivenum status endst
insert netflag endst
storeval place2 eq +0 endst
storeval reclen2 eq +9 endst
dump reclen2 eq mulint of reclen2 count2 ofend endst
dump place2 eq addint of place2 reclen2 ofend endst
comment storeval place1 eq +0 endst
storeval flag1 eq +0 endst
storeval netflag eq +0 endst
storeval somei eq +0 endst

```
open filename for writeread curdri drivenum status endst
dump count2 eq addint of count2 one ofend endst
storeval count1 eq +1 endst
storevar place3 eq place1 endst
storevar place4 eq place2 endst
if count2 eq six then 1
goto label22_ endst
endif 1
goto label1 endst
labelit label22_ endst
storeval place1 eq +0 endst
storeval place2 eq +0 endst
storeval reclen1 eq +11 endst
dump reclen1 eq mulint of reclen1 count3 ofend endst
dump place1 eq addint of place1 reclen1 ofend endst
storeval flag1 eq +0 endst
storeval netflag eq +0 endst
storeval somei eq +0 endst
open filename for writeread curdri drivenum status endst
dump count3 eq addint of count3 one ofend endst
storeval count1 eq +1 endst
storeval count2 eq +1 endst
storevar place3 eq place1 endst
storevar place4 eq place2 endst
if count3 eq five then 1
goto label33_ endst
endif 1
goto label1 endst
labelit label33_ endst
labelit label200 endst
comment message cat ...eof1... endcat endst
labelit label500 endst
comment message cat ...eof2... endcat endst
comment ------------------------------------- endst
labelit labeljoin endst
message cat Completed... endcat endst
endcall
comment ------------------------------------------------- endst
function convert_date is
endcall
function convert_time is
endcall

*

endecrbx.cvb
begin
endecrb endst
```

end

*

```
convdate.cvb
begin
storeval date1 eq char 25-12-2025 endchar endst
storeval date2 eq char 15-07-2024 endchar endst
convertdate of date1 into data1 endst
message anyvar data1 endst
convertdate of date2 into data2 endst
message anyvar data2 endst
if data2 lt data1 then 10
message cat Correct! endcat endst
get somez endst
endif 10
end
```

*

```
convtime.cvb
begin
storeval time1 eq char 03:32:27:pm endchar endst
storeval time2 eq char 02:27:32:am endchar endst
converttime of time1 into data1 endst
message anyvar data1 endst
converttime of time2 into data2 endst
message anyvar data2 endst
if data2 lt data1 then 10
message cat Correct! endcat endst
get somez endst
endif 10
end
```

*

Dedicated to my friend Late Mahendra Srinivas.

EMailID:petcolbaselang@gmail.com.

YoutubeChannel:@srinivasacomputersdarsi-b7d.

-$-

www.ingramcontent.com/pod-product-compliance
Lightning Source LLC
Chambersburg PA
CBHW080553060326
40689CB00021B/4840